On Opposite Tacks

Also by Chester Brigham

Gloucester's Bargain With the Sea:
The Bountiful Maritime Culture of Cape Ann, Massachusetts

The Stream I Go A-Fishing In:
Musical Adventures of Gloucester Schoonerman
John J. Watson

Front Cover

Top: John and Dolly (Wall) Sloan. Detail of photograph of John and Dolly Sloan and friends, c.1915–1918. Gift of Helen Farr Sloan, 1978. John Sloan Manuscript Collection, Delaware Art Museum.

Bottom: Capt. Solomon Jacobs and Sarah (MacQuarrie) Jacobs. Detail of photograph. Cape Ann Museum, Gloucester, Massachusetts.

On Opposite Tacks

When Artist John Sloan

&

Capt. Solomon Jacobs

Crossed Wakes in Wartime Gloucester

CHESTER BRIGHAM

Whale's Jaw
Publishing

Publisher's Cataloging-in-Publication data

Brigham, Chester.
On opposite tacks : when artist John Sloan and Capt. Solomon Jacobs
crossed wakes in wartime Gloucester / Chester Brigham.

p. cm.
Includes bibliographical references and index.
ISBN 978-0-9740778-7-1

1. Gloucester (Mass.) — History — 20th century. 2. Ann, Cape (Mass.) —
History. 3. Sloan, John, 1871-1951. 4. Jacobs, Solomon, 1847-1922. 5. Fishers
— Massachusetts — Gloucester — History. 6. Fishing boats — Massachu-
setts — Gloucester — History. 7. Painting — Massachusetts — Gloucester.
I. On opposite tacks : when artist John Sloan and Captain Solomon Jacobs
crossed wakes in wartime Gloucester. II. Title.

F74.G5 B375 2011
917.44/5 — dc22
Library of Congress Control Number: 2011934397
Copyright ©2011 Chester Brigham
First Printing

Printed in the United States

Whale's Jaw
Publishing

Cover and book design by Barry Rower

Contents

PREFACE

〜

W HEN WRITING *Gloucester's Bargain With the Sea* several years
ago, I looked at how the port's fishing industry was one of
the factors that attracted artists and writers to Cape Ann (along
with the strong beauties of the coast, the remoteness of the area in
the 19th century, and a working population that could take or leave
the summer visitors). I was constantly struck at the contrast between
those most distinctive elements of the Gloucester population, the
fishermen and the artists. How very different they are.

Put them together in a room and you would get very little communication. The summer artists might, out of curiosity, seek to
engage the men of the boats in conversation. The fishermen, less
interested, would keep the wall of apartness impenetrable by responding in gruff monosyllables. It would be no good pointing out
that workers in both vocations produce their output by working with
their hands. The paint-stained hands of the artists would have little
in common with the calloused hands of the fishermen. Each side
would leave the room knowing even less about one another.

How could I compare them? What if I took an outstanding representative of each of the two groups, put them together in a book,
and let them reveal, through their careers, how different (and possibly not so different) they were from one another? Maybe that could
be revealing. I considered a number of candidates from among the
painters and the commercial fishermen. Early on I decided the period I would look at should be that of the sailing schooners, the classic
age of the Gloucester fishermen. Not coincidentally during that era,
late in the 19th and early into the 20th centuries, some of the finest
American artists were also attracted to Cape Ann.

Getting down to individuals, I settled upon John Sloan on the
artist side. Sloan was unquestionably one of the most significant

of American artists, did a great deal of painting in Gloucester for several consecutive summers, and was controversial enough to be interesting. On the fisherman side, I settled on an individual who has never properly received his due. Capt. Solomon Jacobs, down from Newfoundland, was one of the most notable of the schooner captains – some said the greatest – and certainly the most colorful. When I put these two diametrically opposite individuals together in close quarters inside my head, they began to take over the narrative. Both men were in Gloucester throughout World War I. When America finally entered that war, the two responded in very different ways. So they were not only different in their occupations – one an ocean adventurer, the other a creator of images on canvas – but in the way they reacted to the world around them. To explore those responses I would need to follow their careers right from the beginning, and look for contrasts and parallels. That would be my book.

In researching the subject, I have made myself a regular nuisance in the Cape Ann Museum library. Nevertheless, librarian-archivist Stephanie Buck, and her associate Linda Johnson, have been wonderfully patient in making available the library's extensive source materials on Capt. Jacobs and John Sloan. They also suggested avenues of exploration I never would have thought of. Fred Buck, photography archivist at the museum, was equally helpful in unearthing relevant visuals that somehow only he would know about. The museum is a treasure trove of first-rate works by artists who have spent time on Cape Ann, including many that I mention in these pages – not only several fine Sloans, but works by Fitz Henry Lane, Winslow Homer, Stuart Davis, Frank Duveneck, Cecilia Beaux and Charles Grafly, to name some of the most prominent.

The museum possesses those artworks through the generosity of donors. John Sloan said "I regret that the artist must *sell* his work." It is reassuring when fine examples of that work find their way to the walls of a museum to be accessible to the public for generations to come.

Another essential resource for me in Gloucester has been the Sawyer Free Library. There I spent hours viewing microfilms of Gloucester newspapers, consulted the vertical files for clippings on Capt. Jacobs and John Sloan, borrowed a cassette of the 1970s oral history interview with Capt. Michael Clark, and thumbed through relevant art books – *none of which I would have been able to do on the Internet.* If a community doubts the necessity of a bricks-and-mortars library in the current age of Google, its citizens should give thought to all of the largesse, besides inviting stacks of real books, that is available exclusively in a public library. My thanks to Reference Librarian Judy Oski at the library for retrieving tapes and file folders for me.

Whenever I needed information as to births and marriages and deaths and odd details of Gloucester during the period I was interested in, Sarah Dunlap and her associates in the Gloucester City Archives Department practically leaped to the challenge – and invariably found what I was looking for in incontrovertible sources such as vital records, directories and maps. For them, Gloucester's past is very much alive and kicking – and their enthusiasm is contagious.

Rachael DiEleuterio, Librarian, Helen Farr Sloan Library & Archives, at the Delaware Art Museum, assisted cheerfully in locating files of Sloan correspondence for the period of his Gloucester summers – as well as a number of photographs – and making those materials available for review at a convenient location in the museum library. I am grateful, too, to Heather Campbell Coyle, Curator of American Art at the museum, who discussed Helen Farr Sloan's contributions to the museum of John Sloan archival materials and documents relating to other members of The Eight.

My thanks also to those who answered my questions regarding specific portions of the book. Erik A.R. Ronnberg, Jr. – eminent boat model builder who not only brings to his craft superb modeling skills, but shapes his vessels in action, working at sea – shared his thoughts on what influence yacht designer Ned Burgess' concepts had on the design of Sol Jacobs' finest mackerel schooner, the *Ethel B. Jacobs.*

David Dearborn, Research Assistant at the Maine Maritime Museum in Bath, Maine, drew upon the marine shipping records of that museum, a superb institution of all things sea-related to Maine, to document for me the busy itinerary of the down-easter *J.S. Winslow* – including repeated Atlantic crossings – during the years that

Sol Jacobs was aboard, reportedly as second mate.

Margaret McCrae, Curator of the Thomaston Historical Society, found that the Society had no information specifically on the downeaster *General Berry* on which Sol Jacobs sailed as crewman, but did provide details on a similar vessel, the 1,420-ton *John T. Berry* of 1876, also built by Joseph Hill.

Joseph Keefe, Archives Specialist at the National Archives and Records Administration – Northeast Region in Waltham, MA, located and provided to me the complete file on the bankruptcy of Solomon Jacobs in 1911. Gloucester lawyer Robert J. Madruga, son of a local fisherman himself, then reviewed the legal documents in the file, interpreted them in language even I could understand, and suggested scenarios as to what may have triggered Sol's decision to enter bankruptcy court.

Dedicated clock collector Howard Frisch – whose interest in Sol Jacobs had been sparked by Gordon Thomas' accounts of this "invincible" Gloucester captain – was my source for information on the nearly simultaneous donations in 1883 of identical marble clocks by Capt. Sol to the Prospect Street Baptist church, and by Nathaniel Webster to Gloucester City Hall.

This is the second of my books that Barry Rower has designed (he also designed *Gloucester's Bargain with the Sea*). Barry combines art and instinct with a sure command of graphic tools to create a visually rewarding reading environment. With his enthusiasm for a book project and meticulous attention to detail, Barry is a pleasure to work with.

My wife Anthea has contributed in so many ways – commenting wisely, finding unexpected sources and links, proofing, providing encouragement – that any attempt at thanks would be inadequate. She knows she has my constant gratitude.

INTRODUCTION

~~~

THEY HAD steered very different courses up to this point, the two men. One was sailing close to the wind of his ambitions from one direction, the other riding the breeze of inspiration from a different quarter. Each was hell-bent on holding to his heading toward a destiny that lay somewhere over the horizon. Between 1914 and 1918 their courses crossed in the fishing port of Gloucester, Massachusetts. It was then possible to get a good look at the shape and rigging of each as they briefly passed close by one another and then sailed on.

The two men could not have been more unalike. One had spent the better part of his life at sea. The other congratulated himself that he did not become seasick on ferry boats.

One sought his fortunes from the coast of Ireland to the islands off Alaska, north to the Arctic and west to the Pacific. The other never ventured beyond Pennsylvania to the west and Massachusetts to the east.

One needed other men behind him, and challenged and inspired them to follow him. The other worked alone, and sometimes infuriated all around him.

One earned substantial amounts of money three times, and lost it three times. The other had struggled just to survive.

One was devoted to family and to performing charitable actions in a modest-sized community. The other functioned inside a small circle within an impersonal metropolis.

They were also about as far apart in their occupations as possible. Oil and water do not mix, especially when the oil is the oil paint of the artist, and the water the ocean of the commercial fisherman. John Sloan was the artist, and Solomon Jacobs the fishing captain or, more to the point, the ocean adventurer.

Capt. Jacobs was, in anthropological terms, a hunter-gatherer, one who tracks prey and gathers food that he does not plant. He gained his livelihood in intimate proximity with the forces of nature. John Sloan, by contrast, was the product of a later stage in human development when leisure opened opportunities to explore urges of the human mind and emotions. While Capt. Jacobs was concerned with the tangibles of fish and seals, Sloan interested himself with abstractions of color and composition on canvas.

Because harvesting of the seas is primarily manual, and the making of art more cerebral and sensory, art is commonly accorded a more elevated notch on the value scale of human endeavor than commercial fishing. After all, the artists' works appeal to our most discriminating senses and nourish our higher faculties. Together with the output of composers and authors, works of art are valued as the cultural achievements that each age passes on to the next. Even the output of artists who were so boorish they would embarrass a self-respecting fisherman (Caravaggio, Cellini, Jackson Pollock) is valued *in spite of* its creators. Artistic taste involves our optic nerves, memory and emotions. It is complicated.

For most of us, excepting gourmets with educated taste buds, seafood appeals to simple hunger, not to aesthetic discernment. One palate may favor calamari over salmon, but it is a matter of personal choice that does not inspire books of learned advocacy one way or the other. The fisherman offers us dead fish that convert into protein building blocks as we consume them. In consequence he enjoys less prestige and status than the artist.

It should be noted, however, that in times of crisis the ranking is reversed. In the World War I era, where we will be visiting at some length, all young American males were required to register for conscription, but draft boards were lenient toward commercial fishermen who were harvesting from the sea vitally needed foodstuffs. A fisherman, if he were so minded, could apply for exemption under a provision of the draft law that excused "persons whose occupations were necessary for maintaining military or national interests." Artists enjoyed no such dispensation. So when it came down to it, the feeding of stomachs took priority over the nourishing of the senses.

The significant role of fishermen in the food chain gave those toilers of the sea special consideration in World War II as well, when Selective Service State Directors were given authority to recommend draft exemptions for eighteen- to twenty-five-year-old captains of fishing vessels. It has only been in recent times that the federal government's National Marine Fisheries Service has categorized commercial fishermen as criminals by nature, and treated them as guilty of violations of catch limit regulations until proven innocent. The mission of the U.S. Coast Guard has been refocused as well to dealing harshly with fishermen vaguely suspected of engaging in all sorts of illicit activities.

In valuing artists and fishermen, ambiguity creeps into the equation in many respects. Art is the more genteel profession, but notoriously underpaid. John Sloan was dependent upon scraps of illustration assignments or teaching engagements at the fringes of polite society. Capt. Jacobs, by contrast, usually managed to profit nicely by fishing and sealing (with the exception of some disastrous setbacks that would have shriveled a weaker man).

Another anomaly: there is often more in the working life of the fisherman that captures the imagination than there is in that of the artist. The professional artist often exists in the sometimes prickly but generally soft embrace of academia, thrives in an urban environment in which dealers and galleries and collectors proliferate, and socializes in stimulating circles of cognoscenti. The artist escapes from a mundane existence into boundless spiritual adventure through his or her brush..

The commercial fisherman is, by contrast, something of a modern Aeneas. He sets out across the trackless sea, disappears over the horizon, and reappears, often after encounters with monsters of the elements during visits to mysterious capes and banks up the Gulf of Maine and beyond to the eastward. To the fisherman adventure is a matter of everyday routine and only an impediment to gaining enough cash to feed his family. Daring the elements is an unpredictable, and often terrible, adjunct to his trade.

Thus the two men under discussion were fated to be different by their very professions. We pick them up in the summer of 1916, when the opposite tacks they steered were approaching their closest point of convergence. Sloan was a summer resident in Gloucester's art colony, Capt. Jacobs a year-round fixture in the fishing community. It is possible, but unlikely, that they met. There is a greater possibility that they might have passed one another on Main Street because downtown Gloucester was not that big a place, nor is it today. So let us imagine them approaching one another, two figures in the midst of the summer hubbub.

OTHER PASSERSBY are chattering in Yankee crispness or Maritimes brogue, or lyrical Irish, or undulating Scandinavian, or Portuguese from the Azores, or occasionally rapid Sicilian among the few who have recently arrived from that island. Young women share giggling secrets as they breeze along in this season's calf-high skirts that seem daring compared to the hobble skirts of the older women, but will seem downright prim compared to the flapper skirts to follow in a few years.

There are other sounds too, the dull bumping of passing horse-drawn carts and the dinging whine of a trolley, a sibilant steam whistle that might be the train from Boston crossing the trestle a mile away over the Annisquam River (actually an estuary), or the steam ferry *Little Giant* announcing its imminent departure for East Gloucester, or a long blast from the Gorton-Pew fish packing plant calling its workforce back from lunch.

The aromas mixing with the noise are exquisitely varied. They include a blend of fish and bait at various stages of decomposition on the docks, the pungent tar smell of oakum used to caulk the schooners' wooden seams, hints of grease and kerosene, and the farm smell of the horse manure the sparrows are pecking at in the street. Modern olfactory sensors are sadly deprived of the complex bouquet of scents that were then taken for granted.

The two men pass one another with no glimmer of recognition, and scarcely any interest. The taller of the two might glance at the intense, slight of build, middle-aged man with pince-nez, pipe clamped in teeth, city cap and tie, and think, "One of them artist fellas," and pass on without a further thought. While the other, with a sidelong glance at the erect, blue-eyed, leathery ancient striding along, could have a fleeting notion that here is an old sea dog type he might like to paint some day.

Capt. Solomon Jacobs is sixty-nine years old, and has retired from the sea just the year before. In his prime he sailed in down-easters and fished and hunted seals on both the east and west coasts of North America. He had been one of the most successful and certainly the most colorful of the sailing schooner captains during Gloucester's peak years as a fishing port, in the 1870s through the '90s. Then he had over-extended himself and gotten into some financial difficulty. His greatest days might be behind him, but he will still give the town a reason or two to remember him before he is done.

John Sloan is forty-five, almost a quarter-century younger than the captain. His career is, by contrast, on the ascendancy. He has earned a marginal living for himself and his wife as a freelance magazine and newspaper illustrator for the past fifteen years, but is now on firmer ground with a contract to be a salaried art instructor at the New York Art Students League. He also draws and etches prints, and he paints on canvas. His paintings have been shown in exhibitions in New York and across the country since early in the century and have attracted a certain following.

He sold his first painting just a year ago, but it was not of the ones he did early in the century when he was one of the Urban Realists painting the underside of the New York scene with sympathy. Not one of those era-defining paintings of his will sell for another two years.

The disparity between the occupations of the two men is especially profound in 1916. Gloucester's harbor is given over almost entirely to the interests of those who fish the seas, and those who build and supply the vessels, and those engaged in the many trades involved in main-taining and refurbishing the ships. The artists, by contrast, consist of a small, briefly seasonal population huddled sociably on the eastern shores of the harbor, drawn by the ocean-against-granite-ledge scenery and the accidentally appealing scenes of sails and wharves.

The chasm between our two men extends to the way they see this world around them. That will become most evident if we imagine each taking a side street down to the waterfront and gazing out on the har-bor. John Sloan sees the boats as design elements, visually arranging them against the contrasting blues of the sea and the sky and the dark-er forms of Five Pound and Ten Pound Islands in the harbor and the surrounding uplands. His interpretation of the vessels is rudimentary because he has seen them only when they are off-duty – bare-masted, tied up at the piers, or being towed docilely out of the harbor behind a steam tug, until they are well out in the stream and begin to haul their sails up before rounding the breakwater and bending out to sea. To

Sloan the men on those boats are also aspects of design. For him the harbor is essentially raw material for a composition, richly scenic with arresting shapes and colors.

Everything Capt. Jacobs sees in the harbor has its practical significance. He knows each of the vessels tied at the wharves, who owns her, who the master is. From the state of her sails and rigging and deckworks he knows how well she is looked after, how she will respond after catching the wind full-sailed, hull down with lee rail under, knifing through the swells hour after hour, every timber and line straining, every man aboard conspiring with this rearing, plummeting arrangement of wood and sail to speed to the fishing grounds, because only there is the money made. Gazing out over the harbor waters, Capt. Jacobs sees the floor under the water as clearly as he sees the surface, every rock and reef, the shallows to avoid and the deeps where it would be safe to take a schooner drawing nine feet below the waterline. The color of the water and the sky may have limited esthetic significance for him, but it tells, with the wind direction, what the weather promises.

The scene back on Main Street is, on the surface, a typical cheerfully busy summer day, with the commercial fishing interests making room for the sun-seeking vacationers arriving in force as well as others from elsewhere who have come to nourish their talents in arts or crafts. But in the summer of 1916 a certain uneasiness hangs over the apparent normalcy. Most of Europe is locked in a war that has evolved into a stalemate of carnage. So far the width of the Atlantic Ocean has kept that war at bay. But there are disturbing signs that America is being drawn inexorably into the conflict.

America will indeed become a combatant nation the following year, and our two men will react to the reality of war in very different ways. One thing is certain: their responses will be the product of very different but often parallel career narratives, and of deeply held convictions. Their decisions will be firm; because each man, right from the beginning, has met life head-on.

Chapter One
LAUNCHINGS

~~

Of Icebergs and Seal Oil / Of Log Runs and Joinery

Of Icebergs and Seal Oil

SOLOMON JACOBS and John Sloan both began their journeys to Gloucester from near a body of water. But this was hardly a point of similarity, considering the character of the waters involved.

Solomon Jacobs was born in 1847 on one of the most remote shores of the North American continent. He first blinked at daylight in Twillingate, a tiny "outport" on the far northeast Atlantic coast of Newfoundland that is stark, storm-racked and fog-shrouded through much of the year. Twillingate is actually one of an archipelago of small islands at the mouth of the Exploits River where it flows into Notre Dame Bay.

The name Twillingate sounds as if it might have been that of a village of thatched-roof cottages in the Cotswolds. Actually Twillingate was the English corruption of Toulinquet, the name given the place by French fishermen who were reminded of a group of islands off the coast of France near Brest, where bare rock bluffs jut into the sea just as they do at Twillingate.

In Sol Jacobs' early years there was not even an organized municipality at Twillingate, just a few scattered fishing settlements. The houses were built apart from one another; the locals, fiercely self-sufficient, said they liked to keep space between themselves and their neighbors. That apartness applied both to their living arrangements on shore and when they sailed out to fish. With the residents opposed to anything like community spirit, it is not surprising that the citizenry of Twillingate did not sufficiently agree with one another to become a town until 1965.

Despite its location facing the ice-plagued waters of the Labrador Sea, in its early days Twillingate had advantages as a trading station. Its harbor is well-sheltered, and it was convenient to what were then the rich fishing grounds of the Grand Banks. It was also the principal port for trading with the even more remote settlements on the Labrador coast to the north. The cod no longer teem in those waters, though. In 2003, attempting to rebuild the stocks of vanishing fish, the Canadian government imposed a moratorium on cod fishing in the last remaining fishing grounds off Atlantic Canada. Today, apart from some crab and shrimp fishing, Twillingate survives by way of the tourist trade. In the summer months the island has a wild beauty, and the temperature rises to agreeable levels. The average high temperature in July is 72°F, but drops off to 68°F in August. (Solomon Jacobs would later find Gloucester tropical by comparison, where the average high is 82°F in July and 80°F in August – although with the prevailing summer southwesterlies blowing in off the ocean, it feels as if those official averages are seldom reached.)

Taking advantage of what may be its principal natural attraction, Twillingate bills itself as the "Iceberg Capital of the World." In certain years, in late spring and summer, the ice floes march solemnly down Notre Dame bay and make for a grand spectacle offshore. It is a rare and special ecotourism experience for the guests at the town's hostelries. Many visitors also come to observe the sea birds – puffins, plovers, gannets, harlequin ducks and over a dozen varieties of seagulls – that can be viewed from platforms along high trails.

Another attraction is the annual Fish Fun & Folk Festival at the end of July, a family-oriented celebration featuring Newfoundland folk music, street dancing and a craft fair. A recent addition is a beer garden where you can order a lager to wash down a mooseburger.

The fishing on the shoal banks east of Newfoundland had attracted Europeans as far back as 1000 A.D., when Norsemen built a station at what would later be known, in corrupted French, as L'Anse-aux-Meadows on the northern tip of Newfoundland, perhaps as a base for exploration. The settlement is not believed to have endured for long. Some time later the cold curtain of the Little Ice Age descended upon the northern hemisphere and ice blocked the sea route from Europe to Greenland. It would not be until five years after Columbus' voyages far to the south that Europeans once again set foot at least in the vicinity of Newfoundland. The navigator John Cabot (who signed himself Zuan Chabotto in his native Venice) may have landed there in 1497 or perhaps, it is argued, made landfall on Nova Scotia or Labrador instead. The Cabot voyages confirmed what had been fishermen's rumors that there were lands to the west of Greenland.

By the mid-1500s great fleets of French and also Spanish Basque vessels were fishing the Grand Banks. The English joined them in the 1570s, and by 1600 were vying with the French for domination of the Banks cod fishery. After loading salt in Portuguese ports, vessels would make a five-week crossing that would bring them to Newfoundland by April or May. The Europeans set up fish-drying stages along the shore, near the mamateeks, the conical dwellings in the small family communities of the indigenous folk. These were Beothuks, whom the Norsemen had encountered in the neighborhood of L'Anse-aux-Meadows at the beginning of the second millennium. The Norse called them skraelings, their word for aborigines.

The cured fish were returned to the mother ship which set sail homeward when the chill set in come August or September. Nobody wintered over in that time when severe cold continued to freeze the sea lanes as well as the harbors of much of Europe. The cold abated by the mid-1700s, and English trading companies expanded their operations along the Newfoundland shore, shipping back to Europe furs, cod, salmon and sealskins. The most prominent of these enterprises was Slade & Co. In 1753 John Slade of Poole on the south coast of England acquired a vessel and began trading to his own account in Newfoundland. He prospered, and later in the decade established the headquarters of Slade & Co. at Twillingate.

The Slade company recruited experienced fishermen from the West Country of England, that loose designation for the area around the busy port of Bristol down to Penzance at the far southwest corner of Great Britain. The Slade boats brought men to Newfoundland as "fishing servants" in the spring to fish for cod, then returned them home in the fall. In time, some of these itinerant fishermen stayed on, brought their families to join them, and became "livyers," as the permanent Newfoundlanders came to be known. Soon there were 152 of them in Twillingate, and it is very likely that Capt. Jacobs' ancestors were among them. Alternatively, it is conceivable that Capt. Jacobs' ancestors arrived in Newfoundland not from England but from Ireland. Irish Quakers of the Jacobs, Penrose and Harvey families settled in Newfoundland to trade between the island and Waterford, Ireland. However, none of those families are known to have settled in Twillingate. How Sol's ancestry evolved in England's West Country is unknown. The family name of Jacobs was almost certainly patronymic, a family surname derived from a given name. When Englishmen emerging from the Middle Ages began to see the value of having a surname to identify members of a family from one generation to the next, they frequently converted a given name into a family name. Hence the Michaels, Samuels and Adams families. In the Middle Ages the given name "Jacob" was most used in Jewish families, while "James," from the same root, was more common among Christians. With the Protestant Reformation of the 16th century, the trend was to adopt given names directly from the Old Testament, and Jacob began to be heard more often among Christians. Later members of the family of a Jacob would become known as "the Jacobs."

Not surprising in a period of little record-keeping in Twillingate, specific documentation of Capt. Jacobs' family does not appear until 1821. That was when William and Rebecca Jacobs of Twillingate had their son Simon baptized, reportedly by missionaries from the Society for the Propagation of the Gospel. It was a regular practice for missionaries, on periodic visits to the outports, to baptize the un-saved of all ages. The Church of England had built a church and school at the settlement in 1819 but it is unlikely that there was a permanent clergyman. Simon's son Solomon, our Capt. Jacobs, was not born a Canadian. Newfoundland was a separate British dominion in 1847, ruled directly from London. The island long remained apart from what became Canada to the west.

By the time Solomon was six, Twillingate had more of an air of permanence. The Reverend Edward Field, Bishop of the Church of England, visited the parish that year and reported "really almost feeling at home again, a happy English parson." When the bishop visited there were no huts of a native people to jar his impression of an English village. The Beothuk were by then extinct.

Sol's father Simon and his mother Mary Ann (Roberts) had four children, sons Solomon and Jonathan and daughters Lydia and Phoebe. Simon Jacobs executed his will in 1852, apparently a short time before his death, so Sol must have been five or six when his father died. To his wife Simon left the house they lived in at Farmers Arm, along with "all other houses and buildings gardens and lands thereto appertaining and my household furniture goods and chattels my fishing room and all my craft and also all of my cattle." Some of this language was probably legal boilerplate, but Simon did apparently leave a house, maybe a cow or two, and a boat and some fishing gear. As an exception to "all my craft" he left a third-interest in his schooner *Faith* to his brother Thomas, and the remaining two-thirds to Solomon and Jonathan when they reached age twenty-one. Simon provided in his will that Sol's two sisters should have the right to remain in his house so long as they remained unmarried. If one or both remained a spinster, she was to be looked after by the family with "reasonable assistance."

If Mary Ann should remarry, all that Simon bequeathed her would go in trust to Solomon and Jonathan, and devolve to whichever of the two remained at the homestead. Mary Ann did promptly remarry. In 1854 she became Mrs. William Hodder (or Hudder), he a cooper in the village who made and repaired barrels for the fishermen. Mary Ann married Bill Hodder in the Methodist church, and that might well have been the church for her marriage to Simon Jacobs. Methodist missionary activity was strong in the 19th century, and many of the Jacobs clan in Newfoundland were Methodists. There is a Jacobs family Methodist cemetery at Northern Bay in the Bay de Verde District.

From his mother's remarriage Solomon would gain a stepbrother, William Hodder, Jr., who would remain at Sol's side through the adventures at sea over the years to come. As to his education, Sol would have had some familiarity with the church school, but classes there were probably conducted only sporadically. Limited formal education seldom deterred the quick minded, though, and Sol acquired a mastery of the written language that he later deployed as a formidable weapon in legal disputes, frequently on an international scale.

As a son of the Newfoundland shore, Sol would know only one way of life; he would become a fisherman as soon as he was old enough to stand upright in a boat. Fishing at the time was by the time-honored method of baited hook and line. Lead weights would carry the hooks down to the region where the cod congregated. When a cod took the bait, the man at the other end of the line hauled it up, up, over the rail and into the bottom of the boat. One man, one line, one fish. No one had thought of a better way of doing it.

Men fished in small craft, similar no doubt to those largest of the wherries today, the Newfoundland trap skiff. A long, narrow little vessel, often with a wineglass stern, the trap skiff carries one or two gaff-rigged sails, and has a centerboard for easy grounding on a beach. Heading out, the boat that the boy Sol was aboard might pass an inbound vessel. "Arn?" the man handling Sol's boat might call out, enquiring as to whether the others had caught any fish. "Narn," might come the answer, if the others had not caught any, or preferred to keep success to themselves.

It was commonly believed among all fishermen that, if a boy hoped to become a "fitter" or successful master of a fishing boat some day, he must begin to learn the trade at as young an age as possible. As Capt. Joseph W. Collins from Maine put it, "It may ... be stated as a fact that a fisherman never attains to the highest excellence in his profession who has not been accustomed to a sea faring life from early boyhood." That meant going to sea at eight or nine; boys who waited until they were in their teens before being exposed to the life had, it was believed, already been corrupted by the easy life ashore.

Under the rough tutelage of the older fishermen, young Sol would have learned to handle duties on board that became increasingly demanding as he grew and gained strength. In time it would become second nature for him to "lay his hand on any rope in the dark, to steer a vessel at night by the feel of the wind in his face, to ease a vessel in a seaway by an involuntary movement of the hand as it rests upon the helm, to safely enter various harbors, either at night or day, and to know by instinct just what sails to change with varying circumstances." With this early training he would develop quick responses to emergencies, and the composure to make the right decisions when second attempts were not an option.

The apprentice fisherman would also have learned the practical arts of navigating a vessel to where the fish were to be found along the Newfoundland coast, usually within sight of land or in shoal waters offshore. Sol would have first learned to steer from one landmark to the next, then how to relate compass points to the boat's heading, and how to shape a course and measure distance on the charts, and take the bearings of a point of land. To judge the speed of the vessel he would have first learned the old fisherman's way, simply by watching how fast the water flowed past the hull. Later he would master the skill of casting a patent log and counting the knots in the line when it was hauled back in after maybe thirty seconds or a minute.

All that was boat handling and navigation. It would not be lost upon the young fisherman, especially as he grew into his teens, that the men who brought home the most fish were the ones the other men competed to go fishing with. They were the center of storytelling and good laughs and passing a bottle around. And young Sol saw that when the bachelor fishermen were off to a "scoff and a scuff," that is, to a meal followed by dancing, the successful fishermen were the ones who were smiled upon by the best-looking young women in the settlement, sensibly drawn to a good provider.

Sol would observe that one seemingly uncanny talent that distinguished a good fisherman from one who was just average was his ability to sense where the cod would gather to chase the capelin and other small fish. These fed on the plankton teeming in the Labrador Current as it flowed toward the Newfoundland coast. There were those who said that certain fishermen were just plain lucky, or had a sixth sense, or some secret power, or perhaps had made a pact with evil spirits, that told them where the cod would be thickest on a given day. But young Sol soon came to realize that there were no magic incantations involved. It was really a matter of interpreting signs: noting whether the wind was offshore and hence the water warmer which the fish preferred, observing excited activities of storm petrels and gannets over a patch of water, noting the luminescent tracks made by fish swimming alongside the boat at night, developing a minute memory of the ocean bottom especially for wrecks or other objects the fish liked to feed around. Day or night made no difference to the fish, so Sol studied their nocturnal as well as diurnal habits, storing up knowledge of their behavior that in later days would serve him well.

The cod fishery along the Newfoundland shore lasted through the summer, and was the chief enterprise of the Twillingaters. But to survive year round, they needed to be opportunistic in every season. That meant fishing the inland streams for salmon, and trapping beaver for their pelts through the winter. The primary occupation when there were no cod, though, was seal hunting. In February the Atlantic herd of harp seals climbed upon the floes drifting along the northeast coasts of Labrador and Newfoundland, and gave birth to their pups on the ice. In the Twillingate area, when the seals congregated in large numbers to whelp near the shore, men could simply walk out on the ice, shoot the adult seals and drag the carcasses to land. Or they could hunt the seals from small boats.

Unlike the native Beothuk people who had killed seals to eat the meat, the descendants of Europeans were most interested in exporting seal oil that was used for everything from lubricating the gears of machinery to making explosives. The fat was cut from the carcasses, then emptied into vats to be boiled down into oil – a process that was carried on from July into September, and kept the coast settlements thick with smoke and foul odors throughout the summer.

Mature seals yielded much more oil than the pups, the "white noses," which were left to survive until they reached a greater oil-yielding size. (After the 19th century seals came to be valued more for pelts than for oil. In modern day seal hunting, seals that have begun to molt after two weeks are bludgeoned to death by hakapiks, heavy wooden clubs with hammer heads that do not damage the pelts, thus preserving their market value. It is a practice widely deplored, but which continues in order to supply thriving markets for the furs, particularly in Russia and China.)

Twillingaters could consider themselves lucky to have the seals within easy reach. Their neighbors on the southern shores of Newfoundland were off the route of migrating seals. To compete for their share of the seal trade, fishermen of the Avalon Peninsula built small schooners designed to be maneuverable among the ice floes, and set out from St. John's for the whelping grounds in early March. Forty or fifty men would be jammed together below decks under filthy conditions. Then, when they reached the seals, the killing began – the older animals shot and the carcasses dragged back to the vessel. The greatest danger was from the ice that could part and drown a man, or close in on a vessel and crush it, leaving the hunters to starve and freeze hundreds of miles from shelter.

In 1898, Capt. Balfour of the steam sealer *Greenland* sent his men out on the ice despite signs of a storm brewing. The storm did come on and, when the ice shifted, Capt. Balfour could not return to pick up the men. They spent two days and nights on the ice in wind chills of 40 °to 50° below zero. With no shelter the men sang hymns and walked in circles to keep warm because to stop meant almost immediate frozen death. Others, wandering in hopes of finding rescuers, fell through crevices in the ice and disappeared. When the *Greenland* was finally able to reach the men, many would lose fingers and toes, or their feet, to frostbite. Forty-eight men never made it at all. In 1914 alone, 252 seal hunters died, and again many more lost limbs to frostbite.

It was dangerous man's work, and it is unlikely that Sol Jacobs would have shipped aboard a seal boat in his teens. But he probably took part in the "landsmen fishery" – killing seals on the ice off Twillingate harbor. Did the seals have soulful eyes and puppy-like expressions? Any such sentiments would have been lost upon the Newfoundlanders. Here was a resource that was essential to survival in their harsh environment. What's more, the seals competed with them for the cod. And they had a nasty habit of leaping into a small boat and biting a fisherman.

By 1864, economic conditions were bad in Newfoundland. The cod fishery had declined sharply, largely due to a barricading of the coast by sea ice to an extent not seen in the previous twenty years. Exports of dried cod had dropped from 1,138,000 quintals in 1860 to less than 850,000 in 1864. (A quintal was 112 pounds of split and dried codfish ready for market.) The wall of ice devastated the seal fishery as well, and with almost 90% of Newfoundlanders of a population of 162,000 making their livelihood from the fisheries in one way or another, poverty was everywhere. It was especially widespread because the population had increased: in 1864 there were almost five people on Newfoundland for every four who were there in 1857. With no way to earn a living, fishermen and their families survived on government handouts of corn meal and molasses.

The struggles of the fishermen were exacerbated by the sharecropper-like system whereby the merchants advanced food and supplies to the fishermen at high cost in the off season, then paid low prices for the cod when the fishing was good. Many fishing families remained chronically in debt. But the economic collapse of the '60s was sinking all boats; the merchants, too, were in dire straits.

In 1867 Newfoundlanders had a choice between a rock and a hard place. They could remain hard-pinched citizens of a British dominion, or become destitute citizens of a confederation of the Canadian provinces. Delegates met in Charlottetown on Prince Edward Island and, in the course of a boozy convocation, the provinces of Ontario, Quebec, Nova Scotia and New Brunswick voted to approve Confederation, to unite as the federal Dominion of Canada. But Newfoundland refused to join. The island had closer economic ties with England, and even the United States, than with Canada. The islanders did not see Confederation as offering any cure for their own hard times, and Newfoundland remained a separate dominion with its own prime minister. Newfoundland and Labrador would continue in that status throughout Sol Jacobs' lifetime, and for some time thereafter until they agreed to become one of the Canadian provinces in 1949.

But the issue of confederation did not arise until after Sol Jacobs was already long gone from Newfoundland. Conditions in the Hodder household in 1864 would have been no better than among the other families of Twillingate. Sol was now old enough to look after himself, and it appeared unlikely that opportunities for a young fisherman would improve anytime soon. Wise older men on the waterfront warned him that "your paws will never maintain your jaws," which was to say that he would not be able to survive, no matter how hard he worked, under the prevailing conditions.

The question before him was not whether to leave home, but where to go. In the past many Newfoundlanders had migrated south to the "Boston States," by which they meant all of New England. But a move in that direction did not seem like the best option in 1864, with the northern and southern halves of the United States at war with one another.

There was another way out: foreign vessels that put in at St. John's were always looking for deckhands willing to sail for scant wages but secure bunk and board while at sea. So, at age seventeen, Sol Jacobs told his folks he had decided to "give her the long main sheet" – he was leaving Twillingate to go to sea, and likely would not return. Stepfather Bill Hodder would have wished him well: "Fair weather to you and snow to your heels." Sol might have rumpled the hair of the younger Hodder, his half-brother and chum Billy, and said he would send for him by'n'by.

Sol signed on as a hand aboard a British square-rigger loading a cargo of dried cod for a Mediterranean port. His visits back to Newfoundland in the years ahead would be brief, as the master of one American vessel or another. And as a documented American citizen. In his later encounters with Newfoundland fishermen and authorities it became clear that he saw himself as an American sea captain first, and Newfoundlander a distant second.

Of Log Runs and Joinery

ON THE body of water near which John Sloan was born, icebergs were not a problem. Log jams were a more likely hazard in the West Branch Canal that flowed from the Susquehanna River through Lock Haven, a Pennsylvania timber town of scarcely five thousand inhabitants. That number swelled periodically with assorted boisterous loggers and boatmen, as well as the ubiquitous commercial travelers who plied the waterways and railways of 19th century America. When Sloan lived there for his first six years, Lock Haven was the lumber capital of Clinton County.

If there was any similarity whatever between John Sloan's background and that of Solomon Jacobs, it was that the families of each came to North America from the British Isles. Sloan said that the Scottish Presbyterian ancestors of his father, James Dixon Sloan, had been cabinetmakers for generations, and had come to America early in the eighteenth century, settling in Pennsylvania.

When they reached Lock Haven, shouldered by ridges of the Appalachians and distant from the population centers along the coast, they were among their fellow Scots-Irish. These lowland Scots had migrated to Ireland in the 17th century when cheap land was available there as spoils of war, and then to North America a century later. By that time the best lands in the coastal colonies of British North America had already been claimed by expatriate English, as well as some Dutch and Swedes, so many of the newcomers moved west to the Appalachians as frontiersmen. The coastal descendants of the English, relatively even in temperament, viewed their mountain neighbors as contemptuous to authority, argumentative, inflexible in their opinions, and unapologetically individualistic. John Sloan, as he matured, came to fit that profile to a T.

John Sloan's family name, like that of Solomon Jacobs, was patronymic. It is an Anglicized form of an Old Gaelic personal name, Sluaghadhan, which meant leader of an expedition. As a surname Sloan, or Sloane, is widespread in Scotland and Northern Ireland. It was the easy availability of malleable woods that induced the cabinet-making Sloan clan to settle in Lock Haven, and that was where John Sloan was born in 1871. In the 1870s memories of the Civil War would still be raw in the town. Two of the decisive battles – at Gettysburg and Hanover – had been fought in southern Pennsylvania. John Sloan's father had served in the Union Army until he was invalided home with typhoid. As a small boy John would have seen the veterans back in town, some with blank stares, others missing limbs. The darkest side of war would have been impressed upon him early.

John's mother, who taught English at a "young ladies' academy" in Lock Haven, was born Henrietta Ireland. The English relations of her Philadelphia family were prosperous paper manufacturers and stationers in Leeds, the commercial and cultural center of West Yorkshire. They were of the opinion that she had wed beneath her when she married James Sloan. All parties were hopeful that her husband would carry on the family's cabinetmaking business successfully.

But woodworking was no longer a craftsman's trade. Mass production of furniture had come to dominate the industry after the Civil War. Grand Rapids, Michigan, became "Furniture City" in the 1870s, a center of machine-manufactured furniture designed to appeal to Victorian tastes. It became increasingly difficult to convince middle-class families that hand-crafted furniture was superior to factory-built imitations. As another handicap, James Sloan never did have a head for business. His problems were compounded by the crash of 1873. He took out a loan from his brother to save the family company, putting up his and Henrietta's home as collateral. He defaulted on the loan, lost the house, and moved to Philadelphia in 1876 with the household which consisted then of Henrietta, young John, and John's sisters Elizabeth and Marianna.

Through family connections James Sloan took a job as a traveling salesman, selling books and greeting cards for Marcus Ward & Co. But he was no silver-tongued peddler, and his wife's family next set him up in a small stationery enterprise. Business was slow at the shop so James Sloan had time for hobbies. He was always better at working with his hands than with his head. He dabbled in print-making, drawing and painting on china. He was skilled with his hands and with using tools, too, as might be expected of a descendant of woodworkers. That aptitude passed on to son John, who would later relax by crafting cupboards and shelves for what space was available in cramped New York apartments he shared with his wife.

John Sloan said later that he and his sisters knew that his parents had to scrimp, but there was always enough for the basic comforts. And John could plan to go on to higher education. He was home-schooled in his early years. His parents both had a passion for books, and John would later say that he had read his way through all of Shakespeare and Dickens by the time he was twelve. A relative on his mother's side, a paper industry inventor, introduced Sloan to the possibilities of what a pen and an engraver's stylus could do in deftly portraying figures and situations. "My great-uncle Alexander Priestley had a wonderful library with folios of Hogarth and Cruickshank." Sloan became familiar early with Cruickshank's caricatures of English society and Hogarth's fierce satires in the "Rake's Progress" and "Marriage à la Mode" series, the graphic novels of their day.

John left home-schooling for Philadelphia's Central High School in advance of college. Also in the class were Albert Barnes, who would become a wealthy art collector, and William Glackens. Glackens later became a personal and fellow-painter friend of Sloan's for life, although their styles would diverge. Sloan did not get to know Glackens and Barnes well at Central High, though. He was a loner at that age, bookish, with no interest in sports, hunting, fishing or any of the mischiefs that brought boys together.

At home, things were getting worse. James Sloan failed in his stationery business. The anguished father called his sixteen-year-old son aside to tell John that he would have to drop out of school and go to work to help support the family. All plans for higher education were dashed.

A boy typically idolizes his father, and that idol was now tarnished. It was the late nineteenth century, a time in America when opportunities seemed unlimited, when any man with zeal and a desire to succeed was expected to overcome all obstacles and make a success of himself. James Sloan had fallen under the wheels of the economy, and thereafter John regarded his father with kindly pity, perhaps wondering if the wartime typhoid had wrung the spunk out of him. James Sloan became a marginalized figure in the family, lingering on ineffectually. Very likely through the paper industry connections of his mother's family, John took a job as assistant cashier at Porter & Coates, a leading Philadelphia dealer in books and prints. The firm had once published fine editions of Shakespeare and Jules Verne, but by Sloan's time had turned to putting out cheap editions of Horatio Alger's rags-to-riches novels. The teen-age John Sloan found working life there agreeable, more compatible in fact than the discipline of a school. There was time to explore fine books, of which there were many more than in the family library at home. He read Balzac and Zola in translation, and said he gathered from their work, and from that of Dickens, a broad view of life – which he failed to find in the "realistic" – that is, commonplace – novels of American authors like William Dean Howells.

He browsed through collections of etchings by Dürer and Rembrandt, making pen and ink sketches of them that he sold for $5.00 apiece – a handy supplement to his $6.00 a week salary. He would say later that he had "drifted into art as a way to make a living." If so, he did some very purposeful drifting. He studied Hamerton's *Etcher's Handbook* to teach himself how to burn lines into plates with acid. He took freehand drawing classes at night at Philadelphia's Spring Garden Institute. He studied John Collier's *Manual of Oil Painting*, learning how to think in color.

A. Edward Newton, assistant in the Porter & Coates print department, had ambitions to form his own fancy goods company, and lured Sloan to join his staff at the new firm. It proved to be a lateral career move for the young apprentice, with no real advancement and an unexpected job hazard. There were twenty young women in Newton's shop, all painting designs on giftware, and they terrified Sloan who as a young man was socially and sexually awkward. For Newton he designed calendars, "match scratchers," and "etchings of the homes of poets," but still did not earn enough to support himself and contribute to family expenses. So two years later, when he was twenty, John Sloan rented a tiny studio in downtown Philadelphia and set himself up as a freelance commercial artist.

This was the start of his career as an illustrator. For the next twenty-some years that would be how he would think of himself: an illustrator by profession who painted in his spare time in pursuit of self-realization as an artist. Illustration would be the backbone of some of his best work. The fledgling freelancer trained himself to become an accomplished practitioner of the "poster style" popular in the 1890s. He said, "I was fortunate in having been brought up on books illustrated by Walter Crane, who had a fine sense of classical form, a very robust sense of the classical spirit." Crane was an English painter and children's book illustrator who worked in the ornamental style of the Pre-Raphaelites. Sloan learned from Japanese prints, too, and met a Japanese artist, Beizen Zubota, who gave him lessons in brush technique.

Sloan took whatever assignments he could land, designing ads, certificates, flyers. His steadiest client was the Bradley Coal Company. Bradley supplied the coal for the stove in his studio, and a little cash besides, for the streetcar ads he designed for the company in black and white poster style. He wrote the captions, too, in playful verse.

John Sloan's attempt to become self-supporting in his little studio did not work out. One of his uncles on his mother's side tried to be helpful by sending him an introduction to the manager of the Philadelphia Engraving Company. But, struggling as he was, Sloan never made use of the letter. He said later he thought it would "take me away from doing my own work." In convoluted reasoning by which he attempted to conceal from himself his underlying drive to become a painter, he said that it "wasn't that I had ambition to be an artist, but a kind of negative decision — to protect some kind of talent."

In 1892 Sloan finally abandoned his first attempt to survive by freelancing. He landed on his feet, thanks to his streetcar ads for the coal company. They earned him a job in the art department of the *Philadelphia Inquirer*. The twenty-one-year-old who took up his drawing board in the cluttered offices of the *Inquirer* had become very much his own man, independent, opinionated, self-educated, confident in his talent.

Like Solomon Jacobs, John Sloan was a young man on the make. In the case of each there was no father to turn to for affirmation and advice. Sol's father had died. Sloan's father was still alive, but not in any way relevant to his son's ambitions. Sloan and Jacobs were both on their own.

Chapter Two

APPRENTICES TO OBSOLESCENCE

Education Aloft / College of the Artist Reporters

Education Aloft

IN 1865, a year after Sol Jacobs signed on as a hand aboard a British vessel, he was in the port of New York. How had he arrived there? His whereabouts during that year are obscure. Late in life, he apparently told a newspaper reporter that he had crewed on a packet ship of the Black Ball line in the '60s. This seems to be the only time he included any such mention in his *curriculum vitae*. On another occasion Sol said he got his early training from "down east" skippers, presumably on the merchant ships that he sailed in from the time he reached New York until he left the merchantmen for Gloucester. If he had received prior training under the brutal conditions typical of a packet ship, it seems odd that he did not speak of that experience in other interviews.

If indeed Sol did sail on a Black Ball packet in the '60s, he would have found his way to Liverpool, and boarded, say, the *Alexander Marshall*, the *William F. Storer*, the *Hamilton Fish*, or the *Charles H. Marshall*. All were stout square-riggers close to 200 feet in length, and all would be sold out of packet service in 1878 when the Black Ball line finally accepted the impossibility of competing with steamships, and closed down.

In 1864 the sailing packets had long been in their twilight years. The Black Ball line came into being in 1818 when a group of New York textile importers conceived the idea of operating a shipping line between that city and Liverpool with vessels which would sail on dependable, advertised departure dates. The idea appealed to shippers, and soon prime cargo as well as the mails, cabin passengers, and shipments of specie were crossing the Atlantic on Black Ballers and several competing lines of sailing packets.

By the late '40s, the faster clipper ships and more dependable steam freighters were luring away the packet captains. The decisive blow came in 1848 when Samuel Cunard initiated regular steamship service between Liverpool and New York, in direct competition with the sailing packets. Thereafter, the better class of freight and passengers, as well as the mails and specie shipments, jumped ship to take passage on the steamers.

By 1864 the sailing packets had been reduced to carrying a few immigrant passengers in steerage, and low-value bulk cargo. The loss of status led inevitably to a loss of pride. The quality of the officers and crew of sailing packets, and of the vessels, declined precipitously. Packet speeds, which had peaked in the late '40s and early '50s, thereafter lagged as the vessels aged. Captains had to strive harder to maintain schedules, and drove their mates to extract every last ounce of labor from members of the crew. As Herman Melville wrote in his novel *Redburn*, "The crew have terrible hard work, owing to their carrying such a press of sail, in order to make as rapid passages as possible, and sustain the ship's reputation for speed."

In the '60s Sol would have found himself crewmate to a company of "packet rats" whom Capt. Samuel Samuels described as "the toughest class of men in all respects. They could stand the worst weather, food, and usage, and put up with less sleep, more rum, and harder knocks than any other sailors. ... They had not the slightest idea of morality or honesty, and gratitude was not in them. The dread of the belaying pin or heavier kept them in submission." If, indeed, young Sol Jacobs had been a "Johnny Haultight" on a Black Baller, as the newspaper reporter said, he was probably happy to leave his packet ship experience behind him once he reached New York.

He signed on as one of the crew of the American ship *General Berry*. By now, in 1865, 18-year-old seaman Sol would be a seasoned hand aboard a square-rigger, developing his powerful physique as he carried out orders as a deckhand, in such body-building exercises as turning a windlass. He would be perfectly confident aloft now, ready at any hour day or night to hop to at the mate's whistle and scramble up the ratlines to join the other deckhands wrestling with the sails. Always they climbed with the wind behind them, so that the fierce blasts would blow them toward the mast and not into space.

Once a sail was furled up to its yard they made their way out along the footrope under the yard. With one hand on the jackstay, the rail along the top of the yard, they spilled the air out of the sail and lashed it tight against the yard. It was brutal work under the best of conditions, complicated mightily in rough weather when, with the deck veering crazily 90 feet below, they sought to tame a loose sail. A sail was a lethal menace if it flapped out of control, especially when frozen stiff in bitter temperatures and every line and foothold was coated with ice. Judging from the agility aloft he displayed throughout his career, Sol was probably one of those who nonchalantly slid down a stay as the quickest way back to the deck. (Years later, in his 60s in 1909, he was at his ease standing masthead watch when he was master of the auxiliary schooner *Benjamin A. Smith*.)

The *General Berry* had been built two years earlier for Joseph Hill, and was owned by Hill and the Watts brothers, Samuel and James. She was a classic Maine-built down-easter of 1,197 tons. (Tonnage is the measure of a ship's carrying capacity, not its weight.) With larger and deeper hulls, the down-easters were the more practical successors to the celebrated clipper ships of the China trade that were sleek and swift but had limited cargo space. The sail plan of the down-easters was simplified, too, so fewer crewmen were needed to work the vessel. From the close of the Civil War until steam became dominant late in the 19th century, down-easters were in demand as workhorses of trade.

Thomaston was a center of down-easter shipbuilding, and the *General Berry* was built in one of the busiest yards, that of shipbuilder-owner-captain Samuel Watts. Born in 1813, Watts had gone to sea at nineteen, shipping as cook in the brig *Pensacola*. By the time he was twenty-five he was sailing as master of brigs, barks and finally full-rigged ships. Soon he was building his own large vessels, first in association with another leading Thomaston shipbuilder and then together with his brother. They built large ships and schooners for nearly thirty years, all in all launching twenty-four ships, plus a bark and seventeen schooners. Watts was the managing owner of six other vessels as well.

Stately down-easters under Watts management plied the sea lanes to the major ports of Boston, New York, San Francisco, New

Orleans, Liverpool and Antwerp. Samuel Watts prospered, and augmented his shipyard earnings by investing in the railroads being pushed into the American West. By the time of his death at eighty-seven, Samuel Watts was one of the wealthiest and most honored sons of Thomaston. It would not be lost upon young Sol Jacobs toiling on the decks of the *General Berry* that opportunities did exist down in the Boston States for an able seagoing man.

The *General Berry* was named for Major General Hiram Berry, an officer in the Union Army who had been born in Thomaston. General Berry had been mortally wounded at Chancellorsville in 1863. It was said, as is often the case, that he exhorted his troops with a memorable quotation just before he expired. "Have hearts like oak," he beseeched them, "And let the Stars and Stripes wave high." It was no surprise that the next fine vessel based in Thomaston would bear the name of this local hero.

The ship was probably also named with the bark *General Berry* in mind. That splendid vessel, launched in 1847, the year of Sol Jacobs' birth, had carried the American flag into ports across the globe under the command of Capt. Nathan Seavey. A painting in the manner of Joseph Badger shows the *Berry* entering the harbor at Genoa. To his undoubted chagrin, Capt. Seavey had also been in command when the *Berry* was captured and burned by the Confederate raider *C.S.S. Florida* off Maryland's Eastern Shore in 1864.

Seaman Jacobs, on the successor *Berry*, was thus aboard a vessel strongly identified with the sentiments of the North in the Civil War. He would have been regularly reminded by his shipmates that the war, which they called "The Rebellion," was fought by the Union armies primarily to keep the United States whole, as against those who wished to splinter the nation asunder. And, yes, they had fought to end slavery, but that was still a subject of some discussion on board – emancipation was not broadly endorsed by the commercial interests of New England. But the consolidation of the United States had been reconfirmed, and Solomon Jacobs would always sail on American flag vessels thereafter.

The next year, 1866, Sol was one of the crew of the ship *Western Empire*. That great all-wood, all-sail 1,397-ton down-easter, close to 192 feet long, was the largest vessel built in Abner Stetson's shipyard in Damariscotta, Maine. Launched in 1852 she was first based in Boston, sailing for over a decade in the cotton trade for the Pelican Line. When Solomon Jacobs signed on, *Western Empire* called New York her home port, where she was owned by George Howes of that city. Her captain, J. F. Grozier, regularly sailed with his wife in the captain's cabin: eight years earlier their daughter Adella had been born at sea on the *Western Empire*.

Crewman Jacobs was a quick learner under the iron discipline of the merchant marine, and here was his one mention of his on-the-job training: "I got my early training from 'down east' skippers, who tied insubordinate members of the crew to the mizzen mast and lashed them into submission. It was a hard school and thorough one."

Discipline aside, conditions were attractive aboard the down-easters for men like Sol who reveled in the life at sea. The food was good and the officers were fanatical about keeping the vessel in superb sailing condition. Everybody aboard knew that slipshod maintenance of the standing rigging that held up the masts and yards, and the running rigging that controlled the sails, could lead to disaster in a heavy blow. A fine vessel demanded constant care, and the crew members were kept at it, holystoning pine decks with sandstone blocks, oiling the planks, coating them with coal tar, scrubbing them until they shone. Sailing into foreign harbors, Sol Jacobs and his shipmates could take pride in their shipshape American down-easters. Their sails were gleaming white, made of cotton duck. By contrast, most sailing vessels of other nationalities carried dingy-looking flax sails.

In the next record we find of Sol Jacobs, he had moved up in the world. He was now second mate on the *J. S. Winslow*, on what may have been the first voyage of that vessel, to Savannah in 1869, probably for a cargo of cotton. J. S. Winslow & Co. of Portland had built the new 524-ton bark, 128 feet long, at Westbrook, Maine.

The life of the builder and owner, Jacob S. Winslow, had been another maritime bootstrap story like that of Samuel Watts. Born in 1827, Winslow went to sea as a common seaman at fourteen and was master of a brig before he was twenty-one. After several commands for other companies, he built his own bark, the *Philena*, which he named for his wife, and sailed the vessel for six years carrying cargoes to Europe and the West Indies.

Then Winslow came ashore to concentrate on shipbuilding, and eventually built more than a hundred vessels at his three shipyards in and near Portland. He owned a ship chandlery, too, to sell every type of article a down-easter might require at sea. In 1877 he went into politics – as a Republican of course, in Maine in those times. He was twice elected as a representative from Portland to the Maine state legislature.

The *Winslow*, one of the company's fleet of barks painted white from stem to stern, was frequently employed in the cotton trade, now that southern markets were again open to northern vessels. On a route known as the "cotton triangle," vessels sailed out of New York either in ballast or carrying merchandise to southern ports such as Charleston, Savannah, Mobile or New Orleans. There they loaded cotton for transport across the Atlantic to Liverpool, or perhaps to Le Havre for a French consignee. They would then return to New York carrying general freight, and often European immigrants as well.

There were many variations in the routes, depending upon the winds of trade. The itinerary of the *Winslow* with Sol Jacobs as second mate suggests how diverse the peregrinations of a hard-working down-easter might be. The *Winslow* sailed south from Savannah on December 30, 1869 and arrived in Buenos Aires on March 6, 1870. Capt. D. O. Davis was her master, and would continue in command of the vessel for the next five years. Three months later the *Winslow* left the Argentine and made for New York, arriving on July 29th. A month later she shifted to Philadelphia to pick up a cargo for Antwerp. She set sail on September 3rd and, after an Atlantic crossing that took just over a month, arrived in the Belgian port. There she laid over for a month before Capt. Davis cast off and returned across the ocean, arriving in Boston on New Year's day, 1871. Next the *Winslow* sailed to New Orleans to load 1,520 bales of cotton, and departed that port on April 28, 1871, crossing the Atlantic once again to make delivery in Amsterdam on June 12.

By August *J. S. Winslow* was in Teesport, the deepwater port for Middlesbrough, England. It was one of that nation's three largest ports. The vessel departed on August 4th, arriving in New York on September 15. After a quick turnaround she cast off again for Antwerp, arrived and turned around for a run to Boston on December 11, arriving March 30, 1872. It was an unrelenting schedule, with weeks on end on the high seas. Presumably it was after the *Winslow* arrived in Boston in late March that mate Solomon Jacobs decided to make the trip up the shore to Gloucester for a look at the fisheries. If Sol Jacobs had remained with the *Winslow* he might have been assured of steady employment in the carrying trade. The J. S. Winslow Company went on to become one of the most prominent coastal freighting companies on the east coast. By 1910 J. S. Winslow had a fleet of thirty-four schooners, including five of the nine six-masters afloat, several 5-masters, several 4-masters, and a number of "3-stickers." By then, in the age of steam, it was still economical to ship coal and other commodities in these great vessels. Into the early decades of the 20th century the down-easters with their billowing sails continued to be a dramatic sight as they moved majestically along the coast.

But Sol Jacobs had decided that a career in the American merchant marine was not for him. He had gotten into the deep water service ten years too late. Back in the 1850s clipper ships built in the yards of East Boston and New York had been proud symbols of maritime America in ports across the Pacific and the Far East. But during the Civil War the policy of the Confederacy to use armed raiders to destroy Northern shipping was successful far beyond the heavy amount of tonnage sent to the bottom. Insurance rates soared 900% and ship owners responded by placing hundreds of cargo vessels under foreign registry. After the war the U.S. government refused to repatriate those vessels.

Their loss, on top of the toll taken by the Confederate raiders, and the useless condition of many American vessels that had rotted in foreign ports during the war, cut in half the number of merchant ships that had sailed into the world's harbors under American registry before hostilities began. The nation's merchant marine would thereafter operate largely under proxy flags.

Still, many down-easters continued to fly the American banner. These all-sail vessels were floating anachronisms – forced to prove to skeptical shippers that they could carry cargoes at greater profit than steamships. As with the sailing packet lines, owners of down-easter fleets impressed upon their captains the need to economize, and the masters recognized that one expense category where they could realize savings was labor. Hence the goal was to get the most work out of the smallest number of crewmen. It became the age of "bully captains and bucko mates," when domineering ships' officers drove their men hard and brooked no opposition.

In this environment many native Maine crewmen, and those from the Maritime Provinces, rebelled and were attracted to new jobs opening up in industries ashore. Or they traveled farther yet from the sea to seek their fortunes in the beckoning American and Canadian West, where land was cheap and the Indian tribes had been largely subjugated.

Those sailors in the old Northeast maritime labor pool had shared essentially the same language and culture. They were replaced by crewmen from every nation, speaking many tongues. The need for strict discipline intensified and brutal mates were more than willing to oblige. Sol Jacobs did not fit in this environment of sadistic discipline; he would always get the most his crewmen had to offer by challenging them to follow his lead, not by bullying them into resentful obedience.

Sol had been fortunate so far in sailing in good ships under strict but fair captains. But his luck might not hold out on his next voyage. Also, it was unlikely that he could ever own a significant stake in the larger and more expensive vessels entering the coasting trade. Even twenty years before, a one forty-eighth share of a full-rigged ship at Castine was priced at $895, so high as to discourage any but the most affluent investor. The same money would buy full ownership of a good used fishing schooner.

The days when a Samuel Watts or a Jacob Winslow could work his way up from the forecastle ("focsle") to become owner of a fleet of down-easters had passed. It was time for an ambitious, independent-minded, sometimes rashly self-confident young seaman to seek his future elsewhere.

College of the Artist-Reporters

CAPTAINS WATTS and Winslow proved to Solomon Jacobs that it was possible to go from penniless to prominent in a robust

America. John Sloan had no role models as such. A fellow artist who influenced his life and career again and again was Robert Henri. But Sloan always saw Henri as a painter friend, never someone to emulate. They met after Sloan had been hired as one of the staff artists at the *Philadelphia Inquirer*. Here Sloan was finally in his element. For the first time in his life he was among men who thought the way he did. They were irreverent, practical-joking, extravagant personalities who shared a certain smugness in knowing that they were very good at what they did.

The art room of a major newspaper in the 1890s was as important to the success of the paper as the editorial department. It did not matter in the least to the art staffers of the *Inquirer* that the paper's stance on national issues and Philadelphia politics was conservative. That had little to do with the street news the reporter-artists of its art department covered. The *Inquirer* had been a liberal paper before the Civil War, but had leaned increasingly to the right as the century wore on. In 1889 the paper was purchased by publisher James Elverson who adopted the latest printing technology, expanded the staff, initiated a Sunday edition and moved the paper twice to new and larger buildings. It was in this era of growth and success for the *Inquirer* that Sloan worked at the paper.

The young artist-reporters he worked with, skilled in deft, rapid sketching in pen and ink, were dispatched to the scenes of the big-city news stories that sold newspapers: fires, murders, building collapses, criminal trials, street accidents involving runaway horses. Sloan's old classmate from Philadelphia's Central High, Bill Glackens, was a star of the staff. Others were George Luks and Everett Shinn. Glackens was particularly adept as a fast-response artist reporter who could work wonders producing an illustration for a headline story in time for the next edition. He had trained his memory to record every detail in a scene. Back at the newsroom he could retrieve the minutiae of buildings at the site, the position of the murder victim and what he or she was wearing, details of the damage to a trolley car knocked off the tracks, the specific windows of a warehouse from which flames were shooting.

Shinn, who harbored higher worldly ambitions, and Luks, hard-drinking and flamboyant, did not have Glackens' photographic memory, but were capably quick and accurate at capturing a crime scene. While the others were facile and worked rapidly, Sloan was more methodical. The *art nouveau* poster style that he had polished in his streetcar ads for the coal company proved to be eminently suitable for daily feature pages and the Sunday supplement. The editor of the art department gave him time to "work out abstract problems of design, line, arabesques," as Sloan said.

The poster style had originated in France and was reconstituted in England by Aubrey Beardsley to reflect the esthetics of Oscar Wilde. The style made many people uneasy. It was associated with the stylized art of the Pre-Raphaelites and with Bloomsbury Group decadence. Hugh Kenner said that Beardsley was "never quite wholesome," but his sense of line and design was "irrefutable ... rendered with such astonishing technique." Sloan said, "I myself do not care for the kind of decadent and bizarre quality in [Beardsley's] work. I prefer the wholesome kind of humor that comes out in ribaldry." Will Bradley was the foremost American designer in the poster style, integrating elements of *art nouveau* and Japanese block prints into his designs. Sloan was probably familiar with Bradley's work.

Working in the style, Sloan said "I made illustrations for serialized stories, headings for feature articles on the Women's Page, advertisements for such products as Lydia B. Pinkham's tonic, and decorative pictures for the sections on Sports, Vacations, etc." Unlike some of the veteran staff artists who still drew on chalk plates, Sloan drew pen and ink illustrations that appeared as line cuts in the newspaper.

For the first time in his life Sloan was no longer a loner. He was sharing a workplace and a social life with his fellow artists. He and Glackens and other members of the *Inquirer* art department "used to go out on Sundays in the neighborhood of Philadelphia," he said, to try their hand at painting outdoors. Sloan took a night class at the Pennsylvania Academy of Fine Arts taught by Thomas Anshutz, protégé of that founder of the Philadelphia painting tradition, Thomas Eakins. But Sloan soon tired of academic training, of drawing plaster casts under Anshutz.

As a working newspaper illustrator he was attracted by the possibilities of color and form on canvas, but was repelled by the rigid traditionalism that then ruled the academic art world in America. He would subscribe to Anatole France's theory about academies: "Old men hold far too obstinately to their own ideas. That is why the natives of the Fiji Islands kill their parents when they grow old. In this way they facilitate evolution, while we retard its advance by founding Academies."

It was at a party given at the studio of Charles Grafly, then a sculpture instructor at the Pennsylvania Academy of Fine Arts, that Sloan first met Robert Henri. Henri had just returned from a painting excursion to France with Grafly. He was twenty-seven in 1892, just six years older than Sloan, but he already had the cachet of a well-traveled, well-trained artist who was confidently on a trajectory to fame.

Henri had begun his training at the Pennsylvania Academy of Art in 1886. A year later he and Grafly left for Paris where Henri enrolled in the popular Académie Julian. Thus began a love affair with Paris that would take Henri back there twice for a total of six years. In 1891 he had returned to Philadelphia to give courses in landscape painting at the Philadelphia School of Design for Women.

It was said that Henri "taught all day and talked all night," especially after he fell in with the artist-reporter crowd from the *Inquirer*. Henri and the awkward, intense, outspoken young John Sloan took an immediate liking to one another. Sloan told Henri that he painted for amusement with no idea of making art. Henri refused to accept that self-deprecating disclaimer. He said Sloan could be a real artist – his illustrations for the *Inquirer* proved he had the talent. He urged Sloan to paint the everyday life he and the other *Inquirer* artists knew so well as newspapermen: scenes of street life, theatres, restaurants.

Henri said the stuff of art was to be found in the artist's immediate environment – not in musty academic formulas imposed for so long by the National Academy of Design. He talked about the great works of Realism he had seen in Europe – not to be imitated, but to serve as an inspiration for new American works of self-discovery and inspiration. Henri's idols were Manet, Goya, Degas, Renoir, Velázquez, Hals and Rembrandt.

Henri's epigrammatic talk was exhilarating to Sloan and the other artist-reporters on the *Inquirer*, eager for an alternative to Anshutz's conventional art instruction. "What we need is more sense of the wonder of life, and less of the business of making a picture," Henri told them. He fired their imaginations with visions of the artistic life: "I am interested in art as a means of living a life; not as a means of making a living." Heady stuff, and creativity must be accompanied by dramatic agony, the romantic pain these men must be willing to endure to achieve fulfillment: "a work of art is the trace of a magnificent struggle." One element in Henri's teachings was of particular interest to John Sloan: "because we are saturated with life, because we are human, our strongest motive is life, humanity ..." John Sloan would come to put more humanity into his paintings than did his preceptor, but Henri's influence upon him was profound. Years later Sloan would say of Henri, "In Philadelphia in the nineties, there was a group of newspaper artists, plain and rather normal young men making their livings as craftsmen – and we became painters because Robert Henri had that magic ability as a teacher which inspires and provokes his followers into action. He was a catalyst; he was an emancipator, liberating American art from its youthful academic conformity, and liberating the individual artist from repressions that held back his natural creative ability."

Henri began to invite the *Inquirer* illustrators – Sloan, Glackens, Luks, Shinn – to his studio several nights a week where they would draw from a model and he would critique their efforts. They called it the Charcoal Club. Henri was elected president and John Sloan secretary. The Charcoal Club lasted for only a few months, and it would be another five years before John Sloan began to paint seriously. Still, the confidence and optimism inspired by charismatic Robert Henri on the frontier of a new American art would encourage Sloan to believe in his own potential.

After three years with the *Inquirer* John Sloan moved to the *Philadelphia Press* in 1895, where he joined Glackens, Luks and Shinn who had made the move before him. The *Press* was also a conservative newspaper – its editor, Charles Emory Smith, was active in Republican politics. But as with the *Inquirer*, the *Press* art staff was insulated from editorial policy. The art editor of the *Press*, Edward

Wyatt Davis, liked Sloan's *art nouveau* poster style.

Actually, Sloan's poster style work was intrinsically different from that of Beardsley and Bradley. The women in Sloan's poster style illustrations – appearing in the Sunday supplements of the *Press* – were not the unconvincing female images that appeared in the *Yellow Book*. They were, by contrast, distinctly feminine and coquettish. While John Sloan carved a niche for himself as a skilled illustrator in the poster style, *art nouveau* had no real appeal for him. He distanced himself entirely from this vogue in his Urban Realism prints and paintings a few years hence.

And he immersed himself in studying the works of the illustrators he really admired. Significantly, they were the ones most interested in conveying the human dimension. He said, "I rate Hogarth as the greatest English artist who ever lived. ...He found a kind of beauty in life through his interest in real character." Of Théophile Steinlen Sloan said, "I liked the humanism with which he drew people." The French illustrator Steinlen was, like Toulouse Lautrec, famous for his posters of cabaret and music hall performers. He also drew the life of the underclass in Montmartre.

And then there was Honoré Daumier. Daumier's political lithographs were satire at its most scalding. But in his paintings, virtually undiscovered until after his death, Daumier revealed compassion and recognition of the human dignity of his working-class subjects. The French Impressionist Jean-Louis Forain said not long after Daumier died, "Ah – he was different from us. *He had a heart.*" Daumier was a pioneer in Realism, shunned sentimentality, and imbued his paintings with the human warmth that Sloan admired.

Sloan later said that these years at the *Press* were his college years. If so, the social pursuits were distinctly sophomoric. Once a week "the gang" of artist-reporters met at Henri's studio, which Sloan had taken over after Henri left on one of his pilgrimages to Paris. These nonacademic fraternity brothers passed the evenings in fervent discussions, games and elaborate skits as they dined on welsh rarebit lubricated with Falstaffian quantities of beer.

One of the subjects of discussion was inevitably religion, and Sloan stirred things up as an uncompromising free-thinker who espoused the agnosticism of Robert G. Ingersoll, and Darwin's evolutionary theories. Although raised an Episcopalian (the American version of the Church of England faith to which his mother's family adhered), he now dismissed all belief in the supernatural as superstition. In the future he would have little to say about religion, being more engrossed in art and politics.

By 1897, with improvements in photo processing, it became possible for newspapers to reproduce halftone news photos on printing presses running at full speed. The artist-reporters faced the cold reality that soon there would no longer be any market for their pre-photographic skills. John Sloan was not immediately affected because there was still some demand for his Sunday Supplement art. But the writing was on the wall: he could no longer look forward to a future in newspaper illustration.

Chapter Three

REDIRECTED LIVES

~~~

A Born Fisherman / Drawings for a "Light-Weight Dickens"

A Born Fisherman

JOHN SLOAN found himself working in an illustrating specialty that was being overtaken by new methods. Sol Jacobs decided he did not want to commit his future to the declining down-easter trade. Each man needed to make a mid-course correction.

In 1872 twenty-five-year-old merchant seaman Solomon Jacobs swung his sea bag off his shoulder onto the dock in Gloucester. He had decided to go fishing in the Gloucester fleet. The men off the boats that Solomon Jacobs chatted with those first days on shore must have told him he was crazy to give up the relatively comfortable and safe life on a down-easter to go fishing.

No doubt about it, he would be opting for a harder life. The ten or a dozen men – and the captain – in a fishing schooner of the 1870s slept in close quarters in the focsle, worked side by side when on board or as dorymates setting a trawl, were forever sloshing through water and fish gurry on deck. At sea they seldom if ever dried out, had a change of clothes, had opportunity to use a bar of soap or a toothbrush. It was a harshly physical life with fatal chance lurking everywhere, from a swinging boom, a parting stay, a rogue wave towering over the stern, the high prow of an oncoming vessel suddenly lurching out of the fog.

But Jacobs was young and vigorous. He thrived on the outdoor life at sea. And he was at heart a fisherman. He bore the imprint of his fishermen ancestors, and that was the calling in which he had received his essential early training. Life on a fishing schooner held no terrors for him and he liked the looks of these Gloucester boats that had evolved into wonderful vehicles for bringing big trips of fish to market in record time. They were built for speed, carrying impressive amounts of canvas, knifing through the seas handsomely. They had revolutionized the cod and mackerel fisheries, and gave Gloucester a preeminence in the industry that the port would enjoy for the next quarter century.

A case in point was the schooner *Laughing Water* under Capt. Joe Goslin. In eleven trips back and forth to Georges Bank for cod she cleared nearly $18,000. One of the fishermen aboard took home over $1,100 as his share, and the cook a couple of hundred more. Gloucester schooners in the haddock fishery were thriving as well. The *Angie S. Friend*, under Capt. McLain, had "stocked," or earned $7,700 in five months of fishing, paying each member of the crew about $550. These had to be attractive numbers to Sol. And the competitor in him liked the idea of rewards based on effort, rather than the set wages in the merchant marine.

There was no doubt that this town had a place for a man like Sol Jacobs. Gloucester offered more berths for willing fishermen than any other port on the Gulf of Maine, or anywhere up and down the Atlantic coast for that matter. Back in 1862 Gloucester had counted only 317 vessels in the fisheries. Now the harbor teemed with vessels, 517 of which called Gloucester their home port. There were six vessels engaged in foreign trade, towering brigantines among them. Ninety sloops, pinkeys and small schooners shipped goods along the shore in the coasting trade. And there was one yacht.

But the preponderance of the vessels of the port, 420 of them, went after fish. Fishing paid as never before. In the year Sol Jacobs arrived, 1872, the value of fish landed in Gloucester approached $3 ½ million, with cod accounting for over $2 million of the total.

The productivity of each schooner fishing for cod and other ground fish had increased exponentially, thanks to a technological innovation. Up until Civil War days fishing for cod was done by men lining the deck of a schooner and dropping baited lines, just as when Sol Jacobs fished as a boy in Newfoundland waters. But during the 1860s vessel owners turned increasingly to sending men out in dories to lay tub trawls. Each trawl line, buoyed by a wooden tub, was armed with thousands of hooks that yielded far more fish than could be caught the old way. Under the combined influences of tub trawling, refinements in schooner design, and the swelling of demand for fish during the Civil War, the value of fish landings quadrupled between 1859 and 1872.

But there were serious downsides to being a Gloucester fisherman – as newspaper reports of lost vessels and lost men testified. The schooners were dangerous vessels to sail in for a number of reasons. Typically 80 to 100 feet long, 20 or so feet in width, drawing just eight or nine feet below the waterline, they were liable to be knocked over in a gale of wind. Or swamped by a great sea rising over the stern. A year before Jacobs' arrival, 1871, had been one of the most devastating for the Gloucester fleet. Nineteen vessels had been lost at a cost of 140 lives. In one storm on Georges Bank in February of that year, ten crewmen perished when the schooner *Hiawatha* went down, and another eleven died when the schooner *E. L. Cook* sank. Twenty-one fishermen gone, twenty-one empty places at supper tables back in town.

There were more reminders of the power of the sea all around the coast of Cape Ann that year. The shore had been littered with wrecks. The schooner *Jane* from Boston hit on the Squam bar and all hands were lost when their dory overturned. The schooner *William H. Dennis*, from Philadelphia for Salem, struck on rocks outside Rockport harbor on the northeast coast of Cape Ann, and the men aboard were saved by a lifeboat crew at great risk to themselves.

But damn the dangers, damn the rough life. Solomon Jacobs would be a Gloucester fisherman. And he would not settle for doing things the old way. For one thing, he was intrigued by an innovation gaining favor among the Gloucester mackerel boats. When schools of mackerel migrated up the coast each year, the traditional way to fish them was by "jigging," catching the fish individually by jerking hooks at the end of lines tossed over the sides of the vessel. A hundred thousand barrels of mackerel were caught that way by Gloucester boats each year. Think how that catch was expanded by trapping whole schools of mackerel in seine nets! There was nothing Sol could do about the opportunity he perceived in that direction right away, but he could bide his time.

Settling into Gloucester, Sol began to take the measure of a town committed to the fishing industry and to all the ancillary trades supporting the fisheries. Gloucester in 1872 (a year after John Sloan was born in Lock Haven, Pennsylvania) was still a town. But the population had swelled to over 15,000, and the annual town meeting when everybody stood and had their say, and a few would regularly have too much to say, had become unmanageable. In another year or so Gloucester would be incorporated as a city.

In certain ways it was already beginning to feel like a city. Cultural opportunities were spreading from the ship-owning elite to the ordinary citizenry, with the establishment of a free public library as an offshoot of a Lyceum that sponsored eminent lecturers – the likes of Ralph Waldo Emerson, Henry David Thoreau, Edwin Whipple – from out of town.

A new national bank had just been built on Front Street, the principal thoroughfare that would be renamed Main Street. The Irish and Portuguese fishing families now had their first resident priest, and work was begun on Gloucester's first Catholic church. The local newspaper had deplored one side effect of the community's increased urbanity: Middle Street, at the edge of the better neighborhoods, had become notorious for streetwalkers – alarming those citizens who feared that the corruptions of the waterfront were creeping uptown.

But the advantages of the community, cultural and otherwise, were things Solomon Jacobs could become better acquainted with later. His first interest was in learning about the fisheries from men in the business, many of them Nova Scotians or men like himself from Newfoundland, called "Newfies" by the locals (respectfully, if they knew what was good for them). In 1875, three years after Sol Jacobs' arrival, Fitz J. Babson, collector of customs at Gloucester, writing to the Chief of the Bureau of Statistics, gave a succinct appraisal of the attractions of the Gloucester fisheries to men from the British possessions to the north:

> For some years there has been a large immigration of male adults coming from the Provinces to engage in the fisheries of Gloucester, They are mostly young men and unmarried. The superior class of vessels belonging to this port employed in the fisheries, the liberal and excellent quality of provisions provided by the owners, the prompt settlement and payment in cash for the fares obtained in stead of payment

in goods, etc., which is the usual manner of payment to fishermen at other places, the rapid promotion to the command of a fine schooner consequent upon skill and success, all conspire to draw the ambitious young seamen from the Provinces. These immigrants make up to a large degree the crews of our fishing vessels, and hence the loss of life falls principally upon them. If the loss of life were confined to the native population the town, Gloucester could not long maintain the fishing business. ... Of the seven thousand men employed in the fisheries at this port three-fourths are not natives of the town, and for this reason the Provincial fishermen have come direct in vessels to Gloucester rather than by cars [rail coaches], or via Boston and other ports. Very few of these persons return to the Provinces to make their home there again.

Sol Jacobs was one of those whose migration was permanent, and he wasted no time in applying to become a fully accredited American. At the beginning of the following year, January 1873, he went to Boston where he was naturalized a U.S. citizen. Aside from a desire for citizenship in his new country, Sol would be aware that, to be named master of an American-registered vessel, he would need to become a citizen.

Solomon Jacobs took to the life of fishing in a Gloucester schooner with gusto. In his first trip he went as a "hand" in the schooner *Nevada* under Capt. William Lawrence, to Georges Bank for cod. It is said that after two trips he sailed with Capt. Benjamin Wonson, who was catching mackerel with a seine net. Details are lacking, but there were a number of Wonsons who were ship owners and masters in the Gloucester fleet at the time. If the report is true, Sol got his first lesson in handling a mackerel seine under Ben Wonson.

It did not take Sol long to freshen up his fishing skills. After just three years in the Gloucester fleet he was given his first command. At age twenty-six he sailed out of Gloucester harbor as the coolly confident master of the schooner *Sabine*. It was *Captain* Jacobs now, a master mariner, and he would be known as such for the rest of his life.

Now that he was doing well, the notion of a solid mooring ashore had its appeal for a man getting well up in his twenties. He needed a home and a wife. Not just any wife. The ideal spouse for a fishing captain was a woman who could shoulder heavy responsibilities. During her husband's long absences at sea she had to act as his agent in paying bills and conducting business transactions, managing the household (which might include supervising a cook or housekeeper), raising the children. Not the least among her qualifications, he hoped she would be a warm and responsive bed companion when he was at home between voyages.

It was a tall order, but if no sparks were struck between Capt. Jacobs and any of the local belles of Gloucester, there were many young women who spoke his language, literally, arriving regularly from the British Dominions to the north. They were being driven south by poverty in the coastal districts of Nova Scotia and Newfoundland. In the winter of 1867 and 1868 the fishing families of Nova Scotia had been reduced to near famine, and aid from the Crown and institutional charities did little to ameliorate the suffering.

Many of the young women, in groups of twos and threes, were grateful to accept free passage to the Boston States aboard American vessels. They were treated respectfully, and often sailed in company with brothers or cousins who were on their way to join the Gloucester fleet. The women could hope to find employment in Gloucester, and might start keeping company with some young man. More often than not they married their countrymen among the fishermen. They did so with full knowledge that the union might be cut short early if their husband was lost at sea. But those were the risks they had learned to accept growing up in the fishing communities of the Provinces, and it bred a resigned stoicism, a willingness to take life as it came.

Young Capt. Sol Jacobs, already spoken of as a promising new schooner master, would certainly have caught the attention of more than one of the eligible young women who hailed from his part of the world.

Drawings for a "Light-Weight Dickens"

WITH THE collapse of demand for artist-reporters, the Philadelphia crowd had thinned out. Henri married one of his art students, Linda Craige, and went off to Paris. Luks and Glackens had left for Cuba to cover the Spanish-American War, Glackens for *McClure's Magazine*. Glackens paid tribute to the bravery of the 10th

Negro Cavalry Regiment he had observed coming to the rescue of the besieged Rough Riders at the second battle of San Juan Hill. Former Assistant Secretary of the Navy Theodore Roosevelt, organizer and leader of the Rough Riders, was initially grateful and praised the black soldiers. Later he was dismissive, saying the Negro cavalrymen were dependent upon white officers, and that the black noncommissioned officers lacked the abilities of the "best classes" of whites. Glackens' adventure in Cuba almost proved fatal. He ate the miserable food provided to the army mess, suffered hunger when that food ran out at the front, and contracted malaria. His experiences would reinforce his friend Sloan's conviction that war was absurd.

In 1898 John Sloan moved to New York City briefly to take a job with the New York *Herald*. But he did not get along with the paper's art director and a month later was back in Philadelphia at the *Press* where he worked in the newly introduced benday process to etch plates for a series of colored puzzle drawings.

The following year Glackens came through with a generous act of friendship. An English edition of the novels of French author Charles Paul de Kock was to be issued, and Glackens recommended that John Sloan be commissioned to share with him in drawing the illustrations. Sloan was enthusiastic and steeped himself in the culture of the Bourbon Restoration of the early 19th century. He strove for period accuracy in every detail of dress and settings in the fifty-three etchings and fifty-four drawings he completed for the publisher.

Sloan called de Kock "a sort of light-weight Dickens," but the novels were popular at the time. De Kock sometimes caricatured his characters cruelly, as in "Receipt for the Making of a Marriage," in which a matchmaker is having no luck in bringing together a young lady somewhat past her prime, with indifferent looks and a weeping eye, with a too-lanky gentleman who walks with a limp. Matters improve when the narrator provides strong drink in such quantity that the girl and the young man are blinded to one another's faults, and fall in love. There is none of the humanistic sympathy that Sloan admired in de Maupassant, as in de Maupassant's "A Country Excursion," in which a carefully contrived romantic encounter comes to naught, but the characters are portrayed believably and charitably. The De Kock assignments, on which Sloan worked from 1902 to

1904, served him well: working on them he simplified his line and honed a sure, firm touch in etching.

In December 1903, business efficiencies hastened the end of Sloan's career as a newspaper illustrator. The *Press* announced that the paper had subscribed to a syndicated Sunday supplement and no longer had a need for Sloan's feature illustrations. He decided it was time to take final leave of Philadelphia and join his friends in New York City.

Like so many small-town Americans, Sloan was entranced by the electric excitement in the crucible of the arts that was the teeming, alluring Manhattan from the 1890s until World War II – the last remnants of that magic symbolically dismantled when the Ziegfeld Theatre on 6th Avenue was demolished in 1966. Sloan arrived in New York without a job. His parents and sisters back in Pennsylvania might have suggested that maybe, just maybe, John should look for another line of work. But working with paintbrush and pen had gotten into his blood. He was convinced that there was money to be made in New York for an experienced, skilled freelance illustrator. And recognition might even be possible for serious art work that disdained the old academic rituals.

The opportunities were there, and John Sloan was determined that, sink or swim, this was where he would reignite his life … and that of Dolly.

Chapter Four
MATING CALLS

~~~

Eligible Widower / "Ludicrated" Lovers

Eligible Widower

SOMEHOW, IN the social connections between fishermen and women who had migrated down the Gulf of Maine to settle in Gloucester, Sol Jacobs met twenty-year-old Elizabeth McCabe from Halifax, Nova Scotia. One thing led to another and in February 1875 the two went up to Boston (in the coastal terminology you generally go "up" when moving from east to west, and "down" when going the other way, but there is nothing firm or predictable in this usage). Clergyman Henry Cooke pronounced them man and wife. Solomon's age went into the register as twenty-five, but since he was born in 1847, he would have been twenty-eight. Then as later he would give his age variously, as might best befit the occasion.

The marriage, sadly, was brief and tragic. On September 1st of the following year Elizabeth was delivered of a stillborn infant, and she followed the child into the grave a month later. Officially she died of phthisis, an old word for tuberculosis, but there is a good chance that complications from giving birth played a role. There is no hint, from the bare vital records, of the grief that Sol Jacobs must have felt for his young wife and the child she was carrying. The beauty he remembered of her, and her words and love, and their pride in her pregnancy, must have followed him to sea.

But the instinct to compensate for death with new life was strong in the 19th century. A year later, Sol Jacobs would begin to pay court to twenty-two-year-old Sarah MacQuarrie. Her father was John MacQuarrie, son of a Scottish pioneer to Cape Breton. Her mother was Annie MacAskill. Sarah was raised, along with seven brothers and sisters, just north of what was then known as Plaster Cove on the Strait of Canso that separated Nova Scotia from Cape Breton

Island until the strait was later spanned by a bridge. In 1871 the name of the town was changed to Port Hastings to honor Nova Scotia's then lieutenant governor.

Sol was not the type to ever keep a diary, so we can only surmise as to how the romance flowered. Chances are he began to show his interest evenings in the parlor at the boarding house where Sarah was living. As matters progressed the two would find opportunities to sequester themselves in private conversations in a corner. Love is of course unreasoning, but Sol and Sarah no doubt found qualities in the other that were reassuring. Sarah, Sol was pleased to discover, was no flibbertigibbet, fluttering eyelashes at every passing male and talking of nothing but beaus and bonnets. Quite the opposite: Sol could tell that Sarah had a head on her shoulders, and that would be useful for the long haul — if they were to be granted an extended life together.

Sarah took to Sol as well, and on November 1, 1877 they traveled to Boston to say their vows before clergyman James Dunn. Very likely Sarah had family members in attendance. Her sister Jessie had married Edward Haraden of Manchester, the next town on Cape Ann below Gloucester, and they had three children. After she married Sol, Sarah would be comforted to have a sister living close by, plus two nieces and a nephew.

After the ceremony Sol and Sarah took the "cars" back to Gloucester, and Capt. Jacobs must have been well satisfied as they rattled along in the stiff upright seats of the coach. He was making his way in the Gloucester fisheries, had ambitions to do even better, and was about to set up housekeeping with a bride who, judging from all the signs, felt as strongly toward him as he did toward her. It was a good day in the life of Solomon Jacobs.

"Ludicrated" Lovers

WHO WAS Dolly – Anna Maria Wall? That was what Robert Henri wanted to know. What kind of a fix had his friend gotten into, twenty-seven-year-old John Sloan who was so innocent of the ways of women? Shocking news had come to Henri in Paris. A former student of Henri's in New York wrote him to say that

Sloan was living in New York with "a common woman met up on the street."

Henri wrote to Sloan in a stern avuncular manner: "If your scrape is as bad as her letter seems to make it, then, old man, you are in a pretty bad scrape." Man-to-man he added, "Of course I am not so worried about you taking a mistress and all that – Most men do more or less – and a good many come out of it all right. ..." Henri suggested that the best solution might be for Sloan to put some money together and slip over to France to join the Henris. He must save himself for a respectable woman for his sake and the sake of his art.

When Sloan wrote back, he was clearly delighted with his new domestic arrangement, and anything but contrite. Henri's informant was a gossip-monger, he said. Dolly was not someone he had picked up in the street. In fact they had been introduced by a mutual acquaintance well known to Henri: Ed Davis, head of the art department at the *Philadelphia Press*. The gang from the paper's art department had been out for an evening, and Dolly and a friend joined them for drinks at a rathskeller followed by supper at a Chinese restaurant. The evening ended when "I took the little girl perhaps home perhaps not."

This was Sloan's version of how he and Dolly met. He also told Henri in effect that he was not interested in prying into his girl's past because it did not matter to him. That Sloan was apparently able to bed Dolly the first night they met suggests that she was either of flexible virtue, or immediately taken with this sexually awkward young newspaperman. In his letter to Henri, Sloan said the informant who reported that he had taken up with a "woman of the streets" must have heard a ludicrous tale, or had "ludicrated" it herself. Sloan does not outright deny the charge that Dolly had engaged in prostitution. But if she perhaps supplemented her income as a department store bookkeeper with occasional stints in a discreet boarding house/brothel, Dolly abruptly fastened upon Sloan and made him her life's work.

They saw each other regularly over a period of months and "I have brought her to New York and am living steadier and with less dissipation than in the last year & a half." In 1901 Sloan married the four-foot-nine-inch Dolly, whom he appropriately called his "little girl," in the Episcopal Church of the Annunciation in Philadelphia. (Whether their marriage in a church of his mother's denomination was Sloan's idea, or Dolly's, or was coincidental, is anybody's guess.) They survived in impoverished contentment while he was still drawing meager wages from the *Press*.

Dolly Wall, from a struggling Irish family in Philadelphia, was a thoroughly complicated individual. She was a chronic alcoholic with a Jekyll and Hyde drinking personality. When sober she was lively, witty, enthusiastic for causes, warm-hearted and unstinting in her hospitality toward all who crowded into their tiny flat. But after a few drinks Dolly turned argumentative and mean-spirited, distressing Sloan and embarrassing their friends.

The dark side of her character was probably related to some deep-seated neurosis she was seeing a Dr. Collier Bower about. Dr. Bower would put her through a painful series of treatments for the next several years for what Sloan described as her "inward disorder." Sloan said the undefined treatments were "mechanical, and extremely painful."

Dr. Bower was a respected physician who had his practice at 224 South Broad Street in Philadelphia. In 1902 he was elected treasurer of the Philadelphia County Medical Society. The following year he was also house doctor at Philadelphia's St. James Hotel. The famed actress Mrs. Patrick Campbell was a guest at the hotel while starring in *The Sorceress* at the Broad Street Theatre. One evening, as Mrs. Campbell was about to step into her carriage in front of the hotel, carrying her dog Pinky-Panky-Poo under one arm and a bundle of books under the other, she slipped on the icy carriage step and broke her knee cap. The *New York Times* expressed concern that the injury might leave the actress "lame for life." But Mrs. Campbell was fortunate to receive the prompt ministrations of Dr. Bower, and made a full recovery. Sloan would later paint a likeness of Dr. Bower.

Dolly had her problems, but in one respect she was rock solid – her devotion to and belief in John Sloan was unwavering. She sensed there was a true artist somewhere within this bundle of enthusiasms, uncompromising certainties, and flashes of humor. She was not content that he remain an illustrator; she was constantly urging him to paint, and bought him an easel as encouragement. At those weekly parties back when the artist-reporters from the *Philadelphia Press* got together in Henri's apartment for drink, food and amateur dramatics, John Sloan had always been at the center of the hilarity. It was his way of avoiding any one-on-one contact with the girls who were often present. In spite of having two sisters, he was uneasy among women. Then Dolly appeared, reached out, and took him under her wing. For the more than forty years they were together, Sloan openly admired other women both as females and as subjects to paint. But he seems always to have reserved his intimacy for Dolly as long as she lived. They were close, and he depended on her, writing in his diary that he felt aimless without her. "She has a dear way of keeping me going."

Sloan resembled Winslow Homer in one respect. Both were strongly attracted to young women and painted them admiringly, fully appreciating their sensuous femininity. But both artists were, for whatever individual reasons, reticent with females. The difference was that Homer, after some mysterious heartbreak, became reclusive and remained a bachelor. Sloan, on the other hand, was a happily married man, having been gathered to the bosom of his sympathetic Dolly.

John Sloan and Solomon Jacobs each shared a strong marriage that required patience and resignation on the part of their wives. Sarah Jacobs would always have to wonder, especially during a howling night with sleet lashing against the window panes, if her husband would return safely to port. Dolly Sloan would always have to take reassurance from her faith in John's talents as an artist, even when his freelance assignments were not bringing in enough to feed them decently. In the end, Solomon and Sarah were married for forty-five years until he died on his feet, which is the way he would have wanted to go. John and Dolly were man and wife for forty-two years until she suddenly died, which was not the way either of them thought their union would end.

Sarah Jacobs and Dolly Sloan were as much studies in opposites as were their husbands. Sarah enjoyed substantial status in Gloucester as the wife of one of the leading captains in the fishing fleet. It was a precarious position, to be sure, because if her husband failed to return from a fishing trip, as had happened so often to other wives of schooner masters, she would have few resources with which to support herself and their children. Far from allowing herself to put on airs, she must have accepted life with the self-sufficiency bred into women of the New England and Maritimes fishing ports as their only defense against loss and poverty. To the extent that Sol spoke to her of his vessels and where he was off to next, Sarah would listen with interest, but that was his business. Her business was their home and seeing to it that their children went off clean and well fed to school. She took Sol's place in business matters while he was away, writing the checks that came in against his vessels and signing them "Solomon Jacobs by S. M. Jacobs."

Dolly Sloan was an urban woman, beset with the neuroses and vulnerabilities endemic among dwellers in large cities. She shared her artist husband's life fully, participating in heated discussions on esthetic matters with their friends that lasted into the small hours and often with too much to drink. That she could engage the likes of Robert Henri in long, late disputes indicates that her opinions were taken seriously, this little woman of obscure Philadelphia background. Then there was Dolly's big-hearted warmth, her indifference to Sloan's almost willful poverty, her generosity in opening up their cramped studio apartment to lost souls, and the unreasonable joy she took in cooking up memorable meals for many mouths on short notice. Dolly had her problems, but she was as invaluable a partner to John Sloan as Sarah was to Sol Jacobs.

Both women had found compatible mates: Sarah Jacobs with a good provider she could be proud of, Dolly Sloan with a devoted and tolerant man she was convinced would be, with her help, a great artist.

Chapter Five

GETTING UNDER WAY

~~~

Other Men's Boats / Illustrator for Hire

Other Men's Boats

BY THE time they were in their late twenties John Sloan and Capt. Solomon Jacobs both had, through rigorous apprenticeships, learned where their strengths lay and how to put their skills to use. Both had found a female partner for the long haul, although in Sloan's case it may have been that Dolly found him. In any event, both men had their competencies and their contentment and were ready to assault their worlds in earnest.

As to Capt. Jacobs, he quickly made the schooner *Sabine* dance to his tune. From his first trip in the old boat he proved that, like every good schooner captain, he could command the vessel and the men by the sheer force of his spirit and drive. Unlike the merchant service there were no rules of rank aboard a fishing schooner where the master shared the accommodations of the focsle with the crew. Sol's authority rested solely upon the respect he earned from his men through his judgment as master of an ageing but serviceable vessel. The men on the *Sabine* would soon learn that their captain knew what he was about in commanding a schooner.

Sol would make skillful use of navigational aids to supplement his own solid knowledge of the coast. The owner of the *Sabine* might have loaned Sol a compass or two, a clock and maybe a spyglass. It was up to the master to supply the remainder of his navigational gear. Capt. Jacobs probably carried on board Eldridge charts of the New England coast. Although George Eldridge, father and son, based their navigational charts on U. S. Coastal Surveys, the Eldridge charts, lined with linen, were much preferred by go-ahead fishing captains because those charts were well-designed for practical maritime use. Sol would likely have carried Admiralty charts for the coasts of the British Dominions as well. A current copy of *The Farmer's Almanack*, published in Boston, would have been among his papers too – not for long-range weather forecasts of dubious reliability but for the tide charts.

As for apparatus, Sol would most likely have carried a wooden barometer for everyday use, and a brass version for heavy weather. For navigating offshore, by measuring the height above the horizon of stars and planets, he probably carried a quadrant, or a sextant which was more portable, but not an octant which was too expensive. One or two of the crewmen might also have owned a compass which could be a lifesaver in a dory parted from the mother ship, but this was rare.

In the cod fishery, where tub trawling had become the norm, the captain sent his men out in pairs in dories about a half mile apart to set the trawl lines. The routine varied greatly, depending upon factors such as weather and seas, but typically the crew would make a set in the afternoon. Next morning around sunrise they would row back out to their trawl line, haul into the dory the fish that had taken the hooks, and return to the schooner with their catch. Back on the *Sabine*, usually by 8 AM, they would pour down coffee in a restorative mug-up, then set to slitting the innards out of the fish, salting the saleable portions and pitching these into the hold.

In early afternoon Capt. Jacobs would call the men out to bait their trawls again. They would attach a small chunk of bait fish to each of the hooks. If this was to be a "flying set," with the schooner continuing under way, the dories were loaded with the trawls and a pair of men leaped into each dory as it was lowered overboard into the rolling waves. They set off in different directions to set their trawls before returning to the mother ship, before dark if possible.

This could be a nervous time for Capt. Jacobs, when he was like a mother hen fretting to gather his brood. If the weather came on foggy he would ring a large bell that hung from the *Sabine*'s main boom, or sound a horn, to help the dorymen find their way back to the *Sabine*. If a dory was missing somewhere out there he would pace the deck in frustration, and finally fire the swivel gun to recall the men who would otherwise face that often terminal fate of "going astray." Unless they had the good fortune to be picked up by another vessel or managed to row themselves to some distant shore, men separated from the mother ship faced death by drowning, or by hypothermia, or could perish from hunger or thirst. But assuming that all of the *Sabine*'s dories were accounted for, the men arriving back on board could catch some relaxation. It was a sociable time, the crew enjoying the jokes and joshing and fellowship after the lonely hours out in the dories.

Capt. Jacobs brought unflagging zest and vigor to his command, as well as outstanding success in making his trips pay. He steadily refined the encyclopedic knowledge of fish behaviors he had acquired as a young fisherman in Newfoundland. He was, in effect, a practicing ichthyologist. He was expert in the ways and by-ways of fish, and he put that knowledge to profitable use. On one voyage to Georges Bank in the *Sabine* he brought back 17,000 pounds of cod, a mighty haul for any vessel. The Gloucester ship owners must have exchanged meaningful glances. If this young fellow could make money in the creaky old *Sabine*, what couldn't he do in a real vessel?

Recognition came quickly. The firm of Samuel Lane & Brothers signed Sol on as captain of their big new schooner, the 72-ton *S. R. Lane*, launched in 1873, the latest in their fleet of five schooners. There were over fifty fishing firms in town at the time, but seven of these owned a quarter of the fleet of 400 schooners. The Lanes, then, were owners of a modest-sized flotilla. Capt. Jacobs set sail for Georges Bank in the *Lane*, and to the astonishment of all, was rounding back into Gloucester harbor just thirteen days later, hull down with 124,000 pounds of cod and halibut. It was a record for those grounds that stood for years. And to prove his success was no fluke, Sol made more quick, big trips to Georges. The owners were profiting handsomely, as was Capt. Jacobs with the master's share. He had quickly justified the owners' confidence.

The "hands" were happy to sail with this new captain, too. He was hard-driving, all right, but nobody on board worked with more of a will, was more hearty and good natured, or quicker to put himself at risk. Above all, when a schooner crewman could take home a handsome share of the proceeds, he would fight for a chance to sail under that master. According to the shares system that prevailed in the Gloucester fleet, the owners paid for the supplies that went aboard the schooner, and were rewarded for their investment in ship and stores by earning half the profits from a trip. The crew split the other half, with the captain awarded an additional six to eight percent of the take.

Despite his success in catching cod, Capt. Jacobs was still attracted to the potential of the mackerel fishery. Were the boats using seine nets making the most of that new method? He wanted to find out for himself. He asked if he could go after mackerel in one of the Samuel Lane company's other schooners, the ninety-ton *Moses Adams*. The owners were more than happy to accommodate their money-making captain. Judging from the results, they would have no reason to complain: Sol's mackerel catches averaged a value of $14,000 annually over the next several years.

Purse seining was transforming the mackerel fishery, and no one was employing the new method more effectively than Capt. Sol Jacobs. As many as 200 to 300 mackerel could be taken in one haul of the seine net. One day's catch could equal the number of fish caught over several weeks by the old method of jigging. And it was exhilarating work. In *The Fishermen's Own Book* published in Gloucester in 1882 there is a description of a "mackerel catcher" in the era when Capt. Jacobs was fishing in the *Moses Adams*. The vessel has come upon a school of the fish just before sundown:

> The boys were all alive for such sport, and handled the seine boat and net lively, securing 'heavy decks.' The steward had plenty of hot coffee … on hand for just such a lucky strike, and kept the crew well supplied with these refreshments. The moon had risen just as they got their catch on deck, and with a will they turned to and dressed all night. It was a lively time, splitting, gibbing [cutting the gills and part of the gullet out of a mackerel], soaking them out, salting and barreling, and the vessel, with a light wind, pursued her course for old Gloucester, where they got a quick pack out, and replenishing with salt and stores, were soon off again, as every day in the mackereling season counts, and the fishermen like to make the most of it.

When many mackerel schooners were fishing close to one another on Georges Bank, there was always the danger that a sudden gale could raise steep seas in the shoal waters, and that a vessel could drift loose and collide with another, sending both to the bottom in moments. In fog or dark of night the risks were compounded. Nevertheless, the mackerelers were a carefree lot. Also in the *Fishermen's Own Book* there was a light ballad titled "The Merry, Merry Mackerel Catchers":

> Then it's laugh, "Ha! Ha!" and shout, "Hurrah!"
> We are bound for the coast of Maine;
> Our hold is well stored with salt and food,
> In the boat we've a fine new seine.
>
> The sun goes down as we round Eastern Point –
> For Monhegan our course is laid;
> The watch is set, the pipes are lit,
> And a game of cards is played.
>
> A lively lad has a song to sing;
> Uncle Ben has a yarn to spin;
> So pleasantly passes the time away
> Till eight bells when all turn in, …

At dawn they come upon the mackerel:

> Now all is life on the schooner's deck,
> As she ploughs thro' the sparkling brine;
> Her crew in oiled clothes anxiously wait
> For a chance to wet the twine.
>
> "A school! A school" from the foremasthead
> Is the lookout's exciting call;
> "On the weather bow! It's showing red,
> Can't say if it's large or small."
>
> "Come down from aloft! Haul up the boat!
> Out with the dory, tumble up here, cook!
> Work lively, lads – yes, cast her off,
> Pull out, and we'll have a look.

Hold! Way enough! Ah, there they rise –
Good fish! I should say they were fine;
Now gently start her ahead, my boys,
Quick, seine-master, give them twine!

Pull hard, men! Now bend your backs!
Lively! Over with corks, my friend;
That's way enough – take on your oars,
Pass along the dory's end;

Jump to the purse-line, one and all,
Give a long, strong and a steady pull;
The rings are up – yes, take them on;
By Jove! I believe she's full." ...

... All night we worked at split and gib,
Next day they were salted down,
As the sun sank low in the ruddy west,
We made sail for Gloucester town.

This was Sol Jacobs' life in the mackerel fishery, and he exulted in
every minute of it. He rapidly gained repute as one of the most successful, enterprising, and daring skippers in the fleet – a reputation
to which some notoriety was added by exaggerated reports of his
actions in what the Procter brothers called "The Fortune Bay Riot"
in their *Fishermen's Own Book*. After cooler heads prevailed it came
to be known as the "Fortune Bay Affair."

Capt. Jacobs, thirty-one-year-old master of the *Moses Adams*,
sailed into Fortune Bay on the south coast of his native Newfoundland in January of 1878, along with close to two dozen other
Gloucester boats. Their purpose was to fish for herring which they
believed was fully their right under the Washington Treaty negotiated between the U.S. and Britain in 1871.

It was a highly unpopular treaty among the American fishermen, who believed their government had given away far too much
in exchange for very little. The Canadian provincials and the New-

foundlanders were accorded full rights to sell their fish in American markets in competition with fish off American boats. In addition the U.S. had paid $5,500,000 for the privilege of fishing in Canadian and Newfoundland waters for the twelve years the treaty was to remain in effect – a sum far exceeding the potential value of fish the Americans could take from those waters in a dozen years. Of the hefty payment, $1,000,000 was allocated to Newfoundland. The American fishermen also objected as a matter of principle. The United States was, in effect, relinquishing the right of Americans to fish in the waters of those British colonies, a right negotiated by John Adams in the agreements that ended the American Revolution.

Thus the Gloucester fishermen were flabbergasted when, after setting their seine nets to take herring, they were beset by Newfoundlanders who put out from the shore and cut many of the nets. The locals had been profiting nicely from selling frozen and salt herring to the New England fleet, and were upset at losing that trade – treaty or no treaty. They asserted that Newfoundland law banned fishing for herring during the winter months, and most particularly on Sunday.

According to the account in *The Fishermen's Own Book* issued just four years after the "riot," three attempts were made to seize the filled seine net of the *Moses Adams*. And then Sol took action: "Capt. Jacobs and his crew were provided with loaded revolvers, and by threatening to shoot the first man who dared interfere with them, succeeded in keeping the mob at bay until a partial cargo had been secured, when the Newfoundlanders tripped the seine and allowed the remainder of the herring to escape."

A ragtag of fierce sea dogs lining the rail of the *Moses Adams*, all brandishing firearms? It was a colorful, but fanciful, version of what really happened. By the sworn testimony of all who were there, Sol Jacobs, captain of the *Adams*, was the only one who showed a revolver. John Cluett, a fisherman of Fortune Bay, said that "there was a great crowd, and [Capt. Sol] was in an awful rage. He said he would defend his seine if they touched it in a threatening way." Silas Fudge, mate on his father's schooner, was more specific, saying that the American captain "drew a revolver and threatened to shoot any man who touched his property."

Sol did not deny his actions when he spoke with George Snell-grove, Sub-Collector of Customs for the District of Fortune Bay. Snellgrove testified that Jacobs "showed me a revolver and said that he had threatened [the Newfoundland fishermen] with it." But Sol told Snellgrove he only did it to frighten them – he had made sure there were no cartridges in the chambers. So his "awful rage" and drawing of a weapon were a theatrical display. It had the desired effect in bluffing the Newfoundlanders. The *Moses Adams* was the only American vessel that returned to Gloucester from Fortune Bay with any herring.

The Newfoundland and British authorities protested vehemently. The officer in charge of the investigation, Capt. George Sullivan of Her Majesty's Ship *Sirius*, supported the Newfoundlanders unequivocally, reporting that their depositions "distinctly proved that no violence was resorted to until after the exasperating conduct of Capt. Jacobs ... who threatened them with a revolver." British Foreign Secretary Lord Salisbury complained in an outraged tone to John Welsh, U.S. Minister to England, saying that he had read Capt. Sullivan's report and was appalled at the actions of the American captain "who threatened the Newfoundland fishermen with a revolver ..." In what had escalated into an international incident, the official British protest focused on this armed provocation by the American captain placing their loyal Newfoundland subjects in line of fire. There seemed to be conclusive evidence that Capt. Sol had disgraced himself, and his nation, by resorting to deadly force.

At that point the dispute did a dramatic turnabout. On September 28 William Evarts, U.S. Secretary of State, sent an official response to Lord Salisbury by way of Ambassador Welsh in London. Evarts pointed out that the Newfoundland edicts prohibiting fishing on Sunday and taking herring during the winter were provincial rules that were binding only upon Newfoundlanders. He then hinted darkly that, if local laws were to take precedence over the international agreements negotiated between the United States and Great Britain in the Treaty of Washington, perhaps the entire treaty should be revisited immediately.

That was not what the British wanted. They had concluded that the Washington Treaty suited their interests nicely, and were eager to keep the accord in force until it was due to expire in 1885. Lord Salisbury quickly decided that, after all, the Newfoundlanders were the guilty parties. He apologized for the rowdy actions of these uncouth colonials at the fringe of the Empire, and said that he was amenable to paying damages to the American fishermen who had suffered damaged gear and loss of their herring catches. The British made no further mention of Capt. Jacobs' "exasperating behavior."

Thus, after an exchange of diplomatic communications, Sol Jacobs became, instead of an embarrassment to the Gloucester fleet, its hero. He had stoutly defended his rights as an American fisherman under the treaty provisions, refusing to give way when confronted by an angry crowd. His waving a pistol was now seen not as a reprehensible act but a vigorous defense of his rights.

Discussions shifted to how much recompense was due the Americans. The dispute was of such significance as to warrant mention by President Rutherford B. Hayes in his State of the Union Addresses of both 1879 and 1880, in which he looked forward to resolving the issues amicably. Ultimately the American fishermen were awarded $75,000 for damages to their gear and fish lost when their seines were tipped. The owners of the *Moses Adams* demanded $8,586.05, based upon the grievous reports of loss lodged by Capt. Jacobs. However, since the *Moses Adams* had salvaged some of her catch, the award for that vessel was a modest $1,863.60.

The Fortune Bay affair gave birth to the Sol Jacobs legend. The saga would be embellished over time with other accounts – some fact, some fancy – of a Gloucester captain who could not be trifled with, whose daring and audacity was emblematic of the strong-willed, fearless captains of the port.

Sol's return to Gloucester that winter should have been triumphant, but was shrouded in tragedy. He must have struggled over how to break the news to Sarah. He had found a berth for her unmarried thirty-year-old brother James for that trip in the *Moses Adams*, and Jim MacQuarrie had been lost overboard on January 21st, a few weeks after the business in Fortune Bay. Sarah, in her grief over her brother's death, must have been haunted by the thought that one day it might be her husband who would not return.

Before the end of the year, in December 1878, the *Moses Adams* was caught in a gale and sprang a leak too severe for the pumps to keep up with the water rushing in through the seams. Capt. Jacobs had to abandon the vessel at sea. He and his men were rescued "with considerable difficulty" by the bark *Shawmut*. But Capt. Jacobs would not be without a command for long. The Samuel Lane company promptly made him an offer that would elevate Sol, after only five years in Gloucester, to the prestigious rank of a boat-owning captain.

Illustrator for Hire

IN 1904, thirty-year-old John Sloan and his wife Dolly unpacked their belongings in New York again, and this time the move would be permanent. They had found a tiny apartment at 165 West 23rd Street in the Chelsea district. As their one source of regular income they depended on the "word-charade" puzzles Sloan was still drawing in pen & ink for the Philadelphia *Press*. Those barely paid the rent. Launching himself as a new free-lance illustrator in the metropolis, he made the rounds of the popular magazines – *Collier's*, *Harper's Weekly*, *The Saturday Evening Post*, *Munsey's* – showing his portfolio and collaring an occasional assignment. It was a precarious existence, but John took pride in his profession as an illustrator: "I think all real art has an element of illustration in it."

The Sloans found themselves in their element in the maelstrom of early twentieth century New York. The next dozen years would be the most turbulent, and creative, in John Sloan's career. The contrast with settled, self-satisfied Philadelphia could not have been greater. In the 19th century New York had been a crossroads of ocean, river and rail trade. Building on that base entering the 20th century, the city was growing feverishly in every branch of commerce, spawning a largely unplanned agglomeration of skyscrapers, commercial arteries, and housing for a bursting population. The year the Sloans arrived the first subway lines opened and the strings of cars, shrieking around the curves above and below ground, swept commuters to the five boroughs that had been consolidated into the city only a half-dozen years earlier.

Of the crowds swarming the streets it seemed that no one was a native New Yorker. Great numbers were arriving from the rural hinterlands, lured from isolated farm life by the promise of excitement and success in the big city. Other multitudes entered via Ellis Island, speaking in a confusion of mutually incomprehensible languages from the Balkans, Germany, Poland, the south of Italy. The population of the city would more than double in the thirty years following 1890, from 2.5 to 5.6 million.

Sloan and Dolly had a full social life from the moment of their arrival. Members of the old crowd of Philadelphia artist-reporters regularly dropped in: Henri, Bill Glackens, Everett Shinn, George Luks, Ed Davis. After recuperating from the effects of his Spanish-American War assignment Glackens had returned to New York and was free-lancing as a magazine illustrator while painting in his spare time, often beach and picnic scenes.

George Luks resembled the hard-drinking characters in the paintings of Frans Hals, his idol. With Luks it was sometimes difficult to separate reality from the various personae he would assume after a few drinks. To the barroom crowd he might announce that he was prizefighter "Chicago Whitey." That could lead to a scuffle, and Luks might knock someone down, or be floored himself. Sloan or some other friend would help him stagger home to his wife. But besotted and pugnacious as he might be, George Luks was an accomplished magazine illustrator. He also had a solid grounding in technique, having studied in Düsseldorf, London and Paris, following training at the Pennsylvania Academy of Fine Arts. But serious painting was, of necessity, a sideline for him, as it was for Sloan.

When he reunited with the others in New York, Everett Shinn initially worked in the Urban Realism genre in which Robert Henri had inspired them all. Shinn had been a precocious illustrator at fourteen, designing for a gas works company in Philadelphia. He came to know the others when he was studying at the Pennsylvania Academy of Fine Arts. Shinn was, if anything, too versatile. Trim and debonair, he enjoyed success as a playwright and actor as well as an artist. Gaining entrée into café society, he increasingly took his subject matter from the entertainment world in place of the New York underclass. Shinn's canvases often portrayed ballet, orchestral and vaudeville subjects, and he painted theatrical backdrops for the

Ziegfeld Follies.

They all dropped in on the Sloans, and were welcome. Dolly, ever the warmhearted hostess, somehow whipped up satisfying meals from her meager kitchen facilities, then joined in the conversation which, fired by John's nervous energy, would continue into the early hours of the morning. Often as not a guest would flop on the extra cot the Sloans had available, to remain for the night or a week.

Sloan and Dolly were closest to Robert and Linda Henri, who had returned from Paris. Henri had started teaching at the New York School of Art in 1902, where his students included Edward Hopper, Rockwell Kent, George Bellows and Stuart Davis. The two couples frequently spent evenings together in the Sloan flat, Sloan and Henri sketching in the midst of the non-stop earnest conversation.

As much as Sloan was motivated by Robert Henri, and counted him a close friend, Henri remained an enigma. The power of Henri's personality was reinforced by a certain air of mystery about the man. His narrow eyes suggested roots somewhere in the steppes of central Asia, and he said little about who he was or where he had come from. In time it would be revealed that, as Robert Henry Cozad, he had grown up in Cozad, Nebraska, a town named after his father, gambler and real estate promoter John Jackson Cozad. There had been hard feelings between John Cozad and cattlemen opposed to real estate development. In self-defense, Cozad shot one of them to death. He was cleared but, fearing retribution, fled east with his family, all of whom took new names just to be on the safe side. Son Robert assumed the surname Henri, insisted that it be pronounced Hen-Rye, and remained reticent about his past.

He sustained this aura of romantic mystery throughout his years of training and teaching. He studied at the Pennsylvania Academy of the Fine Arts in Philadelphia, and later under Bouguereau at the Académie Julian in Paris. Later Henri taught at the Philadelphia School of Design for Women, then migrated to New York with the other Philadelphians and took his teaching post at the New York School of Art.

John and Dolly were very fond of Linda Henri, but Dolly was not comfortable with the other wives of the group. She felt they looked down on as her as socially inferior. In that first year, 1904, Bill

Glackens had married Edith Dimock, a rare artist of means; she was buttressed by the wealth of her family in New Haven. Everett Shinn at the time was married to Florence Scovel, the first of his many wives. Florence was a Philadelphia Biddle – from an insignificant branch of the family, she said, but nevertheless she was a Biddle. Dolly's problems continued, and in the early years she returned frequently to Philadelphia for extended treatments by Dr. Bower. Then she would be back in New York again with Sloan, once more the caring wife.

Linda Henri, long in poor health, died in 1905. Henri – often argumentative, abrasively sure of himself – was now at loose ends and became a constant visitor at the Sloan apartment, sometimes not leaving until long after midnight. Sloan eventually became irritated with his old friend, but Dolly was understanding – although she and Henri would get into furious arguments, especially after Dolly had been drinking. In May 1908, without a word to his best friend Sloan, Henri married a young newspaper cartoonist, Marjorie Organ, and sailed again for Paris. Sloan and Dolly were not comfortable with Henri's second wife at first, Sloan referring to her in his diary as "H²O" –Henri's 2nd wife named Organ. But later they were on good terms. John and Dolly Sloan were tolerant of their friends' passions and peculiarities.

John Sloan wrote his first diary entry in 1906 and continued the record until 1913. It is remarkable as a chronicle of the artistic and intellectual milieu that flourished in lower Manhattan in the early years of the 20th century. But it is above all a personal document, a continuous first-hand account of an artist's life during some of his most significantly creative years.

On July 28, 1906 Sloan writes "This is Dolly's – my little wife's birthday. She is thirty years old and says she's happy. She makes me so anyway – and lives in a garret studio with me – keeps it clean and fresh and home-like and loves me. May she live to see many many happy returns, is my selfish wish." On August 5, 1911, Sloan and Dolly celebrated their tenth wedding anniversary. "… I know neither Dolly nor I have a whole regret. We have had ruts to jolt us once in a while but it's all happiness."

Sloan confessed that the heavy drinking was not all on Dolly's part. One day he ran into an old friend from the newspaper days and stopped to toss one down. One thing led to another and "I got home ... very drunk indeed and Dolly cared for me like a mother or a mother cat with a wet kitten (only the kitten was wet inside). I felt so rottenly ashamed of myself for forgetting our plans of the evening!" Those plans were for a dinner honoring the mayor of Milwaukee, for which Sloan had paid $2.50 – a big outlay from the Sloan exchequer.

Dolly was indulgent almost to a fault, as she demonstrated when she and John became neighbors of Rockwell Kent and his wife. In 1907 Kent was a student of Henri's, and Sloan had been impressed by his paintings. "These pictures are immense. Rocks and Sea in fair weather and in winter. Splendid big thoughts." Three years later Kent moved his wife and infant son to New York for the winter. Then Kent left to travel alone. Sloan wrote that he believed Kent was going to Gloucester in hopes of working his way to Newfoundland on a fishing vessel .

Kent was going to Newfoundland ostensibly to buy some land and perhaps start an art colony. He had asked Sloan to make the trip with him, but John had no desire to leave Dolly or New York – and thus missed an early opportunity to visit Gloucester (as well as Sol Jacobs' Newfoundland). The true purpose of Kent's journey to Newfoundland was to investigate the possibilities of renewing a relationship with a woman who lived there.

Upon Kent's departure the Sloans agreed to take his wife and the infant into their tiny apartment of "three rooms and a bath." John thought Rockwell, Jr. a "fine and dear" boy, but a nuisance in the cramped space. Kent's wife he judged to be "a rather pathetic figure." She remained silent – they could not engage her in conversation. What's more, she was a vegetarian, and Dolly had to contrive meatless meals for them all. .

Kent's rendezvous in Newfoundland came to nothing. He returned to New York a month later and, to John Sloan's consternation, rented the apartment directly below, whereupon the Kents began borrowing various household necessities. There were other annoyances: soon the entire building was hearing, like it or not, Kent practicing on the flute. One day Kent and his wife stopped by to say that they were off to Carnegie Hall for the evening, and would the Sloans mind looking after the baby – "Just open the door and get it in case of fire!" The Sloans obliged, but the next time the Kents made a similar request Dolly put her foot down. Shame on these people who would go off and leave their own baby! Sloan never let his personal feelings toward Rockwell Kent get in the way of his admiration for the man as an artist – he sought to advance Kent's career at every opportunity.

In his diary Sloan documented Dolly's culinary accomplishments. When she and Sloan hosted a farewell dinner for Robert Henri and the second Mrs. Henri, who were sailing for France in 1910, Sloan wrote in his diary, "The Roberts [friends] and Mr. Yeats we also had at the feast. Very good dinner indeed Dolly turned out of her little cubby hole of a kitchen. ... After dinner Mr. And Mrs. Brewer called, also Sneddon, Bell, Van Wyck Brooks, Mr. Alexander the ex-naval Britisher ... and we had a very pleasant evening together." That was a small crowd. On Thanksgiving they had eleven guests to dinner, for which Dolly roasted a turkey that Sloan estimated was "about twice her size."

The "Mr. Yeats" who appears frequently in Sloan's diary beginning in 1909 was John Butler Yeats, artist and writer, father of William Butler Yeats the Irish poet. The elder Yeats had come to New York in his seventies, low on funds and seeking to make his fortune by painting the portraits of wealthy Americans. He would spend the rest of his life in America, despite the entreaties of his children to return to Ireland.

John Sloan took an immediate liking to John Butler Yeats whom he came to regard as a surrogate father. Yeats, in turn, recognized Sloan's artistic power, and was deeply fond of Dolly. Sloan wrote in his diary of one excursion with Yeats: "Mr. Yeats began in his brightest way to talk and he was a steady warm shower of reminiscences and ideas and kindliness and good humor ..." With his wit and charm J.B. Yeats soon was a magnet for artists, poets and writers who came to dinner at the Petitpas boarding house, owned by the Mlles. Petitpas, three Breton women. The food was atrocious but the company excellent, and the Petitpas sisters, who started with almost nothing, were wealthy when they retired to France after World

War I.

Yeats was the type that Anatole France called "a cultivated and eloquent man [with] acuteness and subtlety of ... mind." Yeats was never the pontificating elder but always fresh and original in his thinking. He was unfailing in his devotion to his two young friends, and talked the wealthy lawyer and art collector John Quinn into buying a complete set of Sloan's fifty-three etchings and drawings for the de Kock novels. Later Quinn would place a standing order with Sloan for a print from each of his future etchings as they were struck.

Splendid old John Butler Yeats presided over the outdoor boarding house dinners at Petitpas, in which John and Dolly Sloan became regulars. One topic tumbled after another in nonstop conversation. No trite remark passed unchallenged, and *bons mots* and illuminating insights were applauded. Others at the long table were the young Van Wyck Brooks who would be a prolific biographer and literary historian; Alan Seeger, bohemian poet; Mrs. Charles Johnson, the Russian niece of Madame Bavatsky, the theosophist, whose Irish husband was working for the *New York Times*; and Fred King, an editor at the *Literary Digest*. John Butler Yeats' famous poet son William Butler Yeats joined the company on one occasion when on a visit from Ireland, and Theodore Dreiser once stopped by, as did Ezra Pound.

It was at Petitpas that J.B. Yeats introduced Eulabee Dix to Robert Henri. Eulabee Dix was in demand both in America and France for her miniature watercolors on ivory. In person she was elegant and striking, and Henri painted her portrait. When she married a New York lawyer, Yeats said "I would not envy the man that she married, for she would be sure to devour him. She has a clinging way like ivy, which we know always kills the tree to which it attaches itself." Yeats' assessment was correct; the marriage was never a happy one.

John Sloan thrived in this dinner table forum of ideas and the arts, among people unconventional in their lifestyles and original in their thinking. He was at one with them because, in addition to his illustration assignments, he was doing real painting. Not much as yet, but enough to become known in the company that assembled at Petitpas as one of those who was bringing a fresh creative spirit to

American art. John Sloan had found a style that suited him in those years, and he was working in it brilliantly.

John Sloan and Sol Jacobs were both at exhilarating moments in their careers.

Chapter Six
EARLY TRIUMPHS

~~

"King of the Mackerel Killers" / "Sloans"

"King of the Mackerel Killers"

IN 1878 Capt. Solomon Jacobs first sailed in a schooner of which he was not only master but part owner. The Samuel Lane company engaged in the practice common among the Gloucester fleet owners of offering their most successful captains the opportunity to buy shares in a vessel. It made good business sense: the company kept its best captains, and those men had the added incentive of participating in the profits from each trip. Sol Jacobs thus moved into the capitalist class with one-quarter ownership of a new fishing vessel built in Bath, Maine, a seventy-eight-foot-long, eighty-ton schooner. Samuel Lane was listed officially as the owner but Capt. Jacobs was given the privilege of naming the vessel. He proudly had her registered in the name of his young wife, and the *Sarah M. Jacobs* joined the Gloucester fleet. Attesting that he was a U.S. citizen, Capt. Jacobs was also officially listed as master of the *Sarah M.*

Entering the ranks of the shipmaster-owners was a momentous step forward for Sol. Gloucester merchant Joseph Proctor said that only one fisherman in a hundred was able to move up in the world, and the only sure route to advancement was to be given command of one of the vessels in the fleet. Now that Capt. Jacobs was not only a master but a part-owner of a new, well-equipped vessel, he had become an accredited member of Gloucester's fishing elite.

Sol wasted no time putting his new vessel to sea. In his first season in the *Sarah M. Jacobs* he caught $19,000 worth of cod. Then he decided to get back to seining for mackerel, where there was greater potential for profit. Eager to get onto the migrating mackerel before the rest of the fleet, on April 16, 1878 he arrived with a trip of fish at the New York market. Only one other boat had beaten him that year. (Capt. Sol knew nothing but success in the *Sarah M.*, but tragedy would visit the vessel in later years when she was in other hands. On February 26, 1886 John Cogan and Thomas Landry were washed overboard and drowned. Cogan left a widow and three children back in Gloucester. Landry was just 19.)

Sol was prospering rapidly, and boat ownership fit well with a determination to shape his own future. The following year, 1879, he became half-owner, along with Dennis Ayer, of the *Edward E. Webster*. The *Webster* was a somewhat bigger schooner than the *Sarah M. Jacobs*, 83 feet long, 98 tons. She had been built in Gloucester in 1875, and as with many of the boats with a fishing history, that history included tragedy. On April 12, 1877 Edward Coles and Howard Powers, visiting their trawl when fishing from the *Webster*, were drowned when upset in their dory on the Grand Banks. A year later, in May 1878, 17-year-old Willis Bateman of Liverpool, Nova Scotia was lost when the *Webster* collided with the schooner *Hereward.*

But Capt. Jacobs was not superstitious, and his achievements in the *Webster* were prodigious. She was the first vessel in the mackerel fleet to arrive at the New York market with a trip of fish in 1879, on April 12th. In 1880 Sol in the *Webster* was again the first to land a trip in New York. He sailed on a Monday and was back on Thursday with 250 barrels of mackerel he had netted seining off Mount Desert Rock, for a value of $1,300. With his skill at finding mackerel and using the latest gear to land them, Capt. Jacobs profited handsomely in the growing demand for iced fish in the New York market, where the first vessel to arrive at the dock could demand the highest prices. There were 150 other New England vessels competing regularly for that prize, but Sol most often claimed top dollar.

The technology of mackerel fishing improved steadily, especially with the introduction of the mackerel pocket or "spiller" about 1880. This was a bag in which newly caught mackerel could be slung alongside the vessel to keep the fish fresh until they could be brought aboard to be dressed and iced.

Seine nets were becoming more sophisticated, too. Through changes in twines and weights, seine makers were offering seines double the size and capacity of those made twenty years earlier, but that weighed no more than the old ones had. These innovations came at a price. A new seine cost $1,000 to $1,500. And seine boats were made bigger and bigger – some up to 40-feet long by 1882. A 36-footer could cost $225, and that was before adding oars, oarlocks and pursing gear. The high costs of the new equipment were compounded by the fact that marine insurance did not cover trawls, seines or seine boats unless the vessel itself was lost. It had become a high-risk, high-investment environment, and by 1882 only one Gloucester schooner in six was owned outright by its master. Sol Jacobs was one of those few independent captain-owners. For those who could afford the upgrades, the rewards were great. These fortunate few were landing annual catches ten times the total of those of the hook-and-line era.

Sol succeeded better than most through his uncanny ability to "think like a mackerel" – and outwit the fish with fair regularity. An example was a year in the early '80s that had been particularly poor for mackerel. Then migrating fish were spied in Massachusetts Bay late in the season, and the fleet eagerly converged upon the scene. One morning a big school appeared, but continually evaded capture, swimming out of the seine nets before the ends could be closed, or "pursed." Toward nightfall Capt. Jacobs appeared on the scene, and seemed to agree with the others that the fishing was hopeless that day. But as the other schooners headed for port, Sol got his men over the side into the seine boat. He had observed that the mackerel had become conditioned to expect the seine net to be cast invariably in the same manner. He reasoned that the fish had learned to dive to safety before the net could be closed to trap them.

Sol altered the routine, confusing the fish which churned in panic as the seine was tightly secured around them. That night Capt. Jacobs' crew bailed enough mackerel onto the deck of the *Webster* to fill 200 barrels. By the next morning the other boats were back at the wharves in Gloucester, with few fish to show for their efforts. Capt. Jacobs, meanwhile, was at T Wharf in Boston where his big catch commanded a premium. It was one of many coups by which Sol earned his repute as "king of the mackerel killers."

These were peak years for the Gloucester fishery. More than 400 vessels were fishing out of Gloucester in 1880, and there were 40 to 50 concerns engaged in the fish business in town. The mackerel fishing was particularly bountiful in the Gulf of Saint Lawrence in 1882. The twenty vessels fishing there averaged 200 barrels of fish each. After one five-week trip, Capt. Jacobs in the *Webster* raced home with 500 barrels of fish in the hold. That year the *Webster* earned $34,229 seining mackerel. The average share for the crew was $959.75; Warren Fowles, with his extra pay of $160 as steward, or cook, took home $1,129.75 for his season's work. In those times that was lavish reward for eight months of fishing. Altogether, between 1878 and 1882, Sol made a number of highly profitable mackerel voyages.

Capt. Jacobs' crew members on the *Webster* would have been a happy lot, sailing on one of the most profitable vessels in the mackerel fleet. The single men would have been able to put up at the best of the forty-five boarding houses in Gloucester, those that provided good fare and a soft bed for $12 a week. (Some houses charged as little as $3 a week, but there you took your chances.) Once at sea and on their way to the fishing grounds, there was time in the focsle for card playing and spinning yarns, often an "Irish bull," an extravagant tale told tongue in cheek. There was the singing, or maybe just reciting, of ballads about some shipwreck, or incidents of a fisherman's life.

There was no consumption of alcohol on board – that was far too dangerous not only for the tippler but for all hands. And some fishermen were proud to be teetotalers ashore as well. On March 3, 1876, after a grand reception at the Reynolds Temperance Reform Club, 400 Gloucester fishermen from the Georges fleet had marched in a procession through downtown Gloucester to proclaim their abstinence, at least from alcohol. The month before, the *Cape Ann Advertiser* printed a list of twenty-two Gloucester vessels manned entirely by temperance men. These were likely from the twenty-five to thirty percent of the fishermen who were married and thought twice about the consequences of arriving home with an unsteady gait and glassy eyes. Many of Capt. Jacobs' crew members were no doubt of the more typical majority who took full advantage of diversions available ashore: there were thirty-two saloons in town, among other facilities for recreation and relaxation, as well as romance-for-hire.

When they put into Canadian or Newfoundland harbors (legally when the Washington Treaty was in effect, or clandestinely in other years), fishermen could look forward to entertaining themselves in a fashion peculiar to the locale. Rowing ashore from the anchored schooner to some Newfoundland outport, crew members might tie up their dory and wander into any house they came to, uninvited. That was the custom. Once inside they would talk to the residents about the subject of interest to all of them – fishing. They are asked if they are filling the fish hold, how their bait is holding out, what weather they have been through. And the locals, the "livyers," ask if the fishermen wish to get up a dance.

Since dancing at that time was one of the favorite pastimes of the fishermen, the answer is yes, and they will be looking to hire one of the houses in the village for a couple of dollars. In the negotiations the Gloucester seamen have no trouble understanding the sea-flavored lingo of the coastal Newfoundlanders. The owner of the house eventually rented for the evening is addressed as "skipper." If he is known as a hard bargainer, the visitors are advised that there is "no getting to windward" of him. The meager furnishings of the abode might suggest that the owner is having to plot a course "very near the wind" because his fishing business is in trouble and his finances are "going to leeward." And if he is a taciturn and silent man, it may simply mean that he has no use for idle talk because "words fill no nets."

News of the dance spreads along the shore, and out of the night, singly and in pairs, the unmarried young women of the neighborhood arrive and take their places side by side on a bare bench. The men off the boat ask for the services of a fiddler but learn that no musician, strictly speaking, is available. However, they are told, so-and-so is a wonder doing "mouth music." This is a traditional form of vocalizing brought over by their ancestors from Scotland, known as *puirt à beul* (literally "tunes from the mouth" in Scottish Gaelic).

This performer is engaged for the evening, and when all are assembled he lets loose, singing lively lyrics that the fishermen cannot understand. They gather from the hooting response of the locals that the theme must be a bawdy one. Soon the performer frees himself from the constraints of language and sings made-up words. After a time there is a call for a square dance or a "lancers," which is a Scottish form of the quadrille. One of the fishermen jumps up to call out the dance figures. By the dim light of a gas lamp the men shuffle about in their boots, attracting the bolder of the girls to partner with them.

The host is all too happy to sell the men a bottle of Newfoundland "screech." This is a home brew, the recipe for which descended from a time when the potent sediment collected from the bottom of barrels of molasses and rum was mixed with grain alcohol. It does not take many sips of screech to liven up the evening's festivities, with the fishermen eventually finding their way back to the ship at four o'clock in the morning.

Capt. Jacobs probably has no objection to his men blowing off steam in this way from time to time. Newfoundland-born himself, he can provide them with some useful local tips. He might, for example, tell a lad what to expect his wedding day to be like if he is smitten by a Newfoundland girl, and is certain she will be a fine wife to take back to Gloucester. The settlement will be decked out with all the bunting that can be found, and the big sealing guns – the ones they use when hunting seals out on the ice – will be fired from morning to night. Then, young fella, Capt. Jacobs might inform the enamored bachelor, when you and your new bride leave the church, you'll be caught up in a fishnet thrown over you both by your wedding party. You won't have no difficulty catching the meaning neither, m'boy – it means you're netted for life!

If Capt. Jacobs stopped by his home shore of Twillingate in the 1880s he would have found little changed. But the community did have a newspaper now. The *Twillingate Sun* had started printing news of the area in 1880 and would continue to publish throughout Sol's lifetime and long after. And in 1885 a telegraph link was established with the outside world.

Now prospering well in the mackerel fishery, Capt. Jacobs acquired another schooner, and this time with no co-owners. Built in Kennebunk in 1884, this was a good sized boat, 98 feet long, 117 tons. Capt. Sol enrolled the vessel officially as the *Molly Adams*, but when he later sent her around Cape Horn he had changed her name slightly as the *Mollie Adams*.

In 1886 Capt. Jacobs, in the *Adams*, had one of his frequent brushes with the Provincial authorities in Nova Scotia. According to an affidavit sworn to by him in that year, he had entered Port Mulgrave in the Straits of Canso on August 31 in need of water. He had encountered heavy weather returning from the fishing grounds and the boat's water tank burst. Capt. Jacobs found his way to the customs house and asked permission of the collector to buy two or three barrels of water, just enough to see him through the voyage back to Gloucester. The collector flatly refused permission, and said that if any purchases whatever in the port were attempted, the *Adams* would be seized.

Capt. Jacobs protested that this refusal, if not a violation of the Washington Treaty, was certainly contrary to human charity. The collector was unmoved, and Sol was obliged to sail on for 500 miles, with only seventy-five gallons of water to ration out among a crew of eighteen men. During the passage, when he came close inshore in hopes of finding water at another port, he was caught in a gale that damaged the vessel, swept $700 worth of mackerel from the deck, and smashed two seine boats. Here, as in claims for damages on other occasions, Capt. Jacobs displayed a dramatic talent for portraying himself the innocent victim of insensitive bureaucrats.

Less than a month later, Capt. Jacobs had a run in with other Nova Scotian authorities who were equally unfeeling. In a letter to U.S. Secretary of State T. F. Bayard, he protested that on September 26, 1886, with it blowing hard and seas running high, he had, at midnight, taken off the crew of seventeen men from the British schooner *Neskilita* that had run aground on the bar outside Malpeque harbor. He fed the rescued men for three days until the wind eased enough that he was able to run into Malpeque. There he was boarded by the Canadian cutter *Critic*, under a Capt. McClennan. Wrote Capt. Jacobs, "He neither offered to care for the wrecked crew, to feed them, nor to give them or myself any help whatsoever."

Nobody on shore would offer any aid to the *Neskilita*'s crew either, so Capt. Jacobs gave the men $60 to pay their way home on the cars, and he staked them to some food to see them on their trip. In addition to his generous outlay, Sol had lost 10 days of prime mackerel fishing time.

Nor was that the end of it, according to the captain's testimony. After feeding so many men, he recounted, his stores ran low once he was at sea. He put into another harbor along the Nova Scotia coast, Port Medway, stated the cause of his dilemma, and asked permission to buy half a barrel of flour and enough provisions for the trip back to Gloucester. Once again the port collector not only refused, but threatened to seize the vessel if Capt. Jacobs bought anything whatever anywhere in Port Medway. Capt. Jacobs was left with no alternative but to sail 300 miles on short rations. Fortunately the weather was good and the wind fair, and he hustled to Gloucester in three days. But he was irate, complaining that "the fishermen are at the mercy of a class of officials hostile to them and their business."

The Nova Scotia port authorities contested Capt. Jacobs' versions of these events, as might be expected. The Canadian government agent in Gloucester promised an investigation by the Dominion government which, he was certain, would exonerate the Canadian port authorities of any charges of "inhumanity." When asked about this, Capt. Jacobs said he was prepared to prove all the statements he had made about the matter, and had sent his sworn testimony to the proper authorities in Washington.

Confrontations with provincial authorities badly frayed relations between Britain's North Atlantic possessions and their former subjects, such as Capt. Jacobs. Sol's name regularly surfaced in these international disputes, and he seemed to thoroughly relish the controversies. When the Canadian authorities denied the captain's claims, saying "his word could not be relied on," prominent members of the Gloucester fishing community rallied to Sol's defense before a hearing of the U.S. Senate Committee on Relations with Canada. It was held at the Hoffman House in New York City in 1889 and chaired by Senator George Frisbie Hoar of Massachusetts. By that time Sol was out West and could not speak for himself, but Gloucester vessel owners and outfitters Sylvester Cunningham and William Pew, along with George Steele who was President of the American Fishing Union, said they were well acquainted with Capt. Jacobs and could testify to his "high character." Pew pointed out that Sol was so well thought of in town that he had been elected a Director of the Gloucester National Bank.

Anecdotal evidence continued to be heard from the Gloucester fishermen that Nova Scotian port authorities, often exercising their own discretion, were barring American fishermen from coming ashore to purchase bait or supplies, even when such transactions were authorized by treaty. As late as 1902, Sol asserted to a reporter from the *Detroit Tribune* that "We will continue to fish where we have rights." He said the fishermen had asked William Moody, President Theodore Roosevelt's Secretary of the Navy, what his warships were doing. "If necessary we will make catches with a battleship alongside to show we mean business."

But in the mid '80s, skirmishes with customs functionaries were only minor irritations to Capt. Jacobs. Earning good money, respected by his fellow captains as an owner of his own vessels and one of the ablest fishermen in the fleet, a solid member of the community with a growing family – Capt. Solomon Jacobs had every reason to feel satisfied with his accomplishments. He would be quick to acknowledge, however, that fishing for a living was an uncertain way of life. And so the next few years would prove.

"Sloans"

OF THE Philadelphia artist-reporters, only John Sloan never studied art in Europe, and that perhaps worked to the disadvantage of his early reputation. Well into the 20th century America's second-class status in the art world made it unthinkable than an aspiring American artist could succeed without exposure to European culture, and instruction at a first-rate European art academy. Even two thoroughly American artists, Winslow Homer and Edward Hopper, spent extended periods upon European soil. Winslow Homer did not study abroad but he did visit Paris and later spent two years in Northumberland painting English fishing families. Edward Hopper made three trips to Paris in the years just after the turn of the century. In the end he developed his own style, uninfluenced by the Fauves and Cubists, but he had been in the midst of the turbulent scene when European art was being turned upside down.

John Sloan said he had not gone to Paris in the early days because he did not want to become a European painter. "I was afraid of being caught in the snares of the art student's life in France – all that business of piling up saucers on café tables with a housekeeper mistress on the side." He mistrusted the French influence that had turned so many American painters like Childe Hassam into Impressionists – what Sloan called "eyesight painting." Hassam had fallen increasingly under the spell of the French Impressionists during the years he and his wife lived in Paris in the 1880s, and when he returned to America in the '90s he was a confirmed practitioner in that style. Sloan did have a high regard for the early French proto-Impressionists, especially Manet, Renoir and Degas. These took as their subjects ordinary people seen working and living in the Paris of Baron Haussmann's grand avenues that alternated with old neighborhoods tumbled together – the cobblestone squares with scruffy cafés remembered with affection in the films of Jacques Tati and in songs like *Sur le Ciel de Paris*. The early Impressionists saw the life of those cafes – and the dance halls and theatres – as the raw material for their art.

Sloan even admired the work of that ultimate Impressionist, Monet. In 1907, Sloan went twice to the Durand-Ruel Gallery in New York to see "Monet's several fine things." Paul Durand-Ruel had introduced French Impressionism to Americans as far back as 1886 when he opened a New York branch of his Paris gallery. Ironically, it was in that year that the Impressionist movement officially expired in France: Monet, Renoir, Sisley and Caillebotte had withdrawn from what would be the final Impressionist Group Exhibition, rather than share wall space with the pointillists Paul Seurat and Odilon Signac.

But few Americans would see French Impressionism in America in the early years – aside from a few wealthy collectors like the Havemeyers who bought the paintings. Mary Cassatt was a friend of George Havemeyer's wife Louisine, and persuaded her to buy works by Degas and Monet on the first of her many buying trips to France. Eventually the bulk of the Havemeyer collection of French Impressionist art went to New York's Metropolitan Museum, but was not exhibited until 1930. Sloan was fortunate to have had an opportunity to see the Monets on view at the Durand-Ruel Gallery as early as 1907.

Sloan's argument was with the America Impressionists who had come to be satisfied with visual effects. Solid forms seemed to evaporate in landscapes suffused with a sunlit haze of color. Artists who worked in this style included William Merritt Chase in his landscapes, as well as Hassam, Frank Benson, Edward Tarbell, Theodore Wendel, Willard Metcalf and John Twachtman. Sloan scorned their use of broken strokes to capture the light and color in a scene. "Don't imitate the color in nature," he said.

Sloan identified more closely with artists who displayed a narrative streak. Especially the most humanistic, like Daumier and Hogarth. Sloan read the European writers, too. He said, "We painted the life we knew as Balzac had drawn the French world he lived in." Balzac had said, "the streets of Paris possess human qualities and we cannot shake off the impressions they make upon our minds." Sloan, similarly, said "we began to paint things of the city because they were interesting as life."

Sloan might have rejected European travel and study, and disdained Impressionism in its later incarnations, but he had equipped himself with a broad, eclectic, cosmopolitan education in painting styles and literature. He was not an artistic naïf when he began to sketch and paint the life of the underclass, mainly immigrants, who occupied the tenements of the Tenderloin district where he and Dolly lived, on the Chelsea side of Broadway between West 14th and 34th Streets.

While surviving on the bread-and-butter work of illustration assignments for *Collier's* and *Century* that kept him and Dolly barely solvent, Sloan was increasingly interested in capturing the life of the city around him he found so invigorating. He walked about the neighborhoods by day, the anonymous *flaneur*, Baudelaire's "gentleman stroller of the city streets," making mental notes of the human comedy to transfer to canvas back at the flat. The neighborhood was all color and noise: German beer gardens, tacky dance halls, gambling parlors, bordellos. He was intoxicated by the New York of that day, what became *his* New York. "Ambiguous," he called it; "evasive, ever changing and always fascinating, like a woman's smile."

He was the benign *voyeur*, gazing upon his neighbors who left their windows open and the shades up in the sweltering New York summer night, or who slept out on the tenement roofs under sooty stars. He witnessed wrenching personal tragedies, and overtures to passion, and poignant vignettes. He said he always had to see some human incident before he wanted to paint a picture, to paint it innocently with "the joy of the painter-poet." He would draw a few lines on the back of an envelope, then later return to the scene to fix in his mind the light and colors.

There were no unkind motives behind his peeping. He said "I never felt the desire to mingle with the people I painted, but observed life as a spectator rather than participant. I think this is the way of the artist who sees and interprets through sympathy. ... I saw people living in the streets and on the rooftops of the city; and I liked their fine human animal spirits. I never pitied them, or idealized them, or sought to propagandize about poverty. I felt with them but did not think for them ... Sympathy with people, I am all for that, but not ideology."

He would create much of his finest, most creative work in this period centering around 1905 and 1906. "It was interest in life and the poetic beauty of things seen when I moved about the city that made me want to paint pictures." At the same time he returned to the etching in which he had developed proficiency when illustrating the novels of Paul de Kock. He produced a series of ten vibrantly perceptive etchings on New York city life of the period that included *Fifth Avenue Critics*, *The Women's Page*, *Turning Out the Light*, and *Roofs*.

Fifth Avenue Critics is Dickensian, with the ample women in the carriage and the Sam Weller coachman. Like *Connoisseurs of Prints* it is nearly a cartoon – which might be expected of a an artist making his way as a commercial illustrator. In *6th Avenue and 30th Street*, Sloan moves beyond the comic cartoon to a human document. Here the blowsy, overdressed, over-age prostitute, emerging for an evening on the streets, is gazed upon by young girls from the tenements who may scorn her, but are dazzled by her smart wardrobe – and may themselves one day see the life of the harlot as their only escape from poverty.

Sloan's finest works of the period are testimonies to the resilient love of life shared by these inhabitants of low-income enclaves of the city. In *Sunday, Drying Their Hair* he portrays the Three Graces as plump, plebeian young women, the ballet of their hair-drying gestures contrasting with the billowing of washing hanging nearby on the roof. *The Hairdresser's Window* has a similar subject. The crowd in the street is entertained by the very visible performance of "Madame Malcomb" seen through a window combing the tresses of a customer. Sloan described in his diary the genesis of the painting: "Walked up to Henri's studio. On the way saw a humorous sight of interest. A window, low, second story, bleached blond dresser bleaching the hair of a client. A small interested crowd about.... Walked out to take another look at the Hair Restorer's Window. Came back and started to paint it."

In *Sunday Afternoon in Union Square* Sloan celebrates the beauty of two young women who are obviously pleased with the attention they are drawing from male passersby, as well as the critical appraisals of two other girls seated nearby. Sloan highlights their outfits in lavender, pink and white, and their blooming flesh tones. He said his motive in painting city scenes like these was to record "bits of joy in human life." Reflecting his cosmopolitan influences, there is much that is European in his work. *Sunday Afternoon in Union Square* could as well have been set in the Tuileries Gardens, with young boulevardiers paying homage to Renoir-ripe demoiselles. The difference is that these are no Parisiennes portrayed with ironic reserve. These are cheerfully sensuous American girls, and Sloan views their allures with humor and good will. It is a richly nuanced American painting.

Sloan said, with some pride, that he had been called the American Hogarth. The Hogarth influence is there in a number of his city prints and paintings, as in *Turning Out the Light*, a scene from one of those tenement windows open to the summer night. But again this is a distinctively American treatment. It is not satire, but an honest celebration of a woman happy in her sexuality, displaying the ample charms she is about to share with the man lying beside her on the bed, as she reaches to envelope them both in darkness.

Sloan did not recognize at the time that he was capturing the essence of a place and a time. He and his fellow Philadelphian émigrés to New York would be forever associated with the portrayal of lower Manhattan street life at the turn of the 20th century. The art world was not ready for that unblinking rendering of city life, and the style was later dismissed as "ashcan school" painting. More impartial critics called the artists American Realists. But if Realism is defined as "the representation of objects, actions, or social conditions as they actually are, without idealization," Sloan was not strictly a Realist. He could be better described as an Urban Humanist. In his art there is more than the surface scene; there is a symbolism that speaks to the viewer at a deeper level. In *McSorley's Bar* there is more than the realism of men standing drinking in a New York tavern. There is dignity and respect and rough fellowship shared by the entire company, the white-aproned waiter as well as the laboring class duo in spirited conversation at one end, and the more elegant patron in Palm Beach hat. All are sharing in the ancient ritual of male camaraderie facilitated by a frothy brew.

Sloan was pursuing his portraits of Tenderloin society in anonymity, but soon his friend Robert Henri would help to gain some exposure for those works. Henri was becoming increasingly prominent in art circles. He even at one time presided over an art academy that bore his name. That was in 1907 when he had forced William Merritt Chase to resign in defeat from the New York School of Art where they were the two most influential art instructors in America. Five years before, Chase had invited Henri to join him on the faculty of what had originally been the Chase School of Art, founded by Chase in 1896. They admired each other's work at the beginning, combining a modern perspective with admiration for masters like Velázquez, Hals and Manet. And both gravitated toward portrait painting.

But they soon split upon issues of the importance of technique, and the relative importance of subject matter. Trained in Munich, like Duveneck and his followers, Chase held that the subject an artist chose was unimportant; what really mattered to make a painting was the degree of professional finish in line, composition and color. He said, "it is never the subject of a picture which makes it great, it is the brush treatment, the color, the form. There is no great art without a great technique back of it."

To Henri, on the other hand, technique was secondary to capturing the reality of the subject and the setting. The differences were evident in their works: Chase's were polished in brushwork and in faithful rendering of the human figure, but lacking in personality. Henri, by contrast, brought out the human qualities of his portrait subjects, even if the work sometimes looked slapdash and the figures not convincingly articulated. Their personalities also clashed. Chase increasingly became the debonair 19th century dandy, while Henri was the enthusiastic apostle of pulsating Realism, urging his students to get out and paint the real life they saw in the streets. Not surprisingly, it was Henri's message and style that resonated with young students like Stuart Davis, Edward Hopper and Rockwell Kent.

In that same year of his victory over Chase, Henri was elected to membership in the powerful National Academy of Design, and the following year was named to the jury for the academy's 82nd annual exhibition. Sloan and others of the Philadelphia crowd might have feared that Henri was going over to the establishment, but he soon reverted to rebellious form. When works submitted by his fellow Urban Realists were rejected, Henri created a furor by resigning from the jury and withdrawing two of his own works from the exhibition.

The following year Henri talked to Sloan about organizing an exhibition of the paintings of their group. The show would be a repudiation of the stifling exclusivity of the National Academy of Design. John Sloan joined in enthusiastically, and they went about organizing what would be the only exhibition of the works of "The Eight." While Henri would generate much of the initial excitement for the group show, proclaiming it a declaration of independence from salon-approved technique in paintings with a moral theme, it was left to Sloan to do much of the legwork of organization. In addition to Henri and Sloan, the other Philadelphians – Glackens, Luks and Shinn – were included, plus three who were hardly Realists in style but shared the independent spirit of the Philadelphians: Lawson, Davies and Prendergast.

Ernest Lawson, from Halifax, Nova Scotia, was essentially an Impressionist. Arthur Davies painted unicorns and floating human figures in an ethereal romantic style. Maurice Prendergast was born in, of all places, St. John's, Newfoundland, but his father's store failed when Maurice was three and the family moved to Boston. Prend-ergast developed there and in Europe a highly individual style in which throngs of faceless people were arranged in bright-colored, tapestry-like settings. Hard-of-hearing and seemingly fragile, Pren-dergast lived in a private world of gentle make-believe – yet was alert to every opportunity to display his works, alone or in groups, and to cultivate potential clients. His brother Charles, an inspired frame-maker, devoted his life to looking after Maurice while the older brother lived, not marrying until after Maurice had died. Maurice Prendergast was still dividing his time between Boston and Europe when he joined The Eight.

William Macbeth agreed to host the show of The Eight at his gallery at 237 Fifth Avenue, the opening scheduled for early in 1908. Advance notices in the press were titillating. *World Magazine* pro-claimed on the cover of its February edition that "New York is hav-ing an art war," incited by "eight rebels who have dared to paint pictures of New York (instead of Europe) and who are holding their rebellious exhibition all by themselves." The critics had their ad-vance viewing and rushed to their typewriters. While many of the reviews were generous and open-minded, a few excoriated the show, deploring its "unhealthy, nay even coarse and vulgar point of view," and calling The Eight "apostles of ugliness." Sloan wrote Henri to say "The *Tribune* has a sermon for us in the morning edition. Ad-vised us to go out and take an academic course, then come out and paint pictures – like all the rest of the saleable things. It is regrettable that these art writers … can command attention in the newspapers. I would rather have the opinion of a newsboy." Sloan's ire would be further fueled by what *Town Topics* had to say about one of his paintings: "I defy you to find anyone in a healthy frame of mind who … wants to hang … John Sloan's *Hairdresser's Window*, and not get disgusted two days later."

The controversy helped to bring in the curious, and Henri wrote to a friend "It was packed like an academy reception from early morn to night." By early February Sloan counted 300 people enter-ing every hour. Altogether about 7,000 visitors crammed into the Macbeth Galleries during the run of the show. And it was a com-mercial success, with total sales valued at over $4,000. Two works by

Davies sold. Two by Henri. One each by Shinn, Luks and Lawson. None by Sloan or Glackens. Yet a jubilant Sloan proclaimed, "We've made a success!" If Sloan had his faults, envy of the good fortune of his comrades in art was not one.

Over the next two years, with Henri absent in Paris, Sloan was the prime mover in booking the paintings from the Macbeth exhibition into the Chicago Art Institute, the Pennsylvania Academy of Fine Arts in Philadelphia, and other institutions across the country from Boston to Cincinnati. Thanks to the energy and persistence of John Sloan, visitors to art museums across the eastern half of the nation saw first-hand what those Urban Realists painting in New York were up to. But while John Sloan could count on his paintings being seen on the road wherever the Macbeth show traveled, his works were not accepted on their own by major institutions. When two of his paintings were rejected by the Carnegie Institute in Pittsburgh he was mildly depressed. "Is the exhibition game lost for me? Oh well, I paint them for myself."

In 1910, to help sustain enthusiasm for the traveling exhibition, Sloan floated the idea among his fellow rebel artists of offering an alternative to the juried exhibitions of the institutes, in which established artists from a previous era presumed to judge young innovators. The insurgents would hold a non-juried show, in which the works of any artist who paid a nominal entrance fee would be shown, arranged by the painters' names in alphabetical order. Members of The Eight and other nontraditional artists formed a loose organization called Independent American Artists, and a committee was formed to organize an exhibition to be held at West 35th Street in April of 1910. The gruntwork, as usual, fell upon Sloan, who was secretary and treasurer.

The 250 paintings, 20 sculptures and 219 prints exhibited on three floors of the building were, predictably, of varied quality. On each side of a Henri might be a submission from an earnest but untalented dabbler. Of all the works displayed only five sold, for a total of $75.00. Sloan would never lose faith in the democratically inclusive concept of non-juried shows. He was not discouraged by the results of this first attempt.

In 1913 the American art world was turned on its ear. The International Exhibition of Modern Art opened at New York's 69th Regiment Armory. The American viewers were stunned by their first exposure to one revolutionary European school after another. They gasped at the Post-Impressionist, Symbolist, Cubist, and Fauvist works that dominated the 1,600 paintings, sculptures and decorative works that lined the vast hall. Thronging the galleries day after day, the visitors hooted at Duchamp's *Nude Descending a Staircase*, but works by Cézanne, van Gogh, Matisse and Kandinsky had power and originality that could not be dismissed. Modern art had shaken the European art world to its foundations, and now this shattering of the old canons had crossed the Atlantic.

Overnight the works by Sloan and the other American interpreters of urban America in the show seemed dated, even conventional, when compared with the bold abstractions and innovations in form and color on display by the Europeans. (To be sure, the furor created by the Armory Show went unnoticed by most Americans who, according to the *Independent* magazine, were obsessed with baseball, the movies, whist, the turkey rot, and the "funny pages.")

Robert Henri was very much aware of the stunning success of the Armory Show, and it left him bitter. He had not played his usual role as impresario of the exhibition – in fact had been shut out by Art Davies and Walt Kuhn, the organizers. Henri would thereafter continue to paint and to teach at the Art Students League, but would play a diminished role in the American art scene until his death in 1929.

Unlike Henri, Sloan had not been dismayed by the Armory Show. On the contrary, he was enthusiastic about much that he saw in the works of the Europeans. The explosive way that van Gogh handled color, for example. And Cézanne's repudiation of the Impressionists, simplifying the forms of buildings and mountains to their geometric essentials. In fact, Sloan had been receptive to the innovations of the Post-Impressionists prior to the Armory Show. A year earlier he had written to John Quinn, "I have not been so dry a reed as to stand unbending against the breeze of brighter color which is sweeping across the field of art." Sloan had been aware, too, of the little-noted revolution under way at Studio 291 on New York's lower 5th Avenue, where photographer Alfred Stieglitz, aided by Albert Steichen, first introduced the works of Rodin, Matisse, Cézanne and Picasso to a puzzled American public in 1911.

The Armory Show eclipsed for a generation the work of Sloan, Henri, Glackens and Luks. The art world, and the gallery-going public, were swept up in enthusiasm for the experiments in color and form and technique embodied particularly in the works of Cézanne, van Gogh, Gauguin and Matisse. In their altered perspectives on reality there was little place for the anecdotal or for social commentary. Or for the humanism that had illuminated John Sloan's city paintings.

Sloan paintings were hung in the Armory Show, but did not sell. That was no surprise. What did surprise John Sloan was that he did actually sell his first painting in that year of 1913. His classmate at Philadelphia's Central High, Albert Barnes, purchased *Nude, Green Scarf*, probably at the urging of fellow classmate Bill Glackens. It was not one of Sloan's rooftop rhapsodies of city life, but it bore his signature.

The purchaser, Dr. Barnes, could well afford to collect paintings. He had co-developed what was hailed as a wonder drug for preventing gonorrheal blindness in infants. He marketed it as Argyrol and made a fortune. Barnes first commissioned Glackens to assemble the rudiments of his art collection. Soon Barnes came to rely, instead, on Paul Guillaume who exhibited the works of Henri Rousseau, Modigliani and Soutine in his gallery on the rue La Boétie in Paris. Under Guillaume's guidance Barnes amassed a superb collection of Post-Impressionist works for his museum in Merion, Pennsylvania to which, grudgingly and infrequently, he admitted a few visitors.

Sloan had mixed feelings about the sale of a painting. "I can't believe it will really come to pass that I sell a painting. I am not at all excited or elated even. I regret that the artist must *sell* his work." Speaking for himself and the Philadelphians, Sloan said "We came to the ... conclusion that an artist who wanted to be independent must expect to make a living separately from the pictures painted for his own pleasure."

Sloan had always been an illustrator by trade; painting was a private journey of the spirit that he pursued to satisfy creative impulses. The jolt he felt at having to part with a painting echoed Camille

Corot's mock dismay at finally selling his first painting when he was over fifty. Pretending to be inconsolable, Corot complained "I have had a complete collection of Corots, and now, alas, it has been broken!"

In the decades that followed, the world would be swept by global economic collapse, two world wars, and genocide on a scale that redefined man's inhumanity to man. The art of those times would seek to express the anguish, often in dark allegorical forms and structures. It would be decades before the early Sloans – those warm, human episodes of human life – would be recognized as powerful records of ordinary people adapting to a new urban America.

John Sloan himself was perhaps too close to his early work to recognize its underlying power and significance. He would later speak dismissively of his urban paintings of his thirties as "Sloans." He would take new directions in Gloucester and Santa Fe, but he would not necessarily move beyond the exuberant warmth of those rooftop anecdotes that spoke so eloquently for their time and place.

Chapter Seven
STRAYING OFF COURSE

~~~

Northwest Passages / The Masses

Northwest Passages

J OHN SLOAN and Sol Jacobs were both reasonable men, but they
could not leave well enough alone. Each veered off course, and
lost considerable headway in so doing. John Sloan, in his 30s, had
been honing an artistic style that combined humanism with increasing proficiency in composition and color. But he became distracted
and, as he would later admit, lost years that he could have better
devoted to painting.

Sol Jacobs went astray in a very different manner. After early
triumphs in the mackerel fishery he undertook a venture that, in ret-
rospect, proved to be far too ambitious. For that he paid a high price.

Mackerel behave in accordance with ocean forces about which
little is known. In the early to mid 1880s the fish had obligingly filled
the nets of Capt. Jacobs and others of the seining fleet (by this time
no one was jigging for mackerel any longer), which redounded to
the prosperity of the fishermen, and to all the trades of Gloucester
dependent upon the vessels.

Then the purse seines began to close on fewer and fewer mackerel, and even Capt. Jacobs, who many believed could think like a
mackerel, was unable to find the fish in the usual hangouts where
they should be gathering as they migrated up the coast. The captain
had much company in chasing those scarce mackerel. From 1881 to
'82 the Gloucester mackerel fleet had increased from 120 to 140 sail.

Sol grew impatient at the sudden lack of cooperation on the
part of the mackerel, and put his fertile mind to considering other
avenues by which he could prosper. It might seem that the logi-
cal alternative would be to pursue other varieties of fish. Cod, for
example. Over five and a half million pounds of cod were landed

at Gloucester in 1887. And over 800,000 pounds of halibut were pitched onto the Gloucester wharves that same year. Surely a fishing captain with Sol's expertise could survive in those fisheries until the mackerel returned. But no, Capt. Sol was looking farther afield. He was wondering if there might not be opportunities in the northern coastal regions on the opposite side of the continent.

Notices were appearing in the *Cape Ann Advertiser* directed at citizens of substance who might be interested in emigrating to the Northwest, or at least investing in the potential of the region. H. H. Dearborn & Co., Bankers, advertised for properties in Seattle, "The Queen City of Puget Sound ... surrounded by fine agricultural and timber land." Dearborn & Co. announced that "We ... select the best-located lots for investors, have titles carefully examined, pay taxes for non-residents, and sell their lots when ordered on commission."

The printing presses for the railroads opening up the Northwest were also touting the wonders of the region, as in *The Northwest* published by the Northern Pacific Railroad. Its premier issue in 1883 bubbled with enthusiasm:

> The development of this immense region [the Northwest] has gone forward with great rapidity of late; but there is so much room in it for people and enterprise, that for at least ten years to come it will be the most attractive field on the continent for new settlement. Farmers, manufacturers, mechanics, miners of coal, iron, gold, silver and copper, lumbermen, cattle raisers, wool growers and business men of all occupations will find there an outlet of escape from overcrowded communities, and abundant openings for their energy, skill and capital.

No mention of fishing here, but Capt. Jacobs could consider the omission favorable to his own purposes. He made some inquiries and learned that the Makah Indians on the Northwest Coast had been fishing for halibut for centuries, but that there was no organized fisheries industry.

According to newspaper stories, Sol said he had taken a trip west in the summer of 1887 to take a look around Seattle and other ports along the coast of what was then the Washington Territory, and that what he saw convinced him that the conditions were promising for developing a fishery. Whether or not he actually made the trip, he would have seen a series of letters in the *Cape Ann Advertiser* in 1886 extolling the potential for sealing, supplemented by halibut fishing, in the Northwest. Sol announced a major undertaking: he would send his two schooners, the *Mollie Adams* and the *Edward E. Webster*, around Cape Horn to fish for halibut and hunt seals along the Northwest Coast.

The vessels cast off on October 27 of 1887, and the town gave the *Adams* and the *Webster* a glorious sendoff. It was the first time since the California Gold Rush thirty-eight years before that an expedition on this scale had set forth from Gloucester, and thousands of people lined the wharves. Capt. Jacobs had seen to it that there would be adequate media coverage: George Procter, editor and co-owner of the *Cape Ann Advertiser*, was there, and so was James Pringle, special correspondent for the *Boston Globe*. Capt. Jacobs announced that he was offering a prize to the first of his vessels to reach the Golden Gate – the *Adams* whose master was Capt. Charles Johnson, or the *Webster* under the command of Capt. John Harris. Both of Sol's vessels were well known on the Gloucester waterfront, especially the *Webster* as the vessel in which Capt. Jacobs had compiled his record catches of mackerel.

Steam tugs towed the two schooners out of the inner harbor past Ten Pound Island where both hoisted their sails and caught the wind, to the hosannas of the multitude along the shore. The *Advertiser* confidently predicted that Capt. Jacobs would "enter into the business with all the vigor which has characterized his career for the past 15 years, in which time he has kept well at the front among our most successful skippers."

Capt. Jacobs had three objectives for his two vessels. They would fish for halibut, yes. But they would also do some trading, and for that purpose carried assorted dry goods, boots, shoes and hardware. They would also engage in seal hunting. Capt. Jacobs had it on good authority that there were huge herds of seals in the Northwest, particularly along the shores of islands off Alaska. True, it was a bitterly cold climate up there, fraught with ice, the turbulent seas often shrouded in fog. But weren't those the conditions that he had been familiar with in Newfoundland from the cradle? Who better than he and some of the other men from the outports to put their sealing prowess to good use in the Pacific? The *Adams* and the *Webster* carried Newfoundland sealing punts built for Capt. Jacobs by the Higgins & Gifford boat shop in Gloucester. They were of a type Sol had seen used successfully out of Twillingate. Built of well-seasoned swamp cedar on a bent-oak frame, these open boats with sharp bows and flaring topsides combined strength with the lightness, speed and maneuverability needed for pursuing seals in open water. They would be the first of their kind seen in the Pacific Northwest, and remained a popular style of seal boat in those waters for years thereafter.

The punts on the *Adams* and *Webster* were to be manned by men who knew how to hunt seals at sea. Capt. Jacobs had sent brother Bill Hodder down to Newfoundland to recruit a score of rugged fellows with solid sealing credentials. The captain and Bill, and Bill's son Capt. Sam Hodder, and the recruited sealers were then to head west by rail. The plan was that they would meet the schooners after the latter had completed their voyages around Cape Horn and up the coast to Washington Territory.

All of Gloucester was excited by the captain's bold vision. He was preparing to leave on his cross-continent train journey when, on Wednesday evening, February 8th, 1888, at Gloucester's Webster House, a group of leading members of the fishing fleet gathered for a "Complimentary Supper tendered by the Gloucester skippers to Capt. Solomon Jacobs." His peers had organized the dinner to wish the captain godspeed in his venture to the North Pacific. The organizers reported that "All the boys fell into line not only with good words but with the $2.00 bills."

The fishing captains brought to the table the hearty appetites of seamen, and dispatched quantities of oysters on the half shell, oyster soup, salmon, fillet of beef, turkey, ham tongue and lamb. After they polished off the final courses of the feast – pies, cakes, ice cream – they settled down with coffee and cigars to hear tributes to their fellow master mariner who was about to depart their company.

William F. Gaffney spoke of the esteem in which they held their "faithful, kind, generous-hearted friend." Capt. Nathaniel Greenleaf was brief and emphatic. He said he hoped for the success of Capt. Jacobs, and called for three cheers (which, it was reported, "were given with a will"). "Vociferous applause" followed Capt. Charles Lawson who cried out, "If Jacobs kills as many seals as he has mackerel, I say god help the seals." Capt. Joseph Smith spoke on a more sober note: "I am sorry that Capt. Jacobs is going away, as he is my friend in every sense of that term. There is no one who feels worse to have him go than I do."

Capt. Jacobs was moved by the kind words of his fellow captains – all vigorous competitors on the fishing banks, but brothers in the courage, ability and audacity of successful masters of fishing schooners. He could only say he would long remember this evening, and was going West only because he hoped to better himself.

Was the captain planning to pick up stakes and move to the Northwest permanently? Did he intend to send back word to have Sarah sell the house on Prospect Street and pack the young household onto a train for the far West? Sarah's opinions at the time are unrecorded, but she would have been reluctant to move west with four children between the ages of one and nine. Nevertheless, she would have been resigned to abide by Sol's judgment.

But the family never did leave Gloucester, and it seems more likely that Capt. Jacobs was planning to remain in Washington Territory only long enough to set up operations. His two schooner crews would catch fish and kill seals, while he set up the mechanisms for shipment of the catches back to the East Coast. He probably intended to supervise the marketing from his base in Gloucester. It was an ambitious scheme, fraught with hazards beyond those that Sol anticipated. Capt. Sol said in his remarks to his fellow captains that he hoped the boys would welcome him back as generously as they were marking his departure.

Capt. Jacobs then took to the rails with his band of fishermen and sealers. In their boots and heavy-duty outerwear they must have presented a colorful contrast to the properly got-out urban types on the main line from Boston to Chicago, among them flashy commercial travelers, as well as mothers in modest traveling attire shepherding their children en route to join husbands somewhere in the West. At the end of the car populated by the fishermen-sealers the smoke would have been thick, with generous contributions from Capt. Jacobs' cigars. And the cuspidors would have been in regular use.

At Chicago Capt. Jacobs' group transferred to the Chicago, Burlington and Quincy Railroad, then often called the "Q," but which would become more familiarly known as the "Burlington." They traveled north to the western tip of Lake Superior to connect with the Northern Pacific for the 1,961-mile trip across the continent to Puget Sound. The Northern Pacific, originally authorized by President Abraham Lincoln to provide a second rail corridor to the West Coast, roughly followed the route blazed by Lewis and Clark. To sell bonds to finance the building of the road, Jay Cooke had lauded the virtues of the region, neglecting to mention the severity of the winters when, as the saying went, there was nothing between the prairies and the North Pole but a barbed wire fence. Skeptics referred with merriment to the railroad's route as "Cooke's banana belt."

Construction had been intermittent, delayed by financial difficulties and Indian unrest, but the enterprise gradually moved forward, with brute labor provided by a workforce of 15,000 Chinese. By the mid-'80s tracks were running all the way to the Pacific Coast, and the Northern Pacific seized upon this milestone to step up its advertising at home and abroad. Land agents publicized real estate for sale on this last great American frontier.

The effectiveness of the publicity overseas would have been evident from the exotic dress and languages of the passengers sharing the coaches with Capt. Jacobs and his party. Beyond Chicago many Scandinavian, German and Czech farming families would be aboard, eventually gathering up their portmanteaus and bundles and leaving the train at snow-swept little stations in North Dakota and Montana, squinting at the prairies endless before them to the horizon. If they had a little to invest they might be on their way to claim their own homesteads, perhaps to combine into agricultural cooperatives with neighbors speaking their language and sharing their old-country ways. Others had been recruited to work the fields owned by large Eastern investor-owners. In time they could hope to make their own way in this new land vast in territory and opportunity.

During the long days as the train swayed along and spewed its great plume of coal smoke into the western sky, Capt. Jacobs and his men would be entertaining one another with anecdotes or personal observations, or gazing out at a landscape hardly less unchanging than the surface of the sea. They might wonder that they saw none of the famous buffalo herds, but those had been cleaned out of this part of the country by parties of sportsmen who had hunted in comfort, firing from the windows of a train. A pity – some in Capt. Jacobs' group would have liked to take a shot themselves to bring down one of those great beasts.

It is possible that they were aboard one of the new vestibule trains that were added to Northern Pacific's Tacoma line in 1888. Before the introduction of these connecting platforms between cars, passengers were virtually imprisoned in the coach they boarded – it was exceedingly dangerous to cross in the open over the exposed steel couplings between cars. The "vestibuled train," as the railroad advertising described it, transformed rail travel by making it safe and convenient to move about from coaches to dining and sleeping cars.

At night the coaches were illuminated by gaslight. It was bitter cold outside on the winter plains, and Sol and the other passengers would appreciate the steam heat, generated by the locomotive, that circulated under the floor of their coach. It was a recent improvement upon the uneven heat provided by stoves formerly mounted at either end of each car.

The landscape changed dramatically as they left the plains and steamed through western Montana Territory (Montana would not become a state until the following year). The locomotive labored up steep grades with a sheer wall of rock on one side and an abyss on the other. The passage through the Rockies culminated in a dramatic climb over Stampede Pass at 3,000 feet. A tunnel nearly two miles in length was under construction through the mountain, but the Stampede Tunnel would not be completed until May 27th. When Capt. Jacobs and his party made their trip, in late winter, the rails still wound upward through the steep pass by way of a temporary switchback.

Grades approached six percent, which meant that the train climbed six feet in every hundred feet it traveled. Only five coaches could make the ascent at one go, and they were hitched to the two largest locomotives in the world at the time, M Class 2-10-0s, one at the front end of the train and one at the rear. In an arrangement known as a decapod, the locomotive's two leading wheels were followed by ten coupled driving wheels. With power going to five of six of the axles, the locomotive had full traction. A brakeman rode the roof of every second car, braced to put all of his strength into a turn of the brake wheel if the train began to slip backward.

Capt. Jacobs' men must have been keenly interested as the train labored upward for an hour and a quarter over the eight-mile detour, winding over timber trestles constructed with virtuoso self-assurance across cleaving ravines. Finally the train reached the summit and the hard-working locomotive boilers could hiss contentedly as they cooled. Once over the pass the train sped on through Washington Territory to reach the Pacific at Tacoma.

But the transcontinental trip did not end there. Capt. Jacobs and his party then had to journey on by steam ferry to Port Townsend at the northeast tip of Washington's Olympic Peninsula, hoping to rendezvous with the schooners he had dispatched around Cape Horn. Sol was relieved to find the *Mollie Adams* already in the harbor. She had arrived on March 3rd, having had a relatively uneventful transit into the Pacific and up the coast, only putting in to take on water at Good Success Bay on Terra del Fuego. But there was no word of the *Edward E. Webster*.

Capt. Jacobs could see that Port Townsend had a broad harbor well protected from storms, with good mooring grounds for his vessels. A large number of square-rigged barks and ships were riding at anchor, having arrived from overseas to deliver goods, then waiting to take on timber felled in the vast forests of the region.

Port Townsend was a pulsating boom town. The Northern Pacific had strongly intimated that Port Townsend was destined to become the western terminus of its transcontinental network, and the other great railroad in the Northwest, the Union Pacific, was projecting a route north to link with that traffic. There was a frenzy of building in the town, with speculators erecting resplendent Victorian mansions on the choicest lots. All on the anticipation that Port Townsend would become a vital cog in the import-export economy of the fast-developing Northwest.

Soon afterward, however, Port Townsend received crushing

news. Instead of reaching Port Townsend, the Northern Pacific was going to terminate its long-haul lines on the eastern shores of Puget Sound, at Tacoma and Seattle. These ports, instead of Port Townsend, were to become the beneficiaries of the transcontinental rail links. The economy of the region did boom as a result, and the population of Washington, first as a Territory and later as a State, would swell from 75,116 in 1880 to 375,232 a decade later. By the late 1890s much of population of bypassed Port Townsend had moved on, leaving it as a footnote to the history of Northwest expansion. Today many of the ornamented mansions remain, monuments to a municipal casualty of westward expansion. In 1888, though, Capt. Jacobs found all of the supplies and equipment he needed for fishing and sealing operations available at the port's piers. He made Port Townsend his base of operations.

Sol became impatient over the failure of the *Webster* to arrive. When he received word of a seal bonanza, he decided fishing could wait. California steamers had reported running through one herd that extended a hundred miles, with the seals "as thick as they could swim." Four days after he arrived in Port Townsend, Sol took the *Adams* on a sealing voyage from off the mouth of the Columbia River, following the seals north. The *Adams* hunted until May 17, but took only 700 seals, not considered a good catch.

Finally in early June, three months after the arrival of the *Adams* in Port Townsend, the *Edward Webster* hove into view in Admiralty Inlet at the entrance to the port. Capt. Harris reported on his voyage to Sol Jacobs, and it was entirely a tale of woe. The schooner had been damaged in a storm off Argentina and had to lay up in Montevideo for repairs at a cost of $5,000. After the *Webster* put to sea again, several of the men developed scurvy, and the vessel limped northward through the Pacific with an ailing crew. By the time the *Webster* finally put in at San Francisco, one man had died and all the others were exhausted. And they knew they had caused great concern among their loved ones. Back in Gloucester the *Webster* had long since been given up for lost. Capt. Harris told the San Francisco papers that the *Webster* was "an old boat" and that "it was a miracle" that he had made it to the West Coast. (The *Webster* was then only eighteen years old and would remain a hard-working and able vessel until, under another owner, she was lost at sea eight years later.)

Although the *Webster* was battered and its crew still recovering, Capt. Jacobs had his fleet together at last, and business could proceed. After his initial lack of success in seal hunting, Sol turned his attention to the halibut. Like their Atlantic cousins, the Pacific halibut were flat fish that swam along the ocean bottom with one side down, both eyes disconcertingly located on the top of their bodies. The Makah Indians of Cape Flattery had harvested the fish from time immemorial by their own version of long-line fishing. They traveled over the open ocean in big cedar canoes and trailed lines made of sinew or kelp hundreds of feet long. The barbs on the hooks that studded the lines were shaped ingeniously to fit the halibut's vertical mouth.

A few white fishermen also fished for the halibut from small boats, basically using the same technique as the Makah. But all that changed when the Massachusetts fishermen arrived. Capt. Jacobs' *Mollie Adams* and the *Edward E. Webster* fished tub-trawling style, each schooner carrying six dories from which two dorymates manhandled the hooked halibut into their dory for transfer to the schooners. Sol's fishermen would discover that these halibut of the Northwest could be more than eight feet long and weigh 700 pounds – not easy for two men to wrestle into a small boat.

Despite the publicity surrounding Capt. Jacobs' expedition to open the Northwest halibut fishery, he was trumped by a competitor. Perhaps word of the captain's plans for exploiting the fishing potential of the Northwest had reached Swampscott, a small port down the shore from Gloucester. In any case, a little 85-ton, 79-foot-long schooner, the *Oscar and Hattie*, owned and commanded by a Capt. Johnson of that town, had set sail for the Pacific close behind the *Mollie Adams* and *Edward E. Webster*. The *Oscar and Hattie* had been built in Essex in 1884 in the Moses Adams yard, and was registered in Marblehead in 1887.

Capt. Jacobs failed to protect his flank. While he was off seal-hunting in the *Adams*, the *Oscar and Hattie*, now commanded by Capt. Silas Calder, went after fish, and reached Tacoma on September 20, 1888 with 50,000 pounds of halibut caught off Flattery Bank opposite Vancouver Island and near the entrance to the Strait of Juan de Fuca. The iced catch from the *Oscar and Hattie* was unloaded at the Tacoma docks and shipped to Boston via the Northern Pacific. Capt. Sol was thus deprived of his goal of being first to enter commercial halibut fishing in the Pacific Northwest and to ship the catch to eastern markets. It was a moment of triumph for the *Oscar and Hattie*, but short-lived. She lost money on that first consignment, sent no further shipments, and was seized for debts the following year. In 1892 the *Oscar and Hattie*, by then British-owned, was impounded by U.S. authorities on the charge of hunting seals in the Bering Sea. This charge may have given rise to the story that Capt. Jacobs was imprisoned for seal hunting in restricted waters. As we shall see, the captain apparently *did* spend some time in a Canadian jail, but as the result of a civil suit.

No doubt incensed at having been out-fished by anybody, Capt. Jacobs took the *Mollie Adams* on three trips to Swiftsure Bank off Juan de Fuca Strait that yielded a total of 145,000 pounds of halibut. He gave glowing interviews to the California newspapers as to how he "caught a quantity of halibut which he shipped in a refrigerator car to New York and other points, where they sold readily and were pronounced excellent." Continued the captain, "The shores of the northern Pacific teem with this fish, and it is only a matter of a couple of days' fishing to load up a vessel, get into port, load right into a car alongside the pier. and ship in all directions."

Sol sent back optimistic reports to the Gloucester press as well, and included a warm testimonial to the quality of the copper paint on the bottom of the *Mollie Adams* supplied by Gloucester's James H. Tarr company: "I cheerfully recommend it to all as an A-1 article." Perhaps fired by Capt. Jacobs' optimistic assessment of the prospects for developing a halibut fishery in the Northwest, two of Gloucester's municipal luminaries, ex-mayor Robinson and Samuel G. Root, took their own fact-finding trip to Seattle.

The truth was, however, that Capt. Jacobs lost money on his shipments of halibut. He was charged $1.25 per ton in freight charges for his first shipment, and $15 a ton for ice – rates that Sol considered grossly out of line. Based on the earlier published prices, Sol had calculated that he would be able to sell Pacific halibut in the Boston and New York markets for eight cents a pound, much lower than the price set by a halibut trust that controlled the Grand Banks supply of the fish. The trust was dominated by the New England Fish Company, formed in 1868 as a combination of eleven Gloucester wholesale fish dealers. The New England Fish Company, and its affiliated Canadian Fishing Company, Ltd., did not take kindly to an interloper selling Pacific halibut at well below their controlled market price. The captain had reason to suspect that the trust, or its agents, were taking steps to inflate his costs of doing business.

At roughly the same time, back in Gloucester, other voices were being raised against the power of the fish wholesaler trusts. At a meeting on the evening of March 19th, 140 of the port's master mariners – present and past captains – formally organized the Master Mariners' Association "for the object of mutual protection from alleged wrongs from which they claim to suffer at the hands of fishing monopolies." Two years earlier, two dozen of the captains of the port had begun to meet, and now, in 1888, an enlarged membership gave the now formally organized association greater standing in the industry.

The Master Mariners' Association was a typical professional organization, uniting in defense of its members' business interests, and at the same time providing comfortable quarters for socializing. On March 22 the members elected officers, and were busy fitting up "in an attractive manner" their rooms in the Ferguson Block on Front Street. By early April generous gifts were being accepted that would render the meeting rooms even more inviting to the members. Joseph W. Collins, formerly a Gloucester schooner master and now author of definitive U.S. documents on the history and state of the fisheries, donated charts and books for the Association's library. And an "elegant marble-top table" was donated by Mrs. Solomon Jacobs (although absent in the Far West, Capt. Sol clearly was casting his support behind the organization). Later that month the members present got down to business at a meeting that deplored the Bayard-Chamberlain Treaty, signed two months before but eventually rejected by the U.S. Senate. In the opinion of the membership at the Gloucester meeting, the treaty was weak in allowing low-priced Canadian fish to enter American markets.

As time passed the Gloucester Master Mariners' Association

would become increasingly devoted to fellowship, especially as the captains from the schooner era aged and sought the company of their remaining peers. They readily got together with other groups as well; in 1895 they took on the town's business men in a series of games of whist (the wily skippers prevailed over the men of commerce). The fact that, in 1888, his fellow captains had organized to protest the abuses of fishing monopolies was of no practical value to Capt. Jacobs. Losing money on costly shipments of halibut, he sold the *Mollie Adams*. It is probable that he intended to sell his two schooners in the West eventually, rather than attempt to round up crews to sail them back around Cape Horn.

After Sol failed in his attempt to establish a Northwest halibut trade, the New England Fish Company stepped in and was soon shipping halibut from British Columbia to Boston via the Canadian Pacific Railway. In November, 1893 the company itself entered the fishery in North Pacific waters, outfitting a small freighter, the *Capilano*, for halibut fishing. Sol had been the trail-blazer, but well-financed opponents seized upon his initiative and made the West Coast halibut fishery a paying proposition.

Stymied in his grand plan of transcontinental halibut shipments, Capt. Jacobs redoubled his sealing efforts. But here again he encountered daunting obstacles. He had sent the *Edward E. Webster* on sealing trips, but the kill off the Washington Territory coast was disappointing. He needed to get to the rookeries where, as in Newfoundland waters, the most profitable kills could be made. On the Fourth of July 1889, after a voyage of 1,500 miles from Port Townsend, he sailed in the *Webster* into the tiny port of Ounalaska (later Unalaska) in the Aleutian Islands, asserting his right as an American fisherman to hunt seals outside the three-mile limit in Alaskan territorial waters. He was promptly advised by American officials that if he attempted any sealing operations in the Pribilof Island rookeries or elsewhere in the Bering Sea, the *Webster* would be seized forthwith by the *Rush*, the American revenue cutter patrolling the area.

Capt. Jacobs found himself in the middle of an international dispute, and that would not have been unusual – he had been involved in many between the conflicting interests of the New England fishing fleet and the Canadian Maritime Provinces and Newfoundland. But here there were multiple interests involved – the United States, Great Britain and its Canadian Pacific territories, the Russians, the Aleut Indians, and the Alaska Commercial Company.

The most formidable of the forces aligned against the captain might well have been the Alaska Commercial Company, whose dominance in the north went back to 1867. In that year, following the U.S. purchase of Alaska for the $7.2 million derided by critics as "Seward's Folly," the Alaska Commercial Company acquired the assets of the Russian-American Company. It thus acquired commercial control over vast expanses of America's new territory. Ten years later the United States granted a lease conferring upon the Alaska Commercial Company exclusive rights to kill seals on the Pribilof Islands, with no restraints other than a limit on the number of seals that could be taken each year.

The U.S. Congress came to regret having given the company *carte blanche*. There were disturbing reports that the Alaska Commercial Company was keeping the native Aleuts in a state of serfdom, that the allowed seal harvest was being exceeded, and that the company was gaining increasing monopoly over the entire Alaskan economy through its trading stations scattered across the territory.

But Congress failed to act. The power of the Alaska Commercial Company was deeply entrenched. And Capt. Jacobs' challenge to its authority was poorly timed. In 1886, three years before his arrival, the sealers *Carolena*, *Onward* and *Thornton*, flying the British flag as Canadian vessels, had been captured by an American revenue cutter and charged with sealing within restricted waters; i.e., waters controlled by the Alaska Commercial Company. The British government protested and the matter went to arbitration.

The American position was that there were no seal breeding grounds on the Canadian Pacific coast (the two seal rookeries in the Bering Sea were the Pribilof Islands belonging to the U.S., and the Komandorski group belonging to Russia). Consequently sealers from Canada could legally conduct only "pelagic" sealing – killing seals at sea. That, said the Americans, was disastrous to the seal population because whelping mothers were killed indiscriminately with the males. And it was wasteful, because only one in seven of the seals shot or otherwise disabled was actually brought on board. Also, the U.S. pointed out, in what seemed a new and uncharacteristic concern for conservation, the seal population was in danger of being overhunted. Indeed, a herd of two million seals in 1882 would decline by more than half to 900,000 by 1890.

All in all, the whole issue of seal-hunting in the Bering Sea had become a highly sensitive matter. Sol Jacobs, true to form, was not intimidated. He did not accept his exclusion from the Alaskan seal hunt without a fight. He protested to the U.S. Treasury Department, arguing that his expedition had left home in Massachusetts to engage in sealing with the full expectation that American vessels would have fishing and sealing rights in what were now the U.S. waters of the Bering Sea.

He asked that, if he took seals south of the Aleutian Islands, he be allowed to run to Unalaska without fear that his vessel would be seized. Once there, he would have his skins counted by revenue officers, whereupon he would proceed to fish for halibut in the Bering Sea. He wished, he said, only to hunt seals as far as the Alaska Commercial Company's official grounds, and then end the season by fishing. Further, he requested permission to take sea otter in Alaskan waters.

The official response was that instructions sent to the revenue officers the preceding year were still in effect. Seals could not be killed except by persons authorized by the Territory of Alaska in waters ceded by Russia. Those authorized persons, of course, consisted exclusively of the Alaska Commercial Company. As for the sea otters – tut, tut, the claimant should know that only Alaskan natives were allowed to kill the passive sea otters that floated on their backs feeding in kelp beds. (Hunted almost to extinction, the sea otter were later protected.)

In defense of his attempts to fish and hunt seals in Alaskan waters, Capt. Jacobs, signing himself "Master of the schooner *Mollie Adams*," wrote eloquently to the United States Senate on May 24, 1889:

> What the fishermen want, and what they ask Congress to do for them, is to give them the right to go into any American waters, except those

immediately adjacent to the Pribyloff Islands, and to fish and hunt for all animals or fish therein, and then so legislate that every poor man in the country may have a cheap supply, which is now forbidden to him by the extortion of the railroads. If we can have the privilege of fishing and hunting unmolested, and can secure the cheap transportation I have mentioned, the fishermen will be encouraged to come out to this coast, and instead of half a dozen schooners, as at present, I venture to assert that within three years there would be a fleet of six hundred sail out of Puget Sound, which would form a means of procuring recruits for our navy as well as a food supply for our people.

Here the captain strikes all the notes that might be expected to resonate with federal officials: patriotism, affordable food for the common man, trained manpower for the Navy, and curbing of the monopolistic railroads. Sol went on to suggest that seal-hunting was a public service, ridding the seas of predatory beasts that competed with humans for fish. He pointed out that Massachusetts offered a dollar bounty for the nose of every seal disposed of.

Despite his claims of law-abiding rectitude, Capt. Jacobs, in a civil suit, admitted indirectly that he had done a bit of seal hunting in the Bering Sea himself. In January 1889 he was sued by an American seal broker at Victoria, British Columbia named Baxter who alleged that Jacobs had defaulted on a contract to deliver to said Baxter the skins of all seals taken by Jacobs' two schooners. Instead, said Baxter, Jacobs had sold the skins to other parties.

Sol did not deny selling the skins, but entered the interesting defense that, inasmuch as seal hunting in the Bering Sea was in violation of U.S. statutes, the contract was not valid. In effect the captain was claiming that he owed Baxter nothing because he, Jacobs, had caught the seals illegally. The Dominion court found for the plaintiff and ordered Capt. Jacobs to pay Baxter $4,161. Sol insisted he was in the right, said he was damned if he'd pay, and was clapped into prison. By some accounts he languished in a Canadian jail for seven months and came out in poor health. Capt. Sol did not confirm or deny that he had served time in Canada; he would only say, probably with tongue planted firmly in cheek, that he had enjoyed the personal hospitality of Mayor Grant of Victoria.

In any event, his western adventures had come to an ignominious end. Sol sold the *Edward E. Webster*, as he had the *Mollie Adams*, for whatever it would bring. Confusingly, the *Gloucester Daily Times* reported, on August 21, 1889, that the *Webster*, under command of Sol's brother Bill Hodder, had run into the harbor at Coal Bay, Unga Island, Alaska "under full sail before a full breeze and heavy sea," when she struck on a sunken reef and soon broke up. That may have been the basis for an entry in the customs records of Seattle to the effect that, in 188?, the *Webster* had struck a hidden reef off Unga Island and was a total loss.

Actually the reports of the demise of the *Webster* were greatly exaggerated. Six weeks after the story in the Gloucester paper, a correction stated that the *Webster* was got off the ledge and repaired. The particulars as to her history and dimensions listed in the *Annual List of Merchant Vessels of the United States* of 1894 leave no doubt that this was the *Edward E. Webster* that Sol Jacobs had owned, and that she was still afloat in that year. She had been sold to become the sealer *E. P. Marvin*, sailing out of Victoria under the British flag, with Capt. Alex MacLean her master. It was not until 1896 that the *Webster-Marvin*, with her crew of twenty-five, was lost on a voyage in the Pacific.

Selling the *Webster* must have made Capt. Sol wince a bit – giving up the noble schooner in which he had scored so many of his fishing triumphs in the Atlantic. Later he filed a $150,000 suit against the U.S. government as a claim for earnings lost when the revenue cutters *Corwin* and *Bear* drove the *Mollie Adams* and the *Edward E. Webster* out of the Bering Sea when he was 120 miles offshore. But he never collected.

All in all, the Northwest venture had cost Capt. Jacobs a fortune – $60,000 (over $222,000 today). Some of his men remained on the West Coast as itinerant fishermen, but by 1891 the captain was back in Gloucester – on his heels financially.

It had been an excursion he might have wished he had thought through more carefully. But it had been an audacious undertaking, an adventure true to the spirit of frontier America. And no matter – Capt. Sol was still in his prime at forty-four. He already had a plan to put the wind back in his sails.

The Masses

SOL JACOBS' detour off course took him 3,000 miles across the continent. John Sloan's corresponding divergence took him only a short walk along Greenwich Avenue in lower Manhattan. There, at No. 91, he reported to his desk as unpaid art editor of the Socialist magazine *The Masses.*

In 1908 John Sloan had declared, "I'm not a Democrat. I'm of no party. I'm for change, for the operating knife when a party rots in power." His focus was then on art, and he would have served his talent better had he not strayed into unfamiliar waters. But Shakespeare scholar Charles Wisner Barrell had been calling on Sloan from time to time, engaging the ever-disputatious artist in discussion. Barrell was a Socialist, and was determined to convert Sloan to his cause.

Socialism was the common currency of political belief in New York artistic and intellectual circles after the turn of the century. John Sloan would meet Socialists at every turn, from editors to authors to women of the Colony Club, all protesting the excesses of unrestrained 19th century Capitalism. Sloan and Dolly would hear again and again how a dozen or so men – notably J. P. Morgan, George F. Baker, James Stillman and the Rockefeller family – held nearly 150 directorships in 111 corporations – in railroads, insurance companies, public utilities. The reformers could claim that this small group of men, with $22 billion under their management, in effect controlled the nation's wealth.

European Socialism was bred by urban and academic ferment. The American version had its roots in Midwest agriculture. Small farmers protested that they were being exploited by banking, railroad and utility trusts dominated by those same few powerful individuals and families who pulled the strings of the nation's economy. This grass-roots unrest fueled the Grange Movement, when scattered farmers, getting together over bean suppers at the Grange halls to discuss feeds and crops, discovered that politicians began to listen to them when they spoke out as an organization against high freight fares and other perceived abuses. The Grangers were a strong element in the Populist coalition which garnered support nationwide to fight the trusts. After the turn of the century the Populists became one of the main groups sympathetic to Socialism, a movement that also drew support from labor unions, immigrant workers and idealistic, reform-minded intellectuals in the East.

John Sloan said he never read Upton Sinclair or Lincoln Steffens, but in his circle he would have been well aware of the indictments made public by these and other muckrakers, condemning the harsh labor practices and indifference to societal needs that had accompanied America's rapid transformation into an industrial and transportation colossus. Sloan, although transplanted into New York urbanity, was at heart the small-town American from Lock Haven, Pennsylvania. He still carried deep within him a belief in simple living and fairness to others. He was humanist in his social thinking as he was in his painting.

Eugene Debs, the leader of the American Socialist Party, seemed to Sloan to be the living embodiment of those values. Unlike the European Socialists who talked revolution, Debs espoused the adoption of moderate methods to achieve fair distribution of wealth and work, and he advocated pacifism as a moral imperative. Debs had been born and raised in the Midwest, quoted Tom Paine and Walt Whitman, and lived with his wife Kate in an unpretentious Victorian house in Terre Haute, Indiana. He was unflinching in his opposition to monopolistic gain, and foresaw an age of glory for the common man under a Cooperative Commonwealth. All that seemed consistent with Sloan's egalitarian humanism. The down-to-earth democratic economics of this creed appealed to many other Americans of the period as well: Socialism would reach its high-water mark in America in 1912 when Debs received 6% of the vote in the presidential election.

In 1909 John Sloan told Barrell that he was in basic agreement with the tenets of Socialism. The following year Sloan joined Branch One of the Socialist Party in New York City. Dolly, loyal as ever, joined with him. In time she would prove herself an even more energetic activist than he. Branch One was known as the "highbrow" branch of the Socialist party in New York. It was the one to which many of the West Side intellectuals belonged, including Sinclair Lewis. John and Dolly attended Socialist meetings and lectures together several times a week, distributed literature and worked for Socialist candidates. Sloan himself ran for office four times on the Socialist ticket from 1912 until 1915, when he ran for a judgeship and was defeated.

John Sloan was always a fervent advocate for whatever cause or belief he was espousing, and he brought that intensity to his new-found faith in Socialism as a cure-all for the inequities rampant in American society. The subject came to dominate his conversations. Always passionate in discussion, he now became intolerant, refusing to listen to arguments contrary to his new and incontrovertible point of view.

He sought to convert Robert Henri to the Socialist cause. But Henri leaned toward the utopian Anarchism of the period which proposed, in some vague way, to replace all governments with voluntary agreements between groups of producers and consumers. (Radical Anarchism was something else again; its bomb-throwing nihilists fueled a national Red Scare.) Sloan also attempted to sway Bill Glackens to Socialism, but Glackens was not in the least politically minded. Sloan's single-track persistence opened a gap between these two old friends that would not be closed for years.

By late 1909 Sloan admitted in his diary that his obsession with Socialism had taken a "monopoly" of him. He wrote that he felt he had "passed the feverish stage," but in fact he would suffer from his political inflammation for several more years. John Butler Yeats wrote to his daughter Lily that Sloan "offends so many people [with his strident Socialism] and so constantly that he will never have any reputation until he is dead."

Sloan's attraction to Socialism intensified when he became associated with *The Masses*. The magazine had been founded in 1911 as house organ for writers' and artists' cooperatives. This was the Golden Age of newspapers and magazines in America, when people relied on the printed word for much of their entertainment and most of their information. Large segments of the public relied on the penny tabloids that flooded the newsstands as media barons William Randolph Hearst and Joseph Pulitzer competed for dominance.

Magazines flourished as well, thanks to a decline in paper costs that enabled publishers to reduce cover prices. The price of wood pulp that had been $366 a metric ton in 1886 dropped to $36 by 1900. Frank Munsey cut the price of his *Munsey's* and *Argosy* magazines to ten cents a copy. *Argosy* he described as offering "good red-blooded fiction for the millions." *McClure's* was forced to follow suit by also cutting its cover price to a dime. Soon 80% of the magazines sold in America were those aimed at the mass market.

Despite the huge popular sale of cheap newspapers and magazines, upper tier magazines like the *Atlantic Monthly, Harper's* and *Scribner's* did well. And periodicals for every niche also found a market. Over 300 Socialist periodicals were being printed in 1912, including thirteen dailies.

Among the left-wing journals that year was *The Masses*, but it was on the verge of collapse. In 1913 the magazine was reorganized by a group that included Art Young, a cartoonist and writer who had reversed his Republican Party affiliation and was penning leftist commentary. Young was joined by painters Charles Allan Winter and his wife Alice Beach Winter. John Sloan was named art editor, and redesigned the magazine with a graphic excellence that stood out among periodicals of the day. During Sloan's years with *The Masses* some sixty illustrators and cartoonists submitted their work without pay, many having been persuaded by John Sloan to contribute their talents. One of these was Stuart Davis, son of Sloan's Philadelphia friend Ed Davis. From the time the younger Davis was seventeen Sloan was convinced that he showed great promise.

The staff of the reincarnated *Masses* gathered in the Winters' studio to plan each issue. On Art Young's advice they recruited Maxwell Eastman to be executive editor, also without pay. The twenty-nine-year-old Eastman had been a Columbia professor until he was fired for his radical views. The others were not aware at first that Eastman was a Marxist with an uncompromisingly radical agenda that would ultimately take the magazine into dangerous political waters. But at the outset all was harmony. There was, in Eastman's words, "the sense of universal revolt and regeneration, of the just-before-dawn of a new day in American art and literature and living-of-life as well as in politics."

Dolly Sloan joined the team that was reorganizing *The Masses*, and brought her bookkeeping experience into play as business manager. Max Eastman remembered her as "a tiny, vital, scrappy, devoted, emotional secretary of socialist locals, organizer of socialist picnics, collector of funds for strikers ..." That mention of strikers referred to the 1912 strike in the textile mills of Lawrence, Massachusetts, during which rioting was fomented by the International Workers of the World, the IWW or "Wobblies." Dolly helped to shelter the children of the strikers, finding families in New York to take them in.

The cause of that strike was rooted in a humanitarian gesture gone wrong: the state of Massachusetts had reduced the maximum 56-hour work week to 54 hours. The mill owners in Lawrence, who were paying their immigrant workers a subsistence-level $7 a week, promptly reduced paychecks proportionately. The irate workers went out on strike, with the IWW and its firebrand leader "Big Bill" Haywood at the fore. Finally, when police and National Guard troops assaulted a group of women and children, public outcry forced the mill owners to back down and restore wages to their earlier level. It was a victory for the IWW, but the violent methods of its leadership terrified the nation. Mary Heaton Vorse wrote an article sympathetic to the strikers that ran in *The Masses*.

After the strike ended Dolly escorted the rambunctious children on the train back to Lawrence, "mothering all 200 of them," John Sloan said. Anarchist Emma Goldman had joined in the protest, and was invited by Dolly to sleep in the Sloans' apartment. But when Goldman returned to the flat after a meeting, it was some time before she was admitted. Dolly had been drinking.

Max Eastman would later claim that *The Masses* was the first literary Socialist magazine. The truth was that it was successor to a little magazine published in Girard, Kansas. Julius Wayland, a Socialist publicist, began issuing *The Coming Nation* as a literary supplement to his political newspaper, *Appeal to Reason*, in 1910. John Sloan and Art Young contributed to *The Coming Nation* and set a high graphic standard with their covers. Walter Lippmann and Sinclair Lewis submitted articles. But Wayland, attempting to publish far from the centers of finance, struggled to secure sufficient financial backing to keep *The Coming Nation* afloat. The last issue appeared in 1913.

With the demise of *The Coming Nation*, *The Masses* was the Socialist magazine of art and ideas for a devoted circle of readers. Its credo was stated by Eastman with profligate use of capitals and disdain for grammar:

> This magazine is owned and Published Cooperatively by its Editors. It has no dividends to Pay, and nobody is trying to make Money out of it. A Revolutionary and not a Reform Magazine; a Magazine with a sense of Humor and no respect for the Respectable; Searching for the True causes; a Magazine Directed against Rigidity and Dogma wherever it is found; printing what is too Naked or true for a money making press; a Magazine whose Final Policy is to do as it Pleases and Conciliate Nobody, and even its Readers – a Free Magazine.

What distinguished the revamped *The Masses* from other radical periodicals was the absence, at first, of heavy-handed propaganda. Eastman proclaimed that "Our appeal will be to the masses, both Socialist and non-Socialist, with entertainment, education, and the livelier kinds of propaganda." As was true of most leftist magazines of opinion, *The Masses* was not read by many of "the masses." As a writer later said, "It was by the radical petit bourgeois for the liberal petit bourgeois."

The Masses thrived in an era of social ferment. Within the next few years Prohibition, women's suffrage, a federal income tax, and direct election of U.S. senators would all become the law of the land. Each issue of the magazine defended strong liberal positions on these and other burning topics of the day: modern art and literature, psychology as a science, social justice in all its forms, the evils of militarism, big business, and institutional religion. There was a strong emphasis on feminism. Articles and poetry celebrated the liberated "New Woman" and advocated birth control, women's rights in marriage, and women's suffrage. Fiction editor Inez Hayes Irwin cordially welcomed submissions that had a strong feminist theme.

Feminism was important to the magazine because the movement to extend voting rights to women in federal elections had been languishing. Theodore Roosevelt's Progressive Party was pledged "to the task of securing equal suffrage to men and women alike." But the Progressives lost the presidential election of 1912, and the Democrats were less committed to women's suffrage. However, when the president-elect, Woodrow Wilson, arrived for his inauguration, he discovered that the issue could not be brushed aside. On March 3rd, 1913, more than 5,000 marchers, mostly women, paraded down Pennsylvania Avenue, marching to the tempos of nine bands, accompanied by twenty-four floats, all in support of the right of the female half of the population to have an equal say on national issues.

Jeering men lunged forward, interrupting the parade, while the police looked the other way. The parade accomplished its purpose, though, of bringing the issue of women's suffrage back to the attention of the nation. (Wilson, arriving for his installation in office, wondered why there were no crowds – and was told they were off watching the women march.) Thereafter there was daily picketing at the White House, and massive demonstrations in which police arrested 500 women for loitering and "obstructing traffic."

The Masses aided and abetted the women's suffrage movement by providing intellectual rationale. But there was one pillar of the feminist movement that received no buttressing from the magazine. The campaign to prohibit the sale of alcohol in every form had marched shoulder to shoulder with the feminists since the days of Carrie Nation and the Women's Christian Temperance Union in the 19th century. In the pre-World War I days, momentum was already under way to line up support for ratification in the thirty-six states needed to pass an amendment to the Constitution banning the sale of all alcoholic beverages.

But *The Masses* did not add its editorial and caricaturing weight to the unstoppable surge of ultra-temperance sentiment. Its contributors tended to agree with those readers who might or might not enjoy a highball while contemplating the great social issues, and believed that this should be a matter of personal choice. There were occasional exceptions: Upton Sinclair became a wartime convert to the crusade for national Prohibition. As for John Sloan, he would not have applauded a shuttering of McSorley's saloon on East 7th Street, that shrine of dignified male sociability which he had celebrated in several paintings. Sloan said "had all saloons been conducted with the dignity and decorum of McSorley's, prohibition could never have been brought about."

John Sloan was enthusiastic about the reincarnated *The Masses* and the appointment of Max Eastman as editor. He said later, "What I liked about *The Masses* was that it had a satirical point of view with life as its subject and a socialist slant." He contributed a few starkly political cartoons, but "while I am a Socialist, I never allowed social propaganda to get into my paintings." Elsewhere he said "I hate war and I put the hatred into cartoons in *The Masses*." He seemed here to be drawing a fine line between his pacifist antiwar stance and the tenets of a Socialist platform.

Sloan's personal version of Socialism was entirely compatible with his good-natured humanism, and that was the tone he and the Winters and Stuart Davis strove to maintain in *The Masses*. They saw no reason why the magazine should be dry and humorless even when espousing such causes as free love, birth control and relieving the miseries of the working classes.

They all painted covers for *The Masses*. Charles Winter painted in bright colors, his designs influenced by Walter Crane, the English illustrator Sloan had emulated for his Bradley Coal Company streetcar posters in Philadelphia in the '90s. Alice Beach Winter's *The Masses* covers took another very different direction, reflecting her lifelong interest in painting children. The covers by twenty-two year old Stuart Davis were distinguished by strong simplicity. If the covers they submitted for *The Masses* reflected very different styles, the four artists shared a deep affinity in their views on the nature and public function of art.

Reformist fervor presented with buoyant urbanity in *The Masses* attracted such prominent contributors from the American intelligentsia as Sherwood Anderson, Amy Lowell, Jack London, Upton Sinclair, Helen Keller and Louis Untermeyer. Looking back years later, those associated with *The Masses* could point to some real achievements, particularly in making the public aware of poor working conditions in factories, and abuses of civil liberties.

But harmony on the staff of *The Masses* was short-lived. Floyd Dell, Chicago editor and writer, was hired by Max Eastman as his assistant. Dell must have been highly valued because he was paid $25 a week – whereas Eastman himself, as well as Sloan and most of the other contributors, were volunteering their talents. Dell wrote later that "At the monthly editorial meetings … the literary editors were usually ranged on one side of all questions and the artists on the other." He remembered that "John Sloan, a very vigorous and combative personality, spoke up strongly for the artists."

The editors all had strong leftist backgrounds. Most radical was John Reed who had aligned himself with the IWW and been arrested (the first of many times) for attempting to speak on behalf of the strikers during a walkout at New Jersey silk mills. Reed would contribute more than fifty articles, reviews and snippets to *The Masses*.

Eastman, Dell and Reed complained that much of Sloan's art in *The Masses* did not properly reflect the miseries of the proletariat. For example, in his drawing *The Return from Toil*, a group of frumpily dressed young women, probably having just finished a shift at a factory, are seen swinging along in high-spirited accord with the world. If they are suffering as exploited workers, it does not show. The ideologues who set editorial policy for *The Masses* were not men likely to see the humor in such situations, and insisted that all text and graphics in the magazine advance the cause of radical Socialism. Sloan began to find that, without his knowledge, new captions had been added to his drawings to better serve political orthodoxy.

In the increasingly stifling environment, Sloan decided that drawing for *The Masses* "no longer was fun." In 1914 and '15 he was providing fewer drawings for the magazine. By 1916 the schism between the freewheeling artists, committed to iconoclastic but good-natured social commentary, and the doctrinaire editors widened. In March the core artists demanded a restructuring of *The Masses* or they would go out on strike. Max Eastman refused to compromise and Sloan, Davis, and Charles and Alice Beach Winter resigned.

Sloan's departure from *The Masses* says much about what Socialism meant to him. He had irritated, and even alienated, many of his friends (including the affectionate and tolerant John Butler Yeats) with his incessant preaching of a new and better world transformed by Socialist ideals. Yet, when he had to declare himself, he came down firmly on the side of compassionate humanism. He wanted to break the dominance of the trusts and the arms profiteers and give the working classes a break, to be sure. He drew a few strongly partisan cartoons. But by and large he envisioned a human comedy in which people behaved like normal life-intoxicated humans while on the march to social justice. When *The Masses* lost its sense of humor, it lost John Sloan.

He became disenchanted with the Socialist Party at about the same time. He had idealized Socialism as a worldwide movement in which, in addition to egalitarian reform, the peoples of all nations would rise up together and refuse to fight wars against one another. But with the outbreak of the war in Europe, Sloan saw how the Socialist parties in Germany and France had quickly fallen in line with each country's nationalistic aims. He became disillusioned with Socialism as a party and a movement.

Sloan remained a pacifist but he had had enough of political activism. He might regret the time lost in tilting at ideological windmills, but he was still in his early 40s. There was time to recover. To explore new surroundings, to challenge himself artistically.

Chapter Eight
SECOND WINDS

~~

The Ethel B. Jacobs / *"A Good Outing"*

The Ethel B. Jacobs

J OHN SLOAN and Solomon Jacobs were both back to square one. Sloan, distracted by ideological enthusiasm, had at the same time lost confidence in his early style and subject matter. He felt he needed to take a new direction. Capt. Jacobs had suffered heavy financial losses in a bold excursion that took him away from the kind of fishing he knew best. He, too, needed to correct course.

Once back in Gloucester, Sol Jacobs had quietly gone about regaining his momentum. With his reputation as a highliner he apparently had no difficulty financing the construction of a new vessel. The *Ethel B. Jacobs* – named for his and Sarah's first child who was now twelve years old – was built in Essex in 1891 by Moses Adams, and registered by Sol Jacobs as the sole owner.

Moses Adams was one of the great Essex shipbuilders of the schooner era. He had been in partnership with Arthur Story from 1872 to 1880, at which point the two went their separate ways. Adams built another eighty-five vessels on his own, and when it came the turn of the *Ethel B.* he was influenced by the new look that Edward "Ned" Burgess was bringing to schooner design. Yacht designer Burgess designed America's Cup victors *Puritan, Mayflower* and *Volunteer* before he turned to designing fishing schooners. He introduced yachting design into the *Carrie E. Phillips,* winner of a fishermen's race in Boston harbor in 1888.

The *Ethel B. Jacobs* may have been designed according to the Burgess canon, but there is little doubt that Capt. Jacobs had much to say in drawing up the specifications. After all those years as the most successful mackerel captain in the fleet he would have firm opinions as to vessel size, sail plan, cabin layout, fish hold capacity and overall workmanship.

Sol wanted a big boat to carry big trips of mackerel. The *Ethel B.* was 108.3 feet long, 24 feet in breadth, 131.75 net tons. Sol wanted speed, and his new schooner would be sleek, trim, her form satisfying to the eye. He demanded that the *Ethel B.* be built to stand up to the severe strains of purse seining and rough weather. To that end he would specify the best of everything in sails, cordage and seine nets, and scrutinize the delivered materials personally to detect any flaws. The *Ethel B.* came into being as a collaboration between designer, builder and owner. The end result would be Capt. Solomon Jacobs' masterpiece.

While the *Ethel B.* was taking shape, Sol agreed to take William Jordan's schooner *Brunhild* [sic] on a fishing cruise to the north. A profitable trip would help replenish his bank account. Unfortunately Sol chose to fish for herring off Newfoundland's Fortune Bay at a time when those waters were closed to local and foreign fishermen alike. It was a transgression that he would compound by an act that was condemned even by his staunchest supporters.

Sol was caught in the act of seining for herring by the Royal cutter *Fiona*, and ordered to depart forthwith and post a bond guaranteeing that he would unload in an American port the herring he had already caught. Agreed, said Sol, but he pointed out to Captain Sullivan of the *Fiona* that to post the bond he would first have to go to the nearest customs house, located at St. Jacques, Newfoundland. Captain Sullivan granted permission, but sent one of his officers along on the *Brunhild* to make certain that Capt. Jacobs would proceed as agreed.

By his own proud admission Sol, despite the protests of the official observer sent aboard the *Brunhild* to oversee his actions, set sail not for St. Jacques, but for the French possession St. Pierre & Miquelon. Sol dropped the protesting officer from the *Fiona* ashore on that remote cluster of islands just off the Newfoundland coast, and sailed for Gloucester. That official found himself alone amid unfriendly islanders all speaking French. There was no British consul, and the inhabitants — who were at odds with the Newfoundlanders over fishing issues — were slow to accommodate the demands of the furious functionary that he be put in touch with his government.

If Sol expected that his treatment of the Newfoundland official would earn him accolades in Gloucester, he was mistaken. This was no longer the 1870s when his gunslinging defense of his rights at Fortune Bay would make him a hero. The Treaty of Washington had expired, and tensions were running high between Nova Scotian fishermen who wanted to be able to sell their fish in American markets, and American fishermen who opposed any return to reciprocity they felt worked all to the advantage of the Provincials. Gloucester schooners had been seized and impounded by British cutters on one pretext or another.

But if accusations and counter-accusations were flying between America and Nova Scotia, Newfoundland was an entirely different matter. Mutual trust and accommodation had been painstakingly nourished between the Gloucester fleet and the Newfoundlanders, who asserted their independence as a Dominion separate from the Canadian Confederation. Gloucester boats were now allowed to resume their purchases of frozen herring for bait in Newfoundland ports, and to sail into those ports at will.

Sol had breached this fragile amity by depositing a Newfoundland-based British officer on unfriendly foreign soil against his will. Some of Sol's fellow Gloucester master mariners, the men in town he respected most, rebuked Capt. Jacobs in plain language. By failing to understand that things had changed since he went West, he had been called to account by his peers.

Sol was chastened. Back in Gloucester he gave his full attention to restoring his good name, and to the building of his new schooner. In fit and finish the *Ethel B.* was one of the most elegant mackerel schooners of the '90s. The cabin was ample, the captain's quarters finished in oak and fitted out with a leather-covered couch, closet, chest and locker. But the luxury was not simply for Sol's comfort. He intended to carry guests and cruising passengers aboard when he was not chasing fish.

The crew facilities of the *Ethel B.* also included amenities that must have struck the crewmen with awe when they first clambered aboard. Each man had an enclosed berth described as "attractive, roomy and well-ventilated." And there were closets for drying wet oil clothes. The cook, the top man in the crew after the captain, had a well-stocked larder and top-quality shipboard culinary facilities. He had everything he needed to provide good food well prepared. That was what kept the crew healthy. And so, they believed, did their way of life. The fishermen were convinced that, working hard on deck and breathing pure ocean air, they were less susceptible to the diseases that afflicted landsmen. Anecdotal evidence seemed to bear them out, but nevertheless crewmen had good reason to fear typhoid fever as well as tuberculosis, the dreaded "consumption" that was the curse of the age. And there were common afflictions such as rheumatism and "dyspepsia," an umbrella term for digestive disorders of one kind or another.

If a member of the crew, or anyone else on board, did suffer an injury or took sick far off shore, Capt. Sol was the doctor. It was one of the responsibilities of a schooner captain to act as ship's physician, and Capt. Jacobs would see to it that the medicine chest in his cabin was replenished before every voyage. A pharmacy in Gloucester, probably M.L. Wetherell or G.H. Blatchford, would stock the chest with a standard assortment of remedies. It was up to Sol to use judgment in dispensing the cathartics, salves, expectorants, cough medicines and liniments prescribed by a book of basic medical advice.

There were times when Capt. Sol did have to take on the role of medical practitioner. One instance was in 1902 when, about to return to Gloucester from Newfoundland in the *Alice M. Jacobs*, he took on a frostbitten Danish fisherman. From the story the man told, it was incredible that he was still alive. He had gone astray from the schooner *A.E. Whyland* in a dory, been forced to swim 300 yards to shore, ran around all night in his wet clothes to stay alive, then trekked three miles breaking deep snow until he found a house. On the trip Sol "doctored him from his medicine chest," and the man arrived in Gloucester tolerably healthy.

The only surgical instrument usually carried in a schooner's medical chest was a lancet; skippers did not relish having to set broken bones or act as surgeons to repair deep wounds. If one of his men was in a bad way, Capt. Jacobs might try to run him in to the hospital at Halifax, Nova Scotia, where seamen could expect to receive medical attention not necessarily forthcoming in their own ports. (If a crewman sailing for one of the big Gloucester fishing companies was landed on an American shore in need of medical attention, he might be turned away from a hospital unless it was an emergency. The fishing company owners were not required to pay hospital dues, the equivalent of modern medical insurance.)

On March 27, 1897 the *Boston Globe* reported on a departure from Gloucester harbor. "Under a smother of canvas kites, the crack schooner *Ethel B. Jacobs*, Capt. Sol Jacobs in command, bowled out of the harbor with a stiff breeze blowing." Sol was, as usual, the first of the mackerel fleet to depart for the south. "Capt. Jacobs' fame as a [mackerel] 'killer' is international. By unanimous consent he is accounted the smartest and fishiest man that ever trod the deck of a Gloucester craft." The *Ethel B.* was about to try out Sol's latest innovation, a seine "which eclipses anything ever known on a seiner before." It was double the size and width of an ordinary seine – nearly a half mile long and 300 feet deep. Made of Scotch flax, a new material lighter than cotton, it promised to be easier to handle and quicker to purse around a school of mackerel.

Wesley George Pierce sailed aboard the *Ethel B.* as cook in those days, and he wrote later in *Goin' Fishin': The Story of the Deep-Sea Fishermen of New England* that, of all the fine vessels he had sailed in, the *Ethel B.* was the best of them all. With her size, she could carry 700 barrels of mackerel. And she was fast. One time when Pierce was aboard, the *Ethel B.* logged 15 knots an hour for six consecutive hours in a heavy sou'wester. Pierce did not know of any other fishing vessel that had matched that performance. In the middle of January 1891, Capt. Jacobs in the *Ethel B.* made the run from Coombs Cove in Newfoundland to Gloucester in under two and a half days, setting a record for schooners under sail. The *Ethel B.* was, as the fishermen said of fast boats, a "slippery piece of wood."

Pierce said "Skipper Sol was a very smart, capable, energetic man, bound to be the first in all that he did. ... He ... made a lot of money, which enabled him to own his vessels, so that he did not have to sail a vessel from a fish firm, for he was his own master and owner [who] always had the latest and best in fishing gear ... [He] very seldom stayed long in the fleet, but would go off by himself, and the next thing heard of him, would be that he was in Boston with a large trip." To be sure, Sol might be overly competitive at times, and exercise some wily stratagems to beat the rest of the fleet to the fish, but nobody could really take offense at this high-spirited schoonerman. An article in *The Fisherman* of 1895 said he was a man possessed of "pluck, push, energy, vigilance, character." There was general agreement that he was "the most daring and intrepid mariner of the Gloucester fishing fleet." The *Ethel B.* under Capt. Jacobs was the best producing vessel in the Gloucester mackerel fleet in 1892, '93, '95, and '96.

Nor did Sol devote the *Ethel B.* exclusively to fishing. As he had planned in the layout of the cabin, he occasionally carried passengers. An undated newspaper clipping relates that Capt. Jacobs had stopped in Gloucester before sailing to the south on a mackerel trip. Sol welcomed on board a Col. Russell of Minneapolis who arrived with his wife and son. The colonel had sailed with the captain the year before and was "eager to repeat" the experience. Also climbing aboard for the trip were Capt. Jacobs' wife Sarah and their son Arthur. Sarah Jacobs was no stay-at-home captain's wife. She did not hesitate to leave their comfortable Prospect Street home to join Sol at sea, and to bring along one of their children.

It says much for the comforts designed into the *Ethel B.* that five passengers, including two young boys, could be accommodated comfortably along with the master of the vessel. Capt. Jacobs' plan for the cruise was to drop off his guests at Old Point Comfort at the southern tip of the Virginia peninsula before continuing on to catch mackerel. The passengers, after a stay at the Chamberlin Hotel, would proceed to Washington to visit the sights.

Capt. Sol was eager to get onto the mackerel, because he had a new piece of gear to try out. For a new 40-foot seine boat, the largest ever built by Gloucester's Higgins & Gifford, he had ordered a five-horsepower gasoline motor to purse the seine. With it Sol would be able to close the mouth of the seine in three minutes, instead of the ten or twelve minutes it took by hand. The mackerel would have much less time to escape the net.

If the *Ethel B.* was superbly fashioned and equipped, she was still an all-sail vessel that demanded the captain's skills to see her through the perils of a fishing cruise. As always, Sol sailed year-round – he was not just a summer mackerel-catcher. It was February 1894 and he was bringing the *Ethel B.* into Gloucester carrying frozen herring from Newfoundland. She jibed her mainsail, and some of the tackle hit Sol in the eye, knocking him down and straining his side. One of the crew, tangled in the main sheet, was nearly carried overboard but escaped with a severe shaking up. And that had not been the only mischance on the trip. During a blow up north, the vessel had her topmast carried away. Later, as she was leaving Gloucester towed by the *Seguin*, she was bumped by the tug and had a portion of her port rail smashed. For Capt. Jacobs and his men it was all in a day's work.

What really made life interesting for Capt. Jacobs was when a competitive challenge presented itself. It was at the close of the mackerel season when again he sailed to Newfoundland to load up on frozen herring that he would bring back to sell in the Boston market for bait. That winter was particularly bitter and the *Ethel B.* was frozen in until March. By the time the captain reached Gloucester at the beginning of April, he learned that most of the mackerel fleet had sailed a week earlier for the southern grounds.

Capt. Jacobs was beside himself – he had a reputation to uphold as the captain usually first to sail south. He worked with his crew night and day offloading the frozen herring and getting the vessel fitted out for seining. In a few days they were ready to put to sea again. Sol spread every inch of canvas. He drove the *Ethel B.* relentlessly until they reached the southern fishing grounds. Joe Cash was one of the crew, and he described to Wesley Pierce what happened:

> So Sol began to yell for us to rouse the [seine] boat overboard, at the same time, he grabbed the wheel and hove the vessel to. "Lively, boys! Lively, now! Hurry an' git th' boat-tackles hooked on," he said, and every man was jumping to do his bidding as we quickly hoisted our boat out and dropped her overboard on the port side. "Hurry, boys! Hurry an' git th' seine hauled onto th' boat!" yelled Sol as he turned the wheel over to the watch and started for the fore-masthead.

Of all the crewmen available in Gloucester, Sol had his pick of the very best for the *Ethel B.*, and they contributed to his success. Wesley Pierce describes one of them:

> Jack Campbell was our seine-heaver, a big, raw-boned, Cape Breton

Scotchman, weighing 250 pounds, six feet and four inches in his sock feet, with a pair of hands on him the size of two good sized hams. The way Jack hauled our seine onto the boat that day was a caution. I never saw anything like it before in my life, for he hauled the seine in hand over hand, just as you would a cod-line, the roller on the rail singing a steady song and never stopping once, until the end of our seine went onto the seine-boat, for Jack Campbell hauled that seine onto our boat in eleven minutes, *a world's record*, so far as I know, for I never heard of any man doing it quicker.

They netted 90,000 pounds of mackerel (about 300 barrels) in one haul of the seine. (Jack Campbell's exploits would be outshone after Sol installed his motorized seine purser.) Wesley Clark continues:

> When the fish had been bailed out on deck, the skipper said: "Let's see how quick we can stow an' ice these fish! Lively now, lads, lively!" We passed them down in bushel-baskets, a steady stream going down both hatches at once, for we all worked fast, every man moving quickly and striving his best to do more work than the skipper, who was working like a beaver himself.

Under way again, the *Ethel B.* overtook every other boat in the fleet making for New York's Fulton Market. She was the first ship in, and the mackerel sold for a good price. Each man of the crew shared $182 for the trip, which gave them bragging rights when they sauntered up to Fishermen's Corner in Gloucester a few days later and compared what they had earned for the trip with men from the other boats. Small wonder a capable mackerel man would prefer to sail with Sol Jacobs, all things being considered.

There were times, though, when Capt. Jacobs allowed his zest for competition to overcome his better judgment. It was August 26, 1892, and a race of the fishing schooners had been scheduled as part of Gloucester's 250th celebration of its original establishment as a town. It blew a gale all day, but the seasoned skippers of the fleet would not let it be said that they backed down just because of a breeze of wind. Not one of them reefed a sail throughout the contest.

The half-dozen contenders, the patricians of the Gloucester fleet, sped out of the view of the harbor spectators in the blinding spray. The first leg of the race took the schooners down to the first mark off Nahant. Approaching the mark, Capt. Jacobs in the *Ethel B.* was ahead of the pack. It would have been prudent for him to lower his mainsail, but Sol saw the other boats crowding in behind him and was determined to maintain his lead. He took a risk and jibed around the mark under full sail. For once, Sol gambled and lost. The *Ethel B.*'s main gaff snapped and he was obliged to take in the flapping mainsail. He was out of contention. But being the proud skipper he was, Sol finished the race, limping home under riding sail. Nobody could fault Capt. Jacobs for not giving his all.

Fishing for mackerel, cod and halibut, sealing, trading – Capt. Solomon Jacobs was ever open to new opportunities. He took passengers occasionally as we have seen. He was even the captain-host of a birding expedition to the far north. *The Osprey*, a short-lived "Illustrated Magazine of Popular Ornithology," carried the following notice in 1897:

> The Frank B. Webster Co. is organizing a party to sail in June for Labrador, Hudson's Bay, and the Arctic regions, returning in about three months. The trip is to be made in the clipper schooner, *Ethel B. Jacobs*, of the Gloucester fishing fleet. Captain Jacobs, the commander of the expedition, is said to be well-acquainted with the coasts of the regions to be visited, and is on friendly terms with many of the Indian and Eskimo chiefs.

The statement that Capt. Jacobs numbered tribal dignitaries among his close friends would have raised some eyebrows among his fellow skippers in Gloucester. But Sol would have ignored any chuckles, secure in the knowledge that he was in distinguished scientific company with the Webster organization. In that same month as the projected expedition to the far north, Frank B. Webster Co., under the patronage of the Hon. W. Rothschild of London, dispatched Mr. C. M. Harris of Augusta, Maine and three associates aboard a schooner on a scientific expedition to the South Pacific. They expected to "do much work in the fauna and flora of the South Sea Islands." If Capt. Jacobs and his party of naturalists made similar contributions to natural science in the North Atlantic, no evidence has as yet come to light.

That same year New England, like the rest of the world, was excited by news of the discovery of gold along the banks of the Klondike River near Dawson City in Canada's Yukon Territory. These were hard times in America, following the double whammy of the Panics of 1893 and 1896. Unemployed men were swarming west toward imagined mountains of gold. In July, early in the Klondike stampede, the *Boston Globe* sent a man to interview that knowledgeable veteran of enterprise in the far Northwest, Capt. Solomon Jacobs, "who knows the field thoroughly, having scoured the grounds for seals with his accustomed energy." Sol, the reporter learned, was planning a venture to the Klondike himself, inasmuch as "he was a firm believer in the wealth of the gold fields."

Asked why he was so confident, the captain said that, when he was bound from the Bering Sea to Seattle on a sealing trip in 1888, he had touched at the mouth of the Yukon River and took aboard two miners for passage to Seattle. They told him that, in two years mining up the Yukon, they had sifted out $40,000 in gold. Sol described the Yukon as "a flat little river, something like the Annisquam ... on the westerly side of [Cape Ann]." But while the sand bars along the Annisquam at low water yielded only clams, the exposed flats of the Yukon sparkled with golden nuggets. More recently, Sol had received a telegram, he said, from the wife of a man he had known in the Northwest, named Stanley. Stanley, it seemed, had gone to the Yukon the year before as a pauper, and returned a millionaire. So Sol said Stanley's wife said.

To make his own expertise available to interested parties, Sol revealed that "I have formed a party of four to start there and have put in $500 to that end, and will cooperate with others who wish to come in." He was looking for investors to subscribe $16,000 to finance the enterprise. "I shall start the four men if need be alone next year and perhaps go myself." It was, said Sol, "an opportunity for ambitious single men not afraid of work and to rough it."

He explained his plans in some detail. There were three routes: one overland through Alberta and Canada's Northwest Territories, one by sea around the Aleutians to St. Michael far up the Alaska coast at the mouth of the Yukon, and the third – which was Sol's preference – by sea to Juneau. "Capt. Carroll will carry [our party] to Juneau from Seattle in his large steamer, the *Argus*." It was then a matter of trekking overland across a series of lakes, and doing so in comfort by hiring Indian labor to carry the baggage. "I know the country and how best to get there," Sol assured his interviewer.

Sol might have had but a sketchy idea of the route from Juneau. It was not simply a matter of crossing "a series of lakes." His prospectors would almost immediately be confronted with the challenge of climbing through deep snows to the summit of 3,500-foot Chilkoot Pass. Having overcome that obstacle, they would receive a less-than-cordial welcome at the Canadian border. The Canadian Northwest Mountain Police (later the Royal Canadian Mounted Police) would confiscate all firearms, collect customs duties and fees, and verify that each would-be miner had with him a year's worth of supplies (about a ton of groceries and other necessities, to be carried on the backs of the Indian porters). The Canadians were not eager to admit adventurers from below their border, fearing that if the Yukon acquired a large population of Americans, the expansion-minded U.S. would proceed to annex the territory onto Alaska.

If Sol's men "not afraid of hard work and to rough it" survived the mountain passes and the Mounties, they would then cross the lakes Sol mentioned, and reach the headwaters of the Yukon River. There they would build rafts or boats and set out on a 500-mile trip down river to Dawson City and ultimately the gold fields. As details of the rigors of the journey filtered back to Gloucester, Sol was hard put to find investors. The four men he had signed up to lead the charge for gold may have had second thoughts as well. When the captain's Yukon trial balloon deflated, he made no further mention of the venture (if he had ever taken it seriously in the first place).

It was fishing that Sol knew best, and in 1899, when the mackerel were again making themselves scarce off New England shores, he turned his attention to the possibility of applying his fish-gathering talents to distant waters – not this time across the continent, but to the other side of the Atlantic. In July he left Gloucester harbor, heading east, and arrived fourteen days later off the Irish coast, sailing the 2,500 miles at close to 180 miles a day – a virtuoso demonstration of the wave-cleaving speed of the *Ethel B.* In no time he had filled 353 barrels with mackerel and shipped them home.

But once again Sol raised international hackles. The resident fishermen of the Irish coast, sailing out of the little harbors of Skibbereen and Dingale, did not like what they were seeing. Here was a Yank scooping up their mackerel, and doing it with that monstrosity, the purse seine, which they were convinced was responsible for the shortage of the fish on the American side of the water. (The Canadian Fisheries Department had forbidden Canadians to purse-seine for herring, fearing that the technology would deplete that fishery.) As when he appeared in the Northwest, Sol's arrival was poorly timed. The Irish mackerel fishery was just beginning to take hold, thanks to the patronage of an English noblewoman who was furnishing the boats. The unexpected presence of Capt. Sol in their waters, raising the specter of foreign competition, provoked indignation.

Responding to the uproar, the English coast guard deployed cutters that kept the *Ethel B.* under close surveillance, daring Capt. Jacobs to intrude within the three-mile limit. Then fate took charge. Sol received word that Sarah was ill, and he rushed back to America to be at her side, leaving the *Ethel B.* under the command of the mate, Sol's friend William Cluett. The *Ethel B.* continued fishing and was sailing into Liverpool with a catch when, according to Cluett, a British pilot was put aboard who ran the vessel onto a reef. Capt. Sol made no subsequent claim to that effect. Apparently what really happened was that the *Ethel B.* was caught in a gale and driven ashore at Derrynane near Abbey Island in southwest Ireland. The crew got off safely, but the vessel was a total loss – its bones on the beach gazed upon by the local fishermen, perhaps with smug satisfaction, for years to come. The *Ethel B.* and all her gear were valued at $14,000. Capt. Jacobs had her insured for $10,000.

Seventeen men from the wrecked vessel were given shelter by nearby residents and advanced the money which enabled them to reach Queenstown. Appeals were still being filed with the U.S. government long afterwards demanding reimbursement. Always relishing a lawsuit for damages, Capt. Jacobs for his part filed a claim of $25,000 against the British government for interfering with the *Ethel B. Jacobs* on the charge that the vessel had been fishing in British territorial waters. The Admiralty subsequently ruled that the action of its navy had been unjustified, but it does not appear that Sol received any recompense.

As with his North Pacific venture, Capt. Jacobs' Irish enterprise was a disaster for him, but helped spawn an industry. Prior to his decidedly unwelcome arrival, the Irish fishermen had marketed their catch fresh in England. When they saw how this Gloucester captain salted his fish and sealed them in barrels for sale to the American market, the scales fell from their eyes. They got in touch with Gloucester dealers. These sent over experienced fish cutters who taught the locals how to split and salt the fish. A mutually profitable market developed. The Irish shipped mackerel suited to American tastes, and the U.S. Congress cooperated by exempting the Irish mackerel from import duties.

Capt. Jacobs had little to show for this latest ambitious venture. And the *Ethel B. Jacobs*, a superb schooner that was so much of his making, was gone. Sol might not have realized it at the time, or even later, but the *Ethel B.* marked the apogee of his career in the age of fishing under sail. He would be an innovator in the years ahead, the first to prove the viability of new technologies for the Gloucester fisheries. But the classic era of fisherman and sail against wind and sea, a confrontation that had endured in its pure state in the port for centuries, would be over forever.

"A Good Outing"

IF SOL JACOBS had recovered his momentum after his Northwest debacle and gone on to new triumphs in the *Ethel B. Jacobs*, John Sloan had determined, after his disillusion with Socialism, to regain headway by finding himself anew. He was now painting fewer of those "Sloans" – his signature paintings of life-in-the-raw on city streets, in restaurants, bedrooms and on the rooftops of the tenements. Those tenements that lined the streets of his old neighborhood in the Tenderloin were giving way to skyscrapers. His subject matter was fading into the past.

In 1914 Sloan decided to get away from New York for the summer, something he had never done before. He had been intrigued by the exuberant coloring and entirely new concepts of space and mass that had been revealed at the Armory Show. Could he apply those insights of the European Post-Impressionists in an American environment entirely unlike that of lower Manhattan? "I decided to save up enough money to have a vacation of several months in the country."

Sloan fixed upon Gloucester as the locale in which he would try out new ideas. Why Gloucester? He had been talked into it. Charles and Alice Beach Winter, fellow artists at *The Masses*, persuaded him to give this distant Massachusetts fishing port a try. The Winters had first come to Gloucester in 1913 when they rented rooms in a guest house on Rocky Neck Avenue. Alice had studied at the Art Students League in New York under John Twachtman and Joseph DeCamp, both of whom had painted in Gloucester, so it is possible that Alice learned about Cape Ann from them. Also, in the late 1890s Charles Winter had studied in Europe with fellow Cincinnatian Edward Potthast. Potthast, best known for his sunny beach scenes, painted in Gloucester soon after 1900, so he also may have influenced the Winters' decision to summer at the port.

Apparently the Winters were sufficiently satisfied with their first summer on Cape Ann that they planned to return the following year, and persuaded John and Dolly Sloan to go as well. Sloan probably listened with at least mild interest to Alice and Charles Winter's talk of the painters who had preceded them to Gloucester. It is unlikely that the Winters would have mentioned, or known of, Fitz Henry Lane, a native Gloucester painter. The remarkable thing about Lane was not that he was the only painter of note produced by the small fishing town up to that time, but that he was so good. After his early years in Gloucester, Lane went to Boston to learn the lithographer's trade, acquired some insights into marine painting from the English artist Robert Salmon, then returned in the 1850s to paint coastal scenes – Gloucester harbor mostly – with reposeful Luminism combined with precise detailing. Highly regarded as a marine painter when he was active, Lane would then be largely overlooked for the next century. It was not until the 1960s, long after Sloan's time in Gloucester, that Lane's achievement began to be recognized. A boom developed in Lane sales that accelerated until his seascapes were selling in the millions by the 1990s.

In the 1870s the first notable out-of-town painters arrived to paint Gloucester harbor. William Morris Hunt was artistically a product of the French pre-Impressionist Barbizon school. Later he taught young women to paint in Boston, and produced at least one landmark painting of Gloucester harbor in the 1870s. Sloan gave no indication that he ever saw that painting. Sloan was familiar with Winslow Homer, though. As he noted in his diaries, he liked all of Homer's work he saw exhibited in New York. It is not known if Sloan saw Homer's 1873 prints of the Gloucester fishermen's children exploring along the waterfront against a background of working schooners (which could have included young Sol Jacobs in his first year aboard a Gloucester boat). It is possible, but also unlikely, that Sloan had seen the watercolors of the harbor that Homer had painted in his 1880 visit.

Next came a surge of summer painters to the area – but not to Gloucester harbor. As early as 1874, William Morris Hunt took his popular Boston art class, all women, for a ten-day painting excursion to Annisquam, four miles north of the harbor on the side of Cape Ann that faces Ipswich Bay and looks toward the distant beaches of New Hampshire and, in clear air, to the Maine coast. A decade later a throng of artists of some note congregated in Annisquam. The somnolent village, long past its days as a coastal trading port, found itself, with some surprise, to be hosting a number of artists who had lived and studied in France. The first was William Lamb Picknell.

Picknell and a dozen other American artists had been setting out from Paris each summer beginning in 1866 to paint picturesque subjects at Pont-Aven, a remote enclave on the coast of Brittany. They trooped out to paint in *plein air*, taking advantage of portable easels and the new oil paints which had only in recent decades been made conveniently available in tubes. This had been a revolutionary advance. In 1841 John Rand, an American portrait painter living in London, invented a collapsible zinc paint tube, replacing paints sold as dry powders or in awkward bladders that had to be punctured. Thereafter artists could concentrate on painting a scene, not on compounding chemicals.

The landscapes of the Pont-Aven artists found a ready market among Americans who at last had a choice for ornamenting their homes with something other than plaster copies of Neoclassical statues of Greek and Roman gods, or sentimental domestic fireside scenes.

Picknell was born in Vermont and raised in Boston. He had studied in Rome under George Inness, and at the École des Beaux-Arts in Paris. Then, at the urging of American painter Robert Wylie, he began painting in the summer at Pont-Aven where the villagers still wore traditional dress – the women in embroidered aprons and high-collared lace *coiffes* head-dresses, the men in felt hats and patterned vests. Wylie could point out that Corot had painted there, as had the English painter Turner. French writers Stendhal, Hugo, and Balzac had also trod the winding coastal paths.

One of his paintings from the summers at Pont-Aven, *The Road to Concarneau*, made Picknell famous, and for its success he owed much to Julia Guillou, owner of the Hotel des Voyageurs. Robert Wylie had been one of her early guests and, it was said, her lover. When Wylie's fellow American artists arrived in Pont-Aven, they all, like him, stayed at the Hotel des Voyageurs.

Wylie died young of tuberculosis, and Mme. Guillou insisted that he be buried in her Catholic family plot, even though he had been a Protestant. Thereafter she became a dedicated patron of the other Americans, who called her *la mere des artistes*. Mme. Guillou supported Picknell and bought his paint supplies at the time he was working on *The Road from Concarneau*. The painting was voted an Honorable Mention in the 1880 Paris Salon, a rare honor for a work by a foreigner. Picknell's style retained form and solidity, not dissolving into pure light and color as in the works of many American Impressionists.

Then Picknell came to Annisquam for the summer. Its snug cottages and pastures sweeping to the shore may have reminded him somewhat of a French coastal village. He arrived as an American artist of distinction – one who had been singled out by the Paris Salon. The Irish artist Thomas Hovenden came too, with his new wife Helen Corson. She also had been an artist at Pont-Aven, and that was where they had met.

Others from the Pont-Aven crowd followed Picknell and Hovenden to Annisquam, some of them prominent, like the Jones brothers who had become friends with Hovenden at Pont-Aven. Hugh Bolton Jones painted landscapes, and Francis Coates Jones, his younger brother, specialized in opulently decorated interiors. Artistic links brought painters of many stripes to the village. Frank Jones was responsible for John Douglas Woodward's presence. Woodward had been introduced to the woman who would become his wife in 1875, Maria Louise Simmons, by Jones who was Maria Louise's cousin. The Woodwards would remain close to the Joneses thereafter. Woodward was successful in painting highly romanticized illustrations of far-away places for travel books, before photography reduced the exotic to the familiar. He and Maria Louise traveled extensively in the Middle East where he painted illustrations for a volume, *Picturesque Palestine.*

Woodward wanted to paint seriously, and when he learned that Frank Jones was going to Pont-Aven, he and Maria Louise went there too for a year in 1883. They took pleasant rooms in an annex that Julia Guillou had added to her Hotel des Voyageurs to accommodate all the artists flocking to the village. Woodward said there were more artists in Pont-Aven "than at any other one place in France." When the Joneses came to Annisquam in the late 1880s, Woodward and his wife joined them there too.

Another painter in the group at Annisquam who had made a career change was Henry Hammond Gallison. After finding no satisfaction first as a doctor, and then as a lawyer, primarily to satisfy his father's hope that he would make something of himself, Gallison devoted the rest of his life to painting. He traveled to Italy and France to study art, and in Paris married a German girl, Marie Reuter. After he returned to Boston his atmospheric landscapes so impressed the art community there that he was made a director of the Copley Society and was voted onto the board of the Boston Art Club. Henry and Marie summered in Annisquam where he could paint by day and they could join the artists' circle in the evening.

William Picknell married Gertrude Powers in 1889, and their Annisquam cottage became a gathering place for the Pont-Aven contingent. To the wonder of the locals, many of these exotic visitors tramped about the lanes in clogs and berets, trying to recreate a French rural ambience in an Annisquam that was quite satisfied to be a salty Cape Ann community. An exhibition of works by the Pont-Aven group, "Pictures at Annisquam," was mounted at the

Williams & Everett Gallery in Boston in December, 1886. That, however, was the high point in Annisquam's brief eminence as host to an art colony. By the 1890s painters of the Pont-Aven group began to seek visual stimulation elsewhere, and many migrated to Rocky Neck on the eastern shore of Gloucester harbor. On one side that point of land faced Gloucester's working wharves, and on the other the outer harbor, alive with schooner sails silhouetted against Ten Pound Island and the Magnolia shore. Among those who departed Annisquam for Rocky Neck were Joseph DeCamp and Augustus Buhler. DeCamp was one of the early Annisquam summer artists in the '80s, but was cut from a very different cloth than the Pont-Avenists. One of Frank Duveneck's "boys," DeCamp was from Cincinnati and studied with the master in that city, then followed Duveneck to Munich, Florence, and finally to Boston in 1883. With Boston as his base he traveled to Annisquam to teach classes in the summer. In the year of the "Pictures at Annisquam" show, 1886, DeCamp was instructing a class of more than twenty young Philadelphia women in the village. By 1901, though, DeCamp had joined Duveneck on Rocky Neck. Very possibly DeCamp's Rocky Neck and Annisquam paintings were seen by his New York student, Alice Beach Winter.

Augustus Buhler, along with Walter Dean, were two artists on Cape Ann – perhaps the only two – who consciously strove to bridge the gulf between working fishermen and professional artists, doing their best to mix oil with water. They made trips in the schooners to experience the working lives of the fishing crewmen, the world of Capt. Solomon Jacobs. Buhler had been studying at the Boston Art Club, then he and his wife moved into a converted fish shack in Annisquam in 1885. He got to know local fishermen, heard their stories, joined them on fishing voyages, and painted them at sea.

Buhler and his wife left in 1889 for two years of study in Paris, then they returned to homes in Boston and Annisquam where he painted, taught, and illustrated for *Harper's Weekly*. Then they, too, moved to Rocky Neck and he painted vintage fishermen types. One such image was purchased by Gorton Fisheries for use as a company logo.

A number of fine painters continued to visit Annisquam. Maxfield Parrish studied there under his father, Stephen, before they both moved on to the art colony at Cornish, New Hampshire. N.C. Wyeth, father of Andrew and grandfather of Jamie, studied under George L. Noyes at Annisquam in 1901. The deaf and charming Maurice Prendergast, that most unlikely member of The Eight, painted in Annisquam while staying with the Williamses in 1902 at their summer home. Fellow-Bostonian Esther (Mrs. Oliver E.) Williams had worked with Maurice in his studio and became a cherished friend with whom he corresponded regularly. Prendergast returned to Gloucester in 1907, 1910, 1916 and 1922, painting local subjects including the long-since-dismantled changing huts at Cambridge Beach in Annisquam.

These were notable exceptions to the artistic exodus from Annisquam. In the summer of 1900 an entire galaxy of significant painters had taken up their summer easels at Rocky Neck, most staying at the Rockaway Hotel. Duveneck and DeCamp were there, Edward Potthast and John Twachtman. Duveneck was now painting light-filled harbor scenes, a far cry from the dark and brooding style of the Munich school that he had once exemplified. He rented two studios in Gloucester so he could study the effects of light both at dawn and at dusk. Ever the disheveled bohemian, Duveneck charmed friends with his *Gemütlichkeit* (his parents had run a beer garden in Kentucky) and enduring passion for painting. His good nature masked the grief he had suffered with the death of his wife, Elizabeth Boott. They had married after a long-delayed love affair that Henry James drew upon for his *The Portrait of a Lady*.

Duveneck reunited on Rocky Neck with John Twachtman who had trained under him in Cincinnati and followed him to Munich and Venice. During his many later years in the muted Long Island Sound light of Cos Cob, Twachtman had become best known for a misty Impressionism. In Gloucester, with its strong forms of rock and vessel shapes and wharves etched against a shouting blue sky, Twachtman's work was more forceful, with firmly delineated forms in structured compositions. Twachtman was popular as a painting instructor, and ranged over Cape Ann with his students, painting *Beach at Squam*, for example, around 1901. (There are no such sand dunes in Annisquam as depicted in the painting – the scene is actually Wingaersheek Beach across the Annisquam River from

Annisquam. Many painters, including Sloan, called those gleaming white sands of Wingaersheek "the Annisquam dunes" in their titles.) There were shadows in Twachtman's life. His wife had left him and taken the children, and he drank. His paintings were not selling and that gnawed at him. His health failed, he died in 1902, and was buried in the park setting of Gloucester's Oak Grove cemetery.

Theodore Wendel came down to East Gloucester regularly from his home in Ipswich just north of Cape Ann on the coast. He would visit his fellow Ohioan Frank Duveneck, sometimes taking over Duveneck's class if the master was absent. Wendel had been with Duveneck in Munich but, after attending the Académie Julian in Paris, became one of the founders of the American art community in Giverny, where he fell under the spell of Claude Monet and became an Impressionist painter of light. In 1897 he married Philena Stone, who was wealthy, and they moved to storied Argilla Road in Ipswich.

Another luminary of American Impressionism, Willard Metcalf, had painted with Wendel in Giverny, and was also in Gloucester in 1895, as was that most eminent of American Impressionists, Childe Hassam. Constantly on the move, Boston-born Hassam had visited Gloucester at least five times during the '90s to paint the harbor and town in the broken-brushwork by which the American Impressionists sought to suggest color infused with light.

Sloan might have found it notable that so many of these artists had painted Impressionistic canvases in Gloucester light. The strains of Impressionism ran deep in the Cape Ann art world. He might dismiss it as "eyesight painting," but American Impressionism had its own enduring aesthetic value. Viewers standing before these sunny, airy, gauzy landscapes found them eminently accessible. The spectators were invited into the indistinct scene and, once in, their imaginations could roam freely. Because observers shared in the "impression" made by the painting, they could repeat the experience without tedium as often as they viewed the work. And many of the paintings were more than visual exercises. The landscapes of New Englanders Metcalf, Wendel and Hassam frequently convey a Transcendental reverence for nature.

By the 1920s and '30s there would be other art enclaves on the outer reaches of Cape Ann. Charles Grafly, Robert Henri's early traveling companion in Europe who introduced John Sloan to Henri, had his sculpture studio among the granite quarries of Lanesville where he gathered about him students from his Philadelphia sculpture classes, Walker Hancock and Paul Manship. Summer artists began to congregate on Folly Cove, and more importantly in Rockport. But all that came after John Sloan's time on Cape Ann.

By the time John and Dolly Sloan agreed to try Gloucester, few of the major artists remained of those who had painted in Rocky Neck around the turn of the century. Still, thanks to Alice Beach Winter, John Sloan would know that he was painting in a setting where many artists had come before. Gloucester was clearly a place where he could take a deep breath and renew himself as an artist.

1914

AND SO it was that in the summer of 1914 John and Dolly Sloan arrived for what would be five consecutive summers in Gloucester. They had rented a little red cottage on East Main Street in East Gloucester. Charles and Alice Beach Winter moved in with them. Thus the main stream of Gloucester summer artists had migrated from Pont Aven to Annisquam, from there to Rocky Neck, and now along the Rocky Neck causeway to the red cottage. There had been many detours from the road to Concarneau.

Another who arrived for an extended visit to the red cottage that first summer was John Sloan's sister Marianna, "Nattie." Nattie had a warm and loving personality that reassured Dolly and nurtured the associations between Sloan and the family back in Fort Washington, the Philadelphia suburb where they were now living. She had written that "Dad" would like to send John some strawberries he had grown, but Nattie had persuaded Dad they would not survive shipment. Dad's needs were modest, Nattie said; occasionally he would buy a little tobacco and charge it to her account.

Nattie was an artist like her brother, painting on canvas and also on lampshades that she sold with some success. John, "your loving brother," wrote her long letters, speaking to her as a fellow artist on matters of art theory. Nattie had not visited the red cottage simply

Gloucester harbor in the 1880s, nearing its peak years as a fishing port.

The crew of the Sarah M. Jacobs, *most of them well-dressed for the photographer, about 1878. Cape Ann Museum, Gloucester, Massachusetts.*

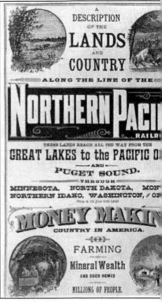

Capt. Sol (standing), urging on rowers in the seine boat as they close on a school of mackerel. Cape Ann Museum, Gloucester, Massachusetts. (above)
Northern Pacific Railroad ad promoting opportunities in the Northwest. (right)

Port Townsend, Washington Territory, became Sol Jacobs' base for his Pacific operations.

Capt. Jacobs' masterpiece, the mackerel schooner Ethel B. Jacobs.
Cape Ann Museum, Gloucester, Massachusetts.

Capt. Jacobs at his ease in the cabin of the Ethel B. Jacobs. *Gulf of Maine Cod project. NOAA National Marine Sanctuaries; Courtesy of National Archives.*

Capt. Sol with binoculars at the ready, and with wife Sarah on board. Cape Ann Museum, Gloucester, Massachusetts.

Capt. Jacobs, aged 62, standing masthead watch on the Benjamin A. Smith. *Cape Ann Museum, Gloucester, Massachusetts.*

The well-attended launching of Gloucester's first auxiliary schooner, the Helen Miller Gould. *Cape Ann Museum, Gloucester, Massachusetts.*

l run of the Helen Miller Gould, *with a few select guests aboard. Cape Ann Museum, .cester, Massachusetts.*

Sol's mackerel steamer, the Alice M. Jacobs – *no beauty, but a money-maker while she lasted. Cape Ann Museum, Gloucester, Massachusetts.*

The Jacobs home on Gloucester's Prospect Street, with Sarah on the porch behind Sol and two of the children. Cape Ann Museum, Gloucester, Massachusetts.

Red cottage children's party, with Dolly at top of steps on right, Sloan with pipe at upper left. Cape Ann Museum, Gloucester, Massachusetts.

"Our red cottage," the Sloan's summer residence on Main Street, Gloucester, c.1918. Gift of Helen Farr Sloan. John. Sloan Manuscript Collection, Delaware Art Museum.

John Sloan and students in his summer painting class, Gloucester, c.1917. Gift of Helen Farr Sloan, 1978. John Sloan Manuscript Collection, Delaware Art Museum.

John Sloan in Gloucester, c.1918. Gift of Helen Farr Sloan, 1978. John Sloan Manuscript Collection, Delaware Art Museum.

John and Dolly Sloan with friends, c1915–1918. Gift of Helen Farr Sloan, 1978. John Sloan Manuscript Collection, Delaware Art Museum. (John and Dolly Sloan at left; Leon Kroll in center; Randall Davey at far right.)

Photograph of John Sloan and friends posing on the front porch of the Red Cottage, Gloucester, 1915, taken by Charles Allan Winter. Gift of Helen Farr Sloan, 1978. John Sloan Manuscript Collection, Delaware Art Museum. (Standing left to right are Dolly Sloan, F. Carl Smith, Alice Beach Winter, Katherine Groschke, Paul Tietjens, John Sloan; seated left to right are Stuart Davis, Paul Cornoyer, and Agnes Richmond.)

The A. Piatt Andrew, *one of the Gloucester schooners blown up by the* U-156 *in* 1918.

WWI poster promoting the "food will win the war" campaign.

WWI poster issued by Herbert Hoover's Food Administration.

German U-boat U-156, scourge of the fishing fleet.

Korvetten Kapitän Richard Feldt, commander of the German submarine U-156.

Gloucester Daily Times.

And Cape Ann Advertiser.

GLOUCESTER, MASS., MONDAY, AUGUST 5, 1918.—6 PAGES.

THREE MORE FISHERMEN FALL PREY TO GERMAN U-BOATS

TO TELL OF Y.M.C.A. WORK IN FRANCE

MEMORIAL TO BRAVE SOLDIER

at Service for Philip Cunningham at the Trinity Congregational Church Yesterday.

THE GREEK HARVEST FESTIVAL FRIDAY

Brilliant Production Will Be Season's Event on North Shore.

CREWS OF CRAFTS LANDED SAFELY AT NOVA SCOTIA

Schs. Rob Roy and Muriel of This Port and Annie Perry of Boston Are Victims of Undersea Raider — German Commander Boasts That He Destroyed Other Gloucester and Boston Vessels Although Story Is Doubted — Attack Made Saturday Off Cape Shore — The Crews Row Ashore at Various Points, and Tell Story of Sinkings.

THE WEATHER.

The litany of frightening reports of fishing schooners sunk by U-boats, this from the front page of the Gloucester Daily Times, *Aug. 5, 1918.*

to enjoy the setting or to paint. She had been summoned by John, possibly because of some crisis with Dolly. John had first come alone to Gloucester at the end of June, while Dolly remained behind in New York. John sent Dolly a postcard from Boston while en route, announcing proudly that he had had "no trouble with seasickness." Inasmuch as Sloan had traveled by sea, he probably arrived in Boston via one of the Fall River Line boats that steamed out from the foot of Warren Street in New York City at 5:30 in the evening. It might have been the *Priscilla*, or *Commonwealth*, or *Plymouth*, all known as floating palaces. An orchestra played in the saloon until the passengers turned in for the night. The vessel steamed out into the open sea, having to take the outer route around Cape Cod because the canal cutting across the base of the cape would not be completed for another two years. After a stop at Newport the boat continued on to Fall River where Sloan and the other passengers disembarked and boarded the early morning 7:10 train for the run to Boston.

In July Dolly was still in New York. Sloan sent her another postcard to say that he had arrived in Gloucester where the weather was cold. Again he could happily report that he had arrived "without seasickness" – which suggests that he taken the steam ferry *Cape Ann* that ran between Boston and Gloucester during the summer months. These are the only accounts of John Sloan's seafaring life, and he seems to have judged his time on the ocean solely in terms of how he fared with nausea.

"I can never tell you what it meant to me to be sent for in your need!" So wrote Nattie to John after her visit to the Sloans in Gloucester that August. Whatever had happened, presumably before Dolly rejoined Sloan in Gloucester, Nattie acquired new admiration and affection for sister-in-law Dolly. After her return to Pennsylvania she wrote to Dolly saying how much she loved her, admonishing her to take care in walking all the way to downtown Gloucester. She was sure that brother "Jack" would be overjoyed with the cake that Dolly wrote she had baked for him. Nattie wrote to her brother that after the visit "I do feel so much nearer and intimate with you and Dolly."

Nattie now felt that she had not valued Dolly enough in the dozen years since she and John had been married: "I love her dearly and never half enough before." With what would seem to be concerns over Dolly's health, Nattie urges John, "And oh, do cherish her, for she is a frail little life, and absolutely yours, and dependent on you for her existence, for as you told me, she is all affection …"

In Gloucester Sloan set out to paint with creative abandon. "The new movements in Art add a lot to one's enthusiasm in work," he said. "[They] have a rather electrifying effect on the general atmosphere, broaden one's horizon, smash moulds and declare liberty."

Gloucester – half fishing industry, half small-town residential and farming dwindling off to inland moors – provided the settings and light he needed for his new direction. Sloan's impression of Gloucester was that it was "one of the old corners of America, built against the Puritan landscape, blue-eyed and rocky." He wrote to John Quinn that, escaping from the summer heat and haze of New York, he was looking forward to "a good outing of works and play and good breathing."

And he went about painting directly outdoors. "Working from nature gives, I believe, the best means of advance in color and spontaneous design." This was something new for John Sloan, except for some brief painting excursions made up the Hudson. He painted coves and distant downtown Gloucester steeples and towers seen across moors behind van Gogh-vivid sunflowers. The bright deep colors of summertime Gloucester sea and sky revealed themselves through Sloan's brushes in landscapes as warm-hued and luminous as any he would paint. Contrary to his earlier practice of basing a painting upon an incident or in making a social comment, he had been convinced by the work of van Gogh and Cézanne that the life of a painting could come from the dynamics of form and color.

He did a few portraits, including *Old Cone (Uncle Sam)* that hangs in the Cape Ann Museum. A study of an unmistakably eccentric man of advanced years, it may have referred obliquely to the Sloans' good friend John Butler Yeats back in New York.

Sloan and fellow-painter Randall Davey had high hopes of attracting students to help pay the bills, but only one signed up in response to the ad they placed in *The Masses* (perhaps not the best media buy for their offering). Frustrated at their lack of success, Sloan scoffed that the Gloucester docks were "littered with Charles

Hawthorne's pupils." Hawthorne was a popular art instructor in the traditional style who taught on Cape Cod.

After that first Gloucester summer Sloan returned to New York with ninety paintings, sixty-four of which he decided were worth keeping.

1915

Ⅰ N GLOUCESTER again for the following summer, John and Dolly were joined in the red cottage by the Davis family. Stuart Davis remembered his own noisy arrival in town. "When I made my initial entrance into this port at eighteen miles per hour, in a classy second hand roadster with two flat tires, I was ambushed by a cop on horseback."

Stuart Davis was only twenty-two, but he was already a creative rebel who had struggled alongside Sloan in the art and political conflicts. He had studied under Henri, placed five watercolors in the Armory Show and, like Sloan, had lately been profoundly influenced by the work of the Europeans. He had been on the board of *The Masses* with Sloan and the Winters, and had been among the dissidents who walked out.

Davis later said of Gloucester, "That was the place I had been looking for. It had the brilliant light of Provincetown, but with the important additions of topographical severity and the architectural beauties of the Gloucester schooner." When Stuart's mother, Helen Stuart Davis, arrived at the red cottage she brought along her other son, Wyatt, who was making his way as a photographer. Stuart's father, Edward Wyatt Davis, had been art editor of the *Philadelphia Press* in the 1890s, overseeing the contributions of Sloan, Glackens, Shinn and Luks. He had introduced Sloan and Dolly and, later when they were all living in New York, Ed Davis and his sculptor wife often got together with the Sloans.

Stuart Davis remembered that, at dinner time in the red cottage, there were eleven around the table – with Dolly the imperturbable hostess. Besides the three Davises and Charles and Alice Beach Winter, the four walls bulged with guests of one creative bent or another. On any given day they might include Paul Cornoyer, elder statesman of the group at fifty-one, who had a summer home in East Gloucester and the following year would be a founder of the North Shore Arts Association. Like Sloan, Cornoyer painted city scenes, but in an Impressionistic style he had honed from studies under William Merritt Chase, John Twachtman and Childe Hassam. Cornoyer was warmly welcomed into the company despite his artistic heresies.

Agnes Richmond also had studied under Twachtman at the Art Students League. She was known for portraits of women, but in Gloucester painted seascapes and harbor scenes.

Leon Kroll, then just over thirty, was already well established, his talent validated by a Grand Prix award in Paris, a one-man exhibition at the National Academy of Design, and paintings hung in the Armory Show. Then as always throughout his career, Kroll would delight in painting the female form, as in landscapes of Folly Cove at the far extreme of Cape Ann in which he incorporated attractive young women.

F. Carl Smith was a California-based portrait painter. On Cape Ann in the summer he was painting shore scenes alongside his wife, Isabel, who was from Cincinnati as he was and, also like him, had trained in Paris. Cincinnati had been an unlikely wellspring of American artists in the 19th century.

Henri's second wife Marjorie visited, too, together with her sister, Violet Organ. Violet traveled often with the Henris and later assisted William Inness Homer in his writing of *Robert Henri and His Circle.*

From outside the painting community came pianist Katherine Groschke, along with her two young nieces. Katherine could chat about music with composer Paul Tietjens, who was comfortably well-off from the success of the 1902 stage adaptation of *The Wonderful Wizard of Oz* for which he wrote the music. Describing evenings in the red cottage, Stuart Davis wrote "Tietjens plays good stuff for the mob every once in a while, and we played at a game of cards call pounce with great gusto." All too frequently, in Sloan's opinion, Charles Winter cranked up operas on the Victrola – what Sloan described as Winter's "Italian wife-beater" music.

With the Sloans in residence the little red cottage saw a volume and variety of permanent guests and visitors that astonished the neighbors. As in their Manhattan apartment, Sloan and Dolly thrived on the interplay of multiple artistic personalities. That was the year John Butler Yeats had been struck by an automobile in New York. Thereafter he would not be able to see well to paint. But he could still talk, endlessly and enchantingly, and Dolly set to on his behalf. When Dolly took up a cause, she was relentless. She and Sloan had taken Yeats into their New York apartment and she pursued a lawsuit for damages on his behalf, enlisting the aid of lawyer John Quinn. She set up lectures for Yeats, and in the years to follow was frequently in touch with Quinn on dates, places, and fees for the popular talks, and on applying the proceeds to pay the old man's board with the Petitpas sisters.

Dolly thought it shocking that no one in John Butler Yeats' family would look after his interests. A year before, when his son William Butler Yeats had arrived on the *Mauretania*, Dolly had confronted W.B. in his hotel room and demanded that he help his ailing and cash-strapped father. The stunned poet, accustomed to deference if not veneration, had shown her the door.

John Butler Yeats reciprocated Dolly Sloan's unstinting friendship with deep, concerned affection. He counseled her that, although she was the wife of a great artist, no one could help her with her personal problems but herself: "You must work out your own salvation."

Preparing for their trip to Gloucester for that summer, John and Dolly had invited Yeats to join them. Dolly touted the benefits of the trip: she would arrange for Yeats to give a lecture in Gloucester, and that would surely help pay his medical bills and his boarding bills at Petitpas. Yeats did not take them up on the offer. He remained convinced to the end that eventually he would find fame and fortune in New York.

Sloan's output was substantial in that summer of 1915. He had seventy-eight paintings to show for his efforts. He painted rapidly and restlessly, striving to capture effects such as a transitory blaze of sunlight on ocean and ledge. He had begun to attract students, too, who joined him on his excursions. In that year a half-dozen hopefuls, all women, gathered to paint under Sloan's guidance, and he was developing the instructing skills by which he would earn a livelihood from that time forward.

1916

THE FOLLOWING year Sloan and Dolly were teetering on the
abyss of poverty as always, but things were definitely looking
up. John now had a regular teaching position at the New York Art
Students League, and was no longer dependent upon irregular illustration assignments to pay the bills. This was also the year that Gertrude Vanderbilt Whitney invited him to mount his first one-man
show, at her Whitney Studio Club at 8 West 8th Street in Greenwich Village. A one-man (or one-woman) show, spotlighting the
work of that artist alone, was of great value in advancing a reputation
– especially for an out-of-favor artist like Sloan who could expect to
be rejected in a juried exhibition.

Millionaire-socialite-sculptor Gertrude Whitney had purchased
four of the paintings of The Eight sold at the Macbeth Gallery exhibition in 1908, when she maintained a studio at MacDougal Alley.
In 1916 she had opened her first gallery in one of the many Manhattan properties owned by her and her husband Harry Payne Whitney
who had inherited a fortune in oil, tobacco and banking interests.
Gertrude, as a Vanderbilt, was even more wealthy in her own right,
and passed her summers comfortably at that most extravagant of
Newport cottages, "The Breakers." Wealth and social position were
not enough: Gertrude Whitney was serious about art. She had studied with Rodin, and had another studio in the elegant Passy area of
Paris, in the XVIth Arrondissement.

The New York art critics were decidedly cool toward the Gloucester paintings that Sloan included in his show at the Whitney Studio Club. Those arbiters of taste had never taken to his unblinking
though genial portrayals of street life, and now did not know what to
make of the artist's new paintings of shore and moor. What's more,
Sloan was an American. In the wake of the Armory Show, works of
art had to bear a European signature to be taken seriously.

Later, when the Metropolitan Museum refused Gertrude Whitney's donation of paintings by The Eight and other American mod-
erns, she simply withdrew her offer and made use of her ample re-

sources. From the modest beginnings of her Whitney Studio Club she built and endowed the Whitney Museum of American Art, and thus was at liberty to display, at her pleasure, the works of artists she admired. She was an influential patron of American artists from 1907 until her death in 1942.

A month following his show at the Whitney Studio Club, John Sloan mounted another one-man exhibition, this at the Hudson Guild Social Center and sponsored by John Weichsel of the People's Art Guild. It was an unexpected invitation because Weichsel, who wrote for *Camera Work*, was an enthusiast for the *avant garde*. He organized modern art exhibitions in restaurants and in New York's immigrant settlement houses. It was likely that the proletarian subjects of Sloan's city paintings earned him John Weichsel's attention. Later Sloan wrote to Weichsel from Gloucester about a series of monographs on American artists that Weichsel was planning. Sloan recommended that he include Glackens, "the most versatile and vital of our painters and draughtsmen," and Maurice Prendergast, "who knew Cézanne's work before any American and loved it."

In April came another coup: an offer for a one-man show at New York's prestigious Kraushaar Galleries. Sloan was sure that this recognition was a direct result of his show at the Whitney Studio Club, and he wrote to Gertrude Whitney to say so: "Due to the prestige which my exhibition at 8 W. 8 established … I have passed through the most successful winter of my career. … Mr. Kraushaar is to handle my etchings and paintings as well – his attention was quite surely attracted to my work by my Whitney Show." The Kraushaars would represent him for years, and from this time forward his paintings began to sell, if only occasionally.

The Kraushaar brothers operated that rarity in the art world, a gallery that specialized in a certain type of painting and persistently exhibited and promoted the major artists in that genre, disregarding the popular taste. Charles Kraushaar, who apprenticed in European galleries, formed his own business in New York in the 1880s, and was soon joined by his brother John. Charles favored works of the Barbizon school, for which there was a ready market, but John promoted French Post-Impressionists like Matisse and Rouault. In New York he became increasingly interested in the work of The Eight as well, and would eventually represent – in addition to Sloan – Henri, Luks, Glackens, Shinn and Prendergast.

Sloan's work in particular was slow to gain public acceptance, but John Kraushaar encouraged the artist and showed his work year after year, decade after decade, determined to educate the public to an American master in their midst. And he never took advantage of an artist, no matter how little demand there might be for his work.

In 1916 Sloan was also intensely involved in organizing and hanging the first exhibition of the American Society of Independent Artists in New York. Like the 1910 Independent American Artists show organized by Henri, Sloan and others of The Eight, this new unrestricted event was inspired by the French Société des Artistes Indépendants which, since the 1880s, had held non-juried exhibitions in Paris that had brought to the fore innovators like Seurat, Signac and Redon. Juried shows were an abomination to artists like Sloan who were their own harshest critics and saw no role for judges, ribbons or ratings.

The American Society of Independent Artists in New York invited submissions from all and sundry. The first exhibition displayed 2,500 paintings and sculptures by 1,200 artists. Inevitably a great deal of inferior art was shown, but peeking from the rubbish were works by Glackens, John Marin, Walter Pach and Man Ray. Glackens was president the first year. Sloan took over the following year and would continue at the helm of the Independents for the next twenty-six years.

In the midst of all this activity, Sloan made an early trip to Gloucester in April, traveling with Randall Davey who was looking for a rental for himself and his wife for the coming summer. Sloan wrote to Dolly from Boston saying that he and Davey had gone to Gloucester in Mr. Smith's car (presumably artist F. Carl Smith), and that it had snowed. Sloan said that he had "glimpsed the Red Cottage in the snow." Accumulating snow is unusual in Gloucester in April, but those were cold years. Two winters later the harbor froze out to the breakwater and townsfolk walked over the thick ice to inspect vessels frozen in around Ten Pound Island.

Dolly had written to Sloan in Boston with news of people who had dropped in at their flat, and closed affectionately with "the same little girl you left is here waiting for her boy." John was sorry that Dolly was not along to "enjoy the good dinner at the Savoy." This was the Savoy Hotel in downtown Gloucester, and they both were familiar with its fare. Davey decided to rent a cottage on Brier Neck for the season, some distance from Rocky Neck but with splendid views of the open ocean. (Sol and Sarah Jacobs had their summer cottage on Brier Neck.)

Later, after John and Dolly had settled into the red cottage for the summer, Sloan was leading his summer students into the moors in search of subjects, and was exploring restlessly in his own painting. In *Gloucester Harbor*, scudding clouds and sails are balanced by the central upright mass of the Gloucester Gas Light Company's coal derrick. The light on Ten Pound Island and toward the far horizon is pure Gloucester luminosity. Sloan painted Dolly small but positive against the ledges, as in *My Wife in Blue*. He described her as "My hardest working model." Dolly would pose without a rest for five hours for Sloan who was "never quite satisfied with the 'likeness' when I paint her."

Sloan was demanding of his sitters, trying their patience as he struggled to capture on canvas the image in his mind. Once he had written, "Why will a man take on all the agony of mind and fatigue of body which results from the struggle to do something decent in paint?" But he was always challenging himself, as when he painted *Town Steps, Gloucester* that year. Here he had to work out the geometry of long diagonals receding in perspective up the wooden steps populated with figures, mostly young women. Sloan said they were "healthy types of the native population." As in most of his Gloucester paintings, he painted them as figures in a landscape, not personalities as when, years before, he had captured episodes from life in New York tenements. The colors are rich, the brushwork vigorous, in the manner of the Post-Impressionists that he admired.

In Gloucester that summer Sloan would begin to try out lesson plans he would use in his classes at the Art Students League. He also kept up correspondence with those who shared his artistic tastes. In the spring he wrote to A.E. (Albert Eugene) Gallatin to congratulate him on his book, *Certain Contemporaries: Notes and Art Criticisms*. Sloan said that Gallatin's critical essays "so little resemble

the destructive verbosities and $10 per column inanities of most of
the art criticism in America." Sloan then corrected himself: "Perhaps
this is over-estimated. I think $5.00 is the rate." The year before,
Gallatin had purchased a set of Sloan's illustrations for the De Kock
novels. To his most recent letter Sloan added, "Let me know when
you are ready to look at my Daumiers." If he had been called the
"American Hogarth," Sloan recognized his debt to Daumier as well.

Gallatin, great-grandson of Albert Gallatin who had been Secretary of the Treasury under Jefferson, was a wealthy collector and
art historian who was sometimes mentioned in the gossip columns
as the most eligible bachelor in New York. He had begun collecting
art a half-dozen years earlier and was buying paintings by American
Impressionists as well as works by the Urban Realists when he purchased his Sloan prints. Later Sloan would have reason to dispute
Gallatin's critical judgments: Gallatin became infatuated with abstract modernism and sold off his Urban Realist works.

During that summer of 1916 Sloan took the opportunity to show
his Gloucester paintings at the first exhibition of the Gallery-on-
the-Moors in East Gloucester, not far from the red cottage. Wealthy
summer residents Emmeline and Charles Atwood had commissioned their friend, Gothic-Revivalist architect Ralph Adams Cram,
to design an exhibition space for artists of Cape Ann who otherwise,
according to Emmeline's observations, could only hope to attract patrons to studios at the ends of wharves and in converted fish shacks.

Cram at the time was the supervising architect for the master
plan he had drawn up for the Princeton campus. Two years before
he was also appointed a professor at the Massachusetts Institute of
Technology, where he would head the architectural department for
seven years. Although he would occasionally stray into art deco and
modernism, Cram essentially held to his belief that the Renaissance
had been a regrettable detour on the march of Western civilization,
and that creative work in the English Gothic idiom was the true path
for academic and domestic architecture. His Gallery-on-the-Moors
was a minor but pure example of this conviction. Visitors would
enter through an imitation old English door and pass through a vestibule painted a deep blue. It was intended to heighten anticipation
as they proceeded into the main gallery. There, the paintings and

sculptures for the exhibition were arrayed beneath hand-hewn and pegged timbers and beams that reiterated the Gothic theme. The Atwoods exercised seigneurial authority over which artists were or were not hung on the walls. Some of the chosen ones would fade into obscurity, but by and large John Sloan was in very respectable company at the first exhibition of the Gallery-on-the-Moors. His friends Randall Davey and Stuart Davis were represented. In a place of honor was *Gloucester Wharves* by sixty-eight-year-old Frank Duveneck. When not at one of his two studios, Duveneck was staying at Mrs. Oakes' cottage on Rocky Neck.

There was a canvas by Charles Hopkinson, *Portrait of Mother and Child*. Hopkinson lived amid wealth nearby in Manchester but supported his large family by the remunerative but stressful business of painting portraits on commission. To relax he painted freshly experimental watercolors of wave-splashed shore in front of his home. He also portrayed his four daughters as they grew, and an oil painting in which he grouped the first three of them was hung at the Armory Show.

There was well-executed traditional statuary on pedestals by Charles Grafly, and by pioneering woman sculptor Anna Vaughn Hyatt, who had her studio at the family compound in Annisquam. Seven years later she would marry Archer Huntington, and their patronage of the arts would crest at Brookgreen Gardens which they created on 10,000 acres in South Carolina to display the statuary of American sculptors.

There were works by other women artists. Cecilia Beaux was a distinguished painter from Philadelphia, but from a very different tradition than John Sloan. She taught portraiture at the Philadelphia Academy of Art for twenty years, and supported William Merritt Chase in his battle of artistic principles versus Robert Henri. Years in Paris during the peak years of Impressionism did not sway Beaux from her devotion to solid composition, and she was much in demand for portraits done in a style similar to that of John Singer Sargent. Beaux had summered at her estate "Green Alley" on Gloucester's exclusive Eastern Point since 1906.

Theresa Bernstein showed *The Little Merry-Go-Round*. The *New York Times* reviewer who covered the show said it displayed her

"racy modern temper." Bernstein had been urged to go to Gloucester that summer by Mrs. Vernon Cook, President of the National
Association of Women Painters and Sculptors. Mrs. Cook told her
that in Gloucester she would "have a lot of beaches to paint." One of
the "Philadelphia Ten" of women artists, Bernstein married William
Meyerowitz three years after the first Gallery-on-the-Moors show,
and the two would be fixtures of the East Gloucester summer art
colony for decades thereafter.

Also in the show were works by Guy Wiggins, best known for
his scenes of snowy Manhattan streets, and by Arthur Wesley Dow
who, like Theodore Wendel, lived in Ipswich. Dow taught Georgia
O'Keefe in New York and was incorporating Japanese techniques
into his renderings of coastal scenes.

And there was a work by the remarkable Jane Peterson who had
risen from poverty to become, in the words of the *New York Times*,
"one of the foremost women painters in New York." Peterson would
concentrate, during that First World War, on painting war scenes to
benefit Liberty Loans and American Red Cross efforts.

The Sloans did not return to New York until the beginning
of October in 1916. Sloan wrote of his regret at having to "leave
Gloucester at her most beautiful moment. These fall days are wistfully beautiful warmish days with a saddening chill in the evenings."

1917

THE FOLLOWING summer saw the second annual exhibition at
the Gallery-on-the-Moors. In its review of the show the *Cape
Ann Shore* singled out for mention works by Impressionist landscape
painter George L. Noyes, Philadelphia Impressionist Martha Walter, Theresa Bernstein, Englishman Henry B. Snell who specialized
in marine paintings, and Boston's Louis Kronberg whose facility as
a painter of ballerinas in the style of Degas was being threatened by
his increasing nearsightedness. John Sloan's two entries were also
mentioned in the review, albeit cautiously. His painting of Niles
Beach was said to "present an individual quality," and his *Urbs in
Rurem* (city brought to the countryside) was "equally pleasing."

Throughout that first summer after America's entry into the European war, art events at the Gallery-on-the-Moors were frequently pre-empted for war relief benefits, as for the French Tuberculosis Soldiers' Relief Fund and the Navy Comforts League. Gloucester was gradually moving toward a war footing, and responding to these pleas for compassionate aid.

At this point Sloan was still roaming about Cape Ann to paint with his students, their rambles not yet impeded by coastal defense measures. However, his access to some choice shore scenery was being denied by new owners. In the summer of 1917 Sloan wrote to Henri, "Gloucester is much the same save on the coast – where the rich, like some pest, have eaten off acres of granite rocks and dunes and walled them in for themselves." At the time the locals were fighting to keep a shore road from being closed by out-of-town owners of the property, a battle the townspeople ultimately lost.

Some of John Sloan's most enduring and endearing oil paintings are from this Gloucester period when he combined a new freedom in color and discipline in form with the human warmth that seemed to reside deep within his brush. Best known is *Gloucester Trolley*. Against the puffy clouds and the solid shapes of the houses is the dynamic flow of humanity from the right in the canvas to the deep red mass of the streetcar, with the motorman stalwart at the controls. The passengers, most of them young, are from Rocky Neck, catching the trolley for downtown Gloucester. And in the foreground is Dolly, about to join the push to board, waving back to John. Lloyd Goodrich said that in these Gloucester paintings Sloan had the "gift of seeing the lyric poetry of everyday reality," and that they are reminiscent of the early French Impressionists.

Another vibrant painting from this summer is *Hill, Main Street, Gloucester*. The scene down the hill toward a curve of buildings has been a favorite of artists. Paul Cornoyer painted it hushed under snow in an oil he called *Twilight in Gloucester*. Charles Winter had painted the scene from the same vantage point. Sloan, in his version, omitted the city hall tower in the distance, apparently deciding it did not belong in his balance of visual elements. His notes, written much later, read: "Down this picturesque dip into town rolls a blue Mercedes, a few years old but full of pep and power. The driver is Randall Davey who painted in Gloucester several summers. The picture is rich in tone and was painted on the spot." The pigeon-scattering speed of the Mercedes down the dusty street is balanced by the unhurried progress of the pair of white horses pulling a wagon up the hill in the opposite direction. On the sidewalk are two of Sloan's healthy young women, not flirtatious as in many of his city episodes, but so wrapped in conversation they are oblivious to the gaudy roadster snorting past them. Again the colors are fresh, rich, vivid.

Randall Davey was, with Stewart Davis, one of the Gloucester friends Sloan was most comfortable with, enjoying late-night parties on the beach. Stuart Davis said, "we have many parties and lots of liquor, lobsters and auto rides." Davis later wrote in detail about one of their evenings.

Cornoyer had taken the Sloans and Carl Smith to dinner at Gloucester's Hotel Savoy. Davis and others went to the movies, and all joined together afterwards, the Savoy diners having put down a few drinks. The women went home by car and the men set out on foot. Davis directed their attention up to a then-abandoned rambling house with a six-story tower on an embankment overlooking the harbor. (It still stands today, in much improved condition.) Davis, Sloan, Cornoyer and Tietjens climbed into the basement, then let Smith and Winter in by the front door.

All found their way through the dark house, to the top of its turret. The police showed up, having been alerted by a neighbor, but decided the tipsy artists offered no threat to the sleeping town. The group continued on their way back to East Gloucester, singing and shouting, Sloan "chasing cats over the roofs of the Gorton-Pew [fish plant] in the moonlight." Davis celebrated the outing in a painting, *New Year's Eve*, and included the donjon of the house in a drawing, *Gloucester Terraces*, of 1916.

Making use of the more vivid colors and disciplined painting routine he learned from the Post-Impressionists, Sloan painted the life and shores of Gloucester with maturing skill in composition, tonality and movement. His landscapes of the period, such as *Sunflowers, Rocky Neck*, are so articulate in composition and color (here with a nod to van Gogh) that they are almost anecdotal: the life of the harbor springs out from them. John Sloan had returned to doing what he did best, reinterpreting the world about him through his paintbrush. In middle life he achieved results that ranked with the finest of his career.

John Sloan's Gloucester paintings and Solomon Jacobs' *Ethel B. Jacobs* - in each case they represented resilient comebacks, revivals of careers that for a time had gone badly astray.

Chapter Nine
SEDUCTIONS OF TECHNOLOGY

~

Power Fishing / Refining the Rainbow

Power Fishing

As THE 19TH century transitioned to the 20th, Americans remained enthralled by invention. Webs of rail corridors had knitted the vast nation together, and now roads were being improved: individuals could be masters of their own routes and timetables once they mastered the controls of the primitive new automobiles. Internal combustion engines had been harnessed to airfoils and were taking to the skies, and no one was really surprised: it had long been expected. This was the age of technology, and America could claim to be at the fore of invention, ever since Thomas Edison had lighted cities with translucent globes in which filaments glowed with no live flames. Edison added to his wonders of invention when he captured arias by Enrico Caruso on phonograph cylinders for posterity – or at least until the fragile wax tubes wore out or shattered. Capt. Jacobs and John Sloan would have the confidence of their age, certain that they could seize upon the potential of some new science.

Sol had lost the *Ethel B. Jacobs*, his finest schooner, when she had been swept onto a lee shore. If there had been any form of supplemental power aboard to resist the force of the wind, the *Ethel B.* might have been saved. The thought must have rankled Sol. The conventional wisdom was that the only kind of power that worked on a fishing schooner was wind power. Everybody knew that petroleum-fueled and steam boiler approaches to combustion power were in use elsewhere. But the Gloucester fleet owners and captains had long resisted the idea of installing auxiliary engines, offering every kind of argument.

Auxiliaries, they said, would be too expensive to purchase and operate, too heavy for a schooner, likely to catch fire and destroy the wooden boat and its cotton sails. Any unnatural power source would disrupt the vessel's sailing characteristics, and steal space that was needed for holding fish. And there was pride: a Gloucester master mariner had made his reputation handling wind-driven vessels in any weather. Putting some foul-smelling motor on board would be a disgrace.

Capt. Jacobs knew all that. At the same time he could see the potential savings in a vessel that could power herself out of the inner harbor without the expense of a tow from a steam tug. One that could get to and from the fishing grounds faster, especially in light airs or against head winds. And be provided with some saving leverage when drifting in wind or currents.

But if he wanted to build some kind of additional power into his next vessel, what were the options? Steam was a leading contender. Side-wheel steamboats had been carrying passengers and cargoes across the Atlantic since the 1840s, and had been replaced by this time with more efficient screw propellers that drove the vessel from under the stern. Steam-powered ferry boats had been running into Gloucester harbor since 1883 when the all-wood *City of Gloucester* arrived from Boston on the first of round trips that she would continue to make for the next forty-three years, mainly carrying freight year-round plus a scattering of summer excursionists. In 1895 the *City* was joined on the Gloucester-Boston run by the more elegant steamer *Cape Ann*. The *Cape Ann* catered more to human cargo (John Sloan, for one, in 1914), but carried some freight as well.

There had long been steam tugboats in Gloucester harbor, too; there were eight in service around the turn of the century when Capt. Jacobs was making up his mind as to a power plant. One former steam tug, *Little Giant*, had retired into the ferry business and was carrying summer visitors from downtown to East Gloucester. John Twachtman had painted *Little Giant* in its later incarnation sometime between 1900 and 1902. Also, cruising off the Long Island and New Jersey coasts, Capt. Jacobs would have seen the steamers used in purse-seining for menhaden (as a Gloucesterman, he would have called those bait fish "pogies"). But the steam boiler and the coal box on those little boats took up far more working space than could be tolerated in the mackerel fishery.

A gasoline engine, the captain decided, would be the answer. He got in touch with Capt. G. Melvin McClain in Rockport. McClain was a much respected designer of schooners such as the *Effie M. Morrissey* (which later went on to a second career as the *Ernestina*). Jacobs told McClain what he had in mind, and emphasized that above all his new schooner should be designed along the proven lines of a Gloucester sailing schooner, without any undue compromises to make room for the auxiliary. In effect, he wanted the best of both worlds: all the characteristics of a classic schooner, combined with the reserve power of a gasoline engine. Mel McClain accepted the challenge, and designed the hybrid vessel that came to be the *Helen Miller Gould*.

In naming the vessel after Miss Gould, Capt. Jacobs was paying tribute to a dedicated humanitarian. When William McKinley declared war with Spain in 1898, Helen Miller Gould immediately donated $100,000 to the United States Treasury. Her motives were humanitarian, not martial. During the course of the war she not only donated generously toward the purchase of military hospital supplies, she visited the camp at Montauk Point, Long Island where wounded and fever-ridden American troops had been evacuated from Cuba. The American public idolized the heroes of San Juan Hill as long as they remained in the abstract. But when they returned as patients suffering from the mysterious contagions of yellow fever and malaria, they were shunned like lepers and confined to the remote camp at the tip of Long Island. When Miss Gould learned that famine threatened the camp, she set out to provide the best of nourishment for the veterans. She sent to the camp a corps of chefs, some from the households of her fellow millionaires in New York City whom she badgered into cooperating.

Intentionally or not, Helen Miller Gould thus did much to compensate for the wrongs of her father, railroad king and stock manipulator Jay Gould. Most likely as far as Capt. Jacobs was concerned, the fact that her father had richly deserved his reputation as a robber baron was neither here nor there. Sol wished to honor a brave and generous woman, and wrote to request her permission to name his new vessel the *Helen Miller Gould*. Miss Gould was happy to oblige, and a year later wrote to Capt. Jacobs that she was sending a set of flags for the boat he had named in her honor.

The *Helen Miller Gould* was built in Gloucester at the John Bishop shipyard in the winter of 1899-1900. The vast majority of Gloucester schooners were built in Essex, but Gloucester also had prominent shipbuilders and John Bishop was one. He turned out 150 vessels "of fine reputation" from 1887 to 1912. A major launching could reliably bring out a big crowd, and on March 29, 1900 more than 3,000 spectators lined the shores of Vincent Cove (long since filled in). The honored guests included Mel McClain, who was gratified that practical experts on schooner design present, including Capt. Jacobs' fellow schooner masters Joseph Cusick and Thaddeus Morgan, admired the fine lines and clipper bow of the big 149-ton, 117-foot-long schooner. The traditional wine bottle was smashed against the bow by Capt. Jacobs' eldest daughter, Ethel. The launching was supervised by John Prince Story, foreman of the yard, and to the satisfaction of all in attendance, *Helen Miller Gould* splashed smoothly into the cove. Amid the cheers there was a fluttering of handkerchiefs. The naming of the vessel after a heroic woman had drawn a large number of women spectators, including members of the Chautauqua Circle who gave their handkerchief salute. (The Chautauqua Literary and Scientific Circle, founded in 1878, is America's oldest continuously operating book club.)

Thus the first fishing schooner that had any kind of auxiliary power was added to the Gloucester fleet. To be sure, at the launching the *Gould* did not have a power plant. That would be added during the fitting-out when a 35-horsepower Globe gasoline engine was installed. Shortly thereafter, that anemic unit was replaced by a 1500-horsepower Globe that could drive the *Gould* at eight knots. Both engines were manufactured by Globe Iron Works in Minneapolis. Innovation had its price: the cost of building and equipping the *Gould* to Sol's requirements came to $23,000, more than twice the cost of a conventional mackerel schooner.

Capt. Jacobs wasted no time in putting the *Helen Miller Gould* through her paces. After a test run down the shore to Beverly with a bevy of favored guests aboard, he set out for mackerel on April 12, barely two weeks after the launching. Two weeks after that he arrived at the New York market with over 200 barrels of fresh mackerel, which he sold at top market price. "We owe the success of the trip to this little engine," Sol told a reporter from New Jersey. "We'd never have come near [the big catch] if we had been solely dependent upon our canvas, for there wasn't a whisper of a breeze blowing when we sighted 'em. That engine is the new fangle in mackerel fishing. It's a thing the other fellows will be running after soon." In reporting the catch, the *Boston Globe* acknowledged that Sol's renown was becoming downright mythic: "Capt. Solomon Jacobs ... is known among the English-speaking people of two continents as the most daring and intrepid master mariner that sails a fishing craft."

Helen Miller Gould was invited to inspect her namesake vessel in New York. She had other engagements, but hoped to step aboard when Sol returned from his next trip. Still unmarried at thirty-two and as eligible an heiress as New York had to offer, Helen Gould remained in that tantalizing state for a dozen more years, finally marrying Finley Johnson Shepard. They would adopt five children, one a foundling who had been abandoned on the steps of Manhattan's St. Patrick's Cathedral.

Capt. Jacobs proved repeatedly that auxiliary power could get him out to the fishing grounds and back again faster and thus more profitably than by wind power alone. When he sailed (and chugged) into Gloucester harbor on September 3rd, the *Gould* was carrying 720 barrels of mackerel, three times the amount of his first trip into New York with the *Gould*. Fish covered the deck and filled the seine boat. The *Gould* broke all seining records that year, stocking $40,660. The lesson was not lost on the other Gloucester ship owners and skippers. They might be suspicious of a schooner spewing smoke and gasoline fumes beneath its sails. But the *Helen M. Gould* was a money-maker, and all had to accept the fact that, like it or not, power was the future of fishing.

The following year, 1901, began just as auspiciously for the *Helen Miller Gould*. Capt. Jacobs, true to form, landed the first mackerel of the season, a substantial fare of thirty-five barrels. The crew was content and in good spirits, as well they might be, considering the good money they were making. But that gasoline contraption growling beneath the deck was slowly altering the time-honored order of life on a fishing schooner. The most disruptive result was the demoting of the cook from his traditional distinction on a schooner as the No. 2 man aboard. Now the member of the crew who was second in importance only to the captain was the engineer, a man of dubious maritime skills who was forever tweaking levers and valves. And that balky early marine engine gave the engineer of the *Gould* and Capt. Jacobs all manner of grief.

The end came with fiery finality. The *Gould* was on a seining trip off the north shore of Nova Scotia. Capt. Jacobs had put in near the eastern tip of Cape Breton at North Sydney which was then enjoying prosperity as a coal refueling port. Also, just two years earlier, it had been designated as the Canadian mainland terminal for ferry service to Newfoundland. While the *Gould* was laid up in North Sydney on October 25, fire broke out in the engine compartment. A leak in the fuel system had gone undetected and was ignited by a spark. The *Gould* probably could have been saved by vigorous firefighting, but the risk of explosion from the volatile gasoline was too great. Capt. Jacobs got himself and all his men off safely, though there was no time to grab any of their personal gear.

Maritime author James B. Connolly wrote of how Sol and the crew looked on in frustration as the *Gould* burned to the water line. Connolly had sailed with Capt. Jacobs on another occasion, and is the sole source for a story that Sol, when chasing halibut and seals in the Pacific in the *Edward E. Webster* and *Mollie Adams*, earned a bit of revenue by also secreting below decks a few Chinese immigrants who lacked documentation. Whether Capt. Sol confided this information to Connolly on a quiet watch, or if it was pure hearsay, cannot be verified.

Word of the destruction of the *Helen Miller Gould* spread quickly, and some in the fleet were confirmed in their mistrust of Sol's power source. Gasoline auxiliaries would continue to be at risk for fire and explosion. It was a danger that would not be significantly reduced until new generations of marine engines were introduced that ran on oil-based diesel fuel. Capt. Jacobs had paid a heavy price for taking a risk on innovation. But, characteristically, he was not deterred. His successes in fishing in the *Gould* convinced him that problems with power were outweighed by the advantages.

Sol began to seriously reconsider that other mode of auxiliary propulsion, steam. The weight and cost of adding a steam plant and its boiler to a traditional schooner made no sense economically. But what if you forgot about classic schooner lines and built a big, fast boat to take full advantage of steam power? That was his thinking behind the *Alice M. Jacobs,* named for the captain's youngest daughter who was now fifteen.

The sequence of events entailed in building a fishing steamer was unfamiliar ground for Sol. He sought out the Keough Brothers in East Boston, known as specialists in this alien sphere of steam engineering. The various parties must have thought the others were speaking different languages when steamboat men Richard & William Keough, sailing captain Jacobs, and master schooner builder Arthur D. Story gathered at the latter's shipyard in Essex. All of them had much to learn – and unlearn.

To be sure, steam vessels had been launched from Essex in the past. In 1881 the steam collier *Vidette* had been built at the John James shipyard. At 191 feet in length and nearly 820 tons she was the largest vessel ever built in those yards fronting on the channel that winds from Ipswich Bay through the marshes to the village. Onlookers at the launching pronounced the *Vidette* unprepossessing. "She was just a great, big, ugly-looking black boat. But she didn't have to be pretty." In 1898, Arthur Story himself had built a steamer, the *Lexington.* She had been commissioned by the state police of Massachusetts to maintain law and order in the territorial waters of the commonwealth.

But a steam fishing boat? That was something new for them all. The design the Keoughs came up with featured a tall smokestack aft and a tiny pilot house forward. But if the classic schooner design had to be abandoned, Capt. Sol insisted that the *Alice M. Jacobs* at least be an honest wooden vessel, framed of oak and tamarack, with mostly pine for the superstructure. Up forward the *Alice M.* had a focsle to house a crew of twenty-six. In the cabin were quarters for Capt. Jacobs and the other ship's officers. One innovation in advance of its day was electric lighting, albeit on a modest scale. Incandescent bulbs, powered by a small dynamo, were used at night when the crew were dressing fish while running for market. Otherwise, as was typical of fishing schooners, the only illumination was provided by oil and kerosene lamps – always a hazard in a wooden ship, especially one rolling in heavy weather.

Down below, besides the fish hold, there were bunkers to hold 100 tons of coal and 40 tons of ice. All of this in a vessel over 141½ feet in length and rated at 220 tons. The *Alice M.* was built to carry a mainsail, foresail and fore staysail, but in function these hark-backs to schooner design were almost vestigial, relegated to minor roles in steadying the vessel and keeping her bow to the wind when fishing.

The launching of the *Alice M.* on March 11, 1902 was the public spectacle that Capt. Jacobs relished. His young son Albert administered the christening blow with a bottle of wine as a thousand spectators looked on, and the *Alice M.* was launched on her side, splashing into the Essex River. Forty guests lined the deck as the steamer was towed around to Gloucester to have her masts stepped. That afternoon she departed under tow to East Boston to have a 300-horsepower steam power plant installed by the manufacturers of the engine, Bartelson & Peterson. In fitting out the *Alice M.*, Capt. Jacobs had occasion to do business with marine suppliers in Gloucester with whom he had not been previously acquainted. P. Stoddart & Co., for example, a firm that specialized in "steam engine yacht work." Capt. Sol bought assorted steam engine supplies and parts from Stoddart throughout the career of the *Alice M.*

In addition to steam technology, Capt. Jacobs incorporated the latest fishery communications into the *Alice M.* When he had been fishing in the vicinity of the South Shoal lightship off Nantucket, he hailed it from time for word on fish sightings. Passing freighters would send that information to the lightship by wireless telegraph. It occurred to Capt. Sol that having telegraph equipment aboard his own vessel would be a great convenience, and provide him with a competitive edge as well. At the time a series of poles and relay stations were being erected along the coast, including a pole that had just been raised 250 feet above sea level on Beacon Hill in Gloucester to capture and pass along messages. Sol contacted the manufacturers of wireless technology equipment, and soon the *Alice M.* was the first boat in the Gloucester fleet equipped to communicate by Morse code over long distances.

"Mackerel by wireless," was how the *Boston Globe* described the operation of the wireless telegraphy gear installed on the *Alice M. Jacobs*. With an operator poised over the telegraph key, Sol could keep track of the movements of migrating fish, as well as the current quotes from buyers in the Boston and New York markets. The system also provided an added margin of safety: Sol could be alerted to hazards, such as fog banks "around Sable Island and other dreaded spots." The *Boston Globe* had no doubt that this was another of Sol's innovations that others in the fishery would soon find indispensable.

Installation of the power plant for the *Alice M.* was completed by April 15th, and that was occasion for another gala event. With Capt. Jacobs at the wheel and, as usual, a contingent of invitees at the rail, *Alice M. Jacobs* steamed from an East Boston dock saluted by other vessels, and left in her wake the gasoline-powered custom-house boat *Dreamer*. After clearing the channel, Capt. Jacobs signaled his engineer to pour on the coal. The *Alice M.* churned along at a satisfying eleven knots back to Gloucester, where an excited crowd was lining the wharves. The word was out that the *Alice M.* had made the run from Boston in record time.

Less than a month later, Capt. Jacobs was on the mackerel off the Carolinas, and he could not have been more pleased with the performance of the *Alice M.* After just nine days he was into the Fulton fish market with 90 barrels of mackerel. The *Alice M.* stocked $41,000 in her first season, breaking all records for mackerel sold.

Nor did Sol allow his costly new steamer to sit idle when the mackerel were not running. In March of the following year, 1903, he ran her into Provincetown to load 286,000 pounds of squid. He then steamed to St. Pierre & Miquelon, skirting ice en route, and sold the squid to French fishermen as bait for their Grand Banks cod fishery. The salt bankers lined up alongside the *Alice M.* to take on all the squid Sol had to offer. Sol concluded matters rapidly. He was eager to return to Gloucester to fit out for seining so he could be first, as usual, on the mackerel. He promised, with probably fractured versions of French and English being exchanged on both sides, to return in three weeks with another cargo of herring. He was discovering that he could attract new markets with the speed and capacity of his big fishing steamer.

The *Alice M.* also demonstrated her value in salvage, rescuing schooners that otherwise would have been lost along with their cargoes. When the schooner *Bertha D. Nickerson* went aground at the Bay of Islands, Newfoundland, Capt. Enos Spinney walked seven miles on the ice down the Humber River hoping to intercept the mail steamer. Back on the *Nickerson*, his crew had almost talked themselves into abandoning the vessel when Sol came along in the *Alice M.*, persuaded them to stay aboard, and towed the *Nickerson* thirty-eight miles to Birchy Cove. Sol put in a salvage claim for $2,000, which was fair enough in view of the $12,000 value of the vessel and its cargo that he had saved.

In 1903 Capt. Jacobs in the *Alice M.* continued to outperform the sail-powered mackerel seining fleet, landing the most fish after the fewest days at sea. If the sailing schooner captains harbored any lingering doubts as to the advantages of power, they were convinced once and for all when Sol Jacobs ran circles around them under steam. He added an exclamation point in September when, after just ten days at sea during which he followed the mackerel east off Nova Scotia, he landed 50,000 pounds of fresh mackerel, and 260 barrels of salt mackerel – the biggest trip of any boat in the fleet up to that time.

Capt. Jacobs invariably invested a fishing cruise with his personal flair. In one instance he took time out to conduct a rescue, and enhanced the occasion with gracious hospitality. Steaming in the *Alice M. Jacobs* on September 14, 1902, he came upon the ferry *Cape Cod* dead in the water off Wood End near Provincetown. To the relief of the uneasy passengers, this smoke-belching fishing steamer, the likes of which they had never seen before, towed the *Cape Cod* to safety in Provincetown.

Sol had performed his rescue. He would have been perfectly justified to simply drop the 360 ferry passengers on the dock and steam away. But that, by the captain's standards, would have been churlish. Sympathetic to the distress of the passengers, Sol invited them all on board the *Alice M.* The steamer set course directly to Boston, where the castaways arrived in good time and with no further inconvenience. The grateful handshakes and winsome smiles were acknowledged modestly by this Gloucester sea captain who had done his duty, and then some.

Capt. Sol was less amiable in his dealings with functionaries who interfered with his fishing. The *Alice M.*'s steam boilers had a great appetite for coal, and this occasioned another of Sol's frequent run-ins with Canadian authorities. In February of 1902, off Halifax, he sent a wire to that port requesting permission to land and purchase coal. The Royal Collector of Customs flatly refused, on the grounds that he was not allowed to issue fishing licenses to steam vessels. Sol continued along the coast as his store of coal diminished, and he was also turned down by the port authorities in Sherburne and Canso. Then the Port Mulgrave Customs Collector granted Sol a license. It was quickly canceled, though, when the collector's superiors sternly pointed out to the functionary the error of his ways.

Capt. Jacobs protested indignantly to the U.S. consul in Halifax, who stepped into the brouhaha. The consul listened to the Canadian authorities who insisted that their directives prohibited the granting of fishing licenses to steamers. The U.S. consul reviewed the directives, and pointed out to the Provincials that no such restriction was even mentioned in their official instructions. Capt. Jacobs had been virtuously correct in his requests to enter Canadian harbors, and had been egregiously wronged by the various port authorities.

Sol would not have long to savor any righteous sense of vindication. Late in that year, just twenty-one months after her launching, the *Alice M.* was wrecked. Capt. Jacobs had sent her north under the command of brother Bill Hodder. Hodder was at the wheel in a December gale east of Cape Ray, Newfoundland with the temperature below zero. The long, awkward fishing steamer struck on the reefs of Durant Island and rapidly began to break up in heavy seas. A dory was put over the side but was quickly swamped. A second met the same fate. The third floated, and one of the crewmen, Austin George, jumped in carrying a line and rowed the dory to shore in the numbing cold, freezing his fingers and ears. He tied the line fast to a rock, and the other crewmen pulled themselves to the island in other dories.

All were safe. But their ordeal was just commencing. They dragged a dory three and a half miles across the uninhabited island to the side facing the mainland. They then rowed themselves to shore and were rescued. All suffered frostbite. After breaking up, the *Alice M. Jacobs* caught fire, and there was little left to salvage. The loss was equivalent in value to that of four conventional fishing schooners: $40,000. It was the largest single loss to the Gloucester fleet up to that time. It had been Bill Hodder who had been in command when the *Edward E. Webster* ran aground on Unga Island in Alaska, and now he had been master when the *Alice M. Jacobs* was lost. But Sol could not fault Hodder for the destruction of the steamer in a raging gale. In any event, Sol was always loyal to his half-brother Bill.

Sol continued to be plagued by the unreliability of the early auxiliaries. In 1905 when he went master of the *Veda M. McKown* for its Gloucester owner, Fred L. Davis, he put into Provincetown for gasoline to fuel the auxiliary engine. Somehow, during the refueling, 120 gallons of gasoline escaped into the cabin and the hold. The errant fuel was pumped out, and the boat aired out for forty hours. Then Sol set out to sea. The *McKown* was seven miles offshore, a crewman lit the binnacle lamp, and all seemed well. Then the cabin exploded in flames. Sol ordered most of the crew off in the seine boat, then he and four volunteers who remained on board attempted to douse the fire. The engine was still working and Sol ran for Provincetown, fighting the flames all the way in. Once the burning vessel was seen entering P-town harbor, other vessels rushed to aid in extinguishing the fire.

Capt. Sol – and the other skippers operating gasoline auxiliaries – came to realize that gasoline fumes were always an insidious threat. But despite all the early problems – fires and explosions, mechanical problems with engines and shaft alignments and stuffing boxes – it was clear that powered vessels had come to stay. Sol had proved that vessels under power could get to and from fishing grounds more quickly, especially in calm weather or with headwinds. Furthermore, in designing a new boat the expense and weight of topmasts, long main booms, heavy main gaffs and full sailing rig could be dispensed with. Bowsprits could be shortened or eliminated altogether.

Again Capt. Jacobs had been the pioneer, had seen his own venture fail and cost him dearly, and been left to watch others succeed along a path he had blazed. He was cheered only by knowing that he had been first, he had shown them the way.

As Sol had said about the auxiliary in the *Helen Miller Gould*, an engine was "the new fangle in mackerel fishing." And, indeed, it did become "the thing the other fellows came running after." From 1905 on, standard practice was to include provision for an auxiliary engine in every vessel built for the Gloucester fleet. By then, fifty-nine-year-old Capt. Jacobs was not ordering any new boats. Henceforth he would let younger men take the glory – and the risks – of breaking new ground. He had had his fling with the technologies of the future, and suffered the disappointments, as well as the satisfactions, of a pioneer.

Refining the Rainbow

JOHN SLOAN's infatuation with technology was on a more modest scale than that of Sol Jacobs. Sloan did not mechanize easels or invent a steam-powered paintbrush. But he did become enamored of a scientifically rationalized color system that he was convinced would change the way artists used paint.

He once said, "I get an attack of enthusiasm once in a while that lasts me for several years." One of these attacks led him into Socialism. Another was his espousal of the Maratta pigment system. As so often in Sloan's career, and in that of the other members of the Philadelphia crowd, the original impetus came from Robert Henri. On June 13, 1909, Sloan recorded a visit from Henri and his wife and noted "H. is full of a scheme of color, a new set of pigments made by a man named Maratta." In an entry two weeks later Sloan wrote. "Mr. Maratta ... called today and gave me a very interesting demonstration of the working of the colors. I feel that they are important and I ordered a set."

Sloan's visitor, Hardesty Gilmore Maratta, after indifferent success as a painter in Chicago, had decided that his true talents lay in marketing pigments. He developed a system of color harmonics and manufactured a corresponding line of premixed colors. Sloan became a convert to the underlying theory of the Maratta system, which was based upon theoretical parallels between art and music. "The palette is an instrument that can be orchestrated to build form," he said. "If we stumble around in colors we are like a musician who would have to tune every note on the piano each time he sits down to play or compose."

In 1911 Sloan wrote in his diary, "I wish, so does H[enri], that we had studied music harmony. The colors and musical scale are perfectly parallel. A color can be made 'dominant' and chords can be determined as in music." In other words, colors were to the eye what musical tones were to the ear.

It was an attractive analogy that had long intrigued speculative thinkers. Throughout the Middle Ages the seven notes identified by the Greeks in the diatonic scale were being associated with colors. In the 17th century Sir Isaac Newton devised a color wheel in which he identified seven primary colors, which conveniently matched the seven notes of the diatonic scale. Newton cautioned that his color wheel applied only to mixtures of light, not to paint, but elegant color wheel refinements for use by artists appeared regularly after his time.

In the fecund creative environment of the early 20th century, various theories were being advanced that drew parallels between painting and music. Roughly at the same time that Maratta was introducing his system, a Canadian, Percyval Tudor-Hart, propounded the theory that the twelve colors in a standard color wheel corresponded to the twelve notes in the chromatic scale that had become the tonal currency of iconoclastic composers of the day like Arnold Schoenberg and Alban Berg. With his "Synchromism," Tudor-Hart went beyond relating color and musical scales: he discerned significant "hollow and bump" curves in color and sound, and sought to define form and space in terms of warm and cold colors.

It is generous to call Synchromism a movement inasmuch as Tudor-Hart seems to have attracted only two followers, Stanton Macdonald-Wright and Morgan Russell, both Americans, who studied under Tudor-Hart in Paris. Their first showing of paintings which reflected the Synchromist rationale was held in 1916, but apparently without great success because Russell abandoned the concept in 1916. Macdonald-Wright continued to paint using color scales throughout his long career as a familiar presence in the Los Angeles art scene. If Sloan and the other converts to the Maratta color scheme were aware of Synchromism, they never mentioned it. All of the music-color theories were based on the belief that absolute color corresponded to absolute pitch, that just as musical notes were measured in vibrations per second, colors could be measured in wavelengths across the visible spectrum. Unfortunately the analogy was not exact. In Western music, musical notes are fixed frequencies defined around a central note, *A4*, that vibrates 440 times a second, no more and no less. But colors are less precise: red in the visible spectrum can range from 620 to 750 nanometers, and vary in frequency from 400 to 484 terahertz.

Such fine points were dismissed as quibbling by Sloan and Henri and their fellow enthusiasts for the Maratta System. Charles Winter was the chief proponent and explainer of the theory. Thus it was as more than a friend, fellow artist and fellow ex-staffer on *The Masses* that Winter joined Sloan at the red cottage in 1914 and for the summers following. Sloan and Winter, along with Randall Davey, devoted long hours to experimenting with wheels and pyramids of harmonizing colors.

The challenge was to select a battery of shades and tones they could assemble onto their palettes for a given painting. Winter introduced Sloan and Davey (and Henri and George Bellows back in New York) to the Dudeen color triangle, which they found more useful than the color wheel as a structure for relating pigments. The Dudeen color triangle was an adaptation of Scottish physicist James Clerk Maxwell's diagramming of relationships within the color spectrum. Winter elaborated on the Dudeen triangle in a book he was writing with the help of Sloan. The book was never completed (the manuscript resides in the library archives of Gloucester's Cape Ann Museum). Winter was a painter, not a physicist, and the concepts behind the Dudeen triangle were picked apart by later investigators.

Theory aside, Sloan found that thinking of his palette as a musical keyboard of pigments had practical application, and regularly put the system into practice for his painting sorties in Gloucester. One lesson he had taken away from the Armory Show was that the European Post Impressionists were disciplined workmen who painted every day, and often outdoors, weather permitting. Sloan found this a liberating regimen: instead of waiting for an inspiration, he began to choose his setting and immediately decide what he wanted to achieve. "I would … walk a mile or so until I saw some kind of subject that had exciting plastic rhythms and color textures that could be the starting point of a theme."

Then he would return to the cottage and prepare his palette. He said that he and Winter and Davey had worked out "an arsenal of 48 tones, each in three shades." They put them all in separate stock jars, and "from these we could rapidly select a particular palette." Sloan would then return with his painting equipment to the scene that had appealed to him, perhaps the same or next day. "Sometimes I made two pictures a day, working with various set palettes that gave me control over the color orchestration."

When Sloan's artist sister Marianna visited at the red cottage in 1914, her brother bombarded her with rationale for the Maratta system, and afterwards he wrote her at length about the theory, illustrating a letter with diagrams to explain a "diatonic dominant palette." He said "God Bless the Maratta Colors. I can think in these! When I paint a thing I know where I got the pigment I used. I know how I made it. I have some common sense idea of what I'm doing."

Sloan was all enthusiasm for the Maratta System when, on October 4, 1916, a reporter for the *Gloucester Daily Times* wrote about calling in at John Sloan's studio for an interview as part of a series he was writing on artists in Gloucester. John and Dolly must have been thinking about returning to New York – in early October the nights would be getting chilly in the red cottage. The *Times* man found the studio "hospitable, with spice cakes." (Dolly had no doubt provided something right out of the oven for her husband's guest.) Ushered into the studio, the reporter found himself surrounded by "serious paintings" and sketches. He had no difficulty in drawing out the artist. Throughout the interview Sloan held forth animatedly upon one subject: the virtues of the Maratta system. With Maratta's pre-mixed battery of pigments, he explained to the reporter who was no doubt struggling to take it all down, "we could plan color chords, similar in some ways to those of music."

Sloan continued on the same theme with his Gloucester art students, telling them "I think it is very important for the artist to have a working knowledge of the use of the palette. The palette is an instrument, like a piano or a violin. In the hands of a master it may be a complete orchestra." Should his students begin to think of themselves as Maurice Ravels on canvas? Perhaps. Sloan asserted that the great painters had orchestrated their palettes, whether or not they were familiar with theories of color harmonies. Rembrandt, he said, would balance an area of neutral color "as a foil for the palpitating color changes of the other surfaces." Renoir's paintings were usually dominated by a red color-texture, plus subtle themes of other colors, like yellow and green, that could be followed throughout the design. All of Titian's and Rembrandt's pictures were "painted in the orange scale ... with other color notes used as accents." Sloan particularly admired Delacroix for his experimentation with the optical qualities of color, and his care in approaching each subject with a specially designed palette of colors of specific intensities.

For all his enthusiasm about color triangles and harmonic analogies with music, John Sloan never let the Maratta system override his artistic judgment. He used it as a practical template for organizing the combination of color tones most satisfying to the eye, but kept his options open. He said, "If the limited palette I had chosen to work with proved inadequate to get the kind of plastic realization I wanted, I could always open the palette up ..." He freely deviated from the regimen to achieve the results he was striving after. Sloan said "I painted hundreds of landscapes, portraits and other subjects [using the Maratta-Dudeen system] – and no two of them have the same color scheme."

For several years Sloan made use of Maratta-Dudeen principles in organizing his palette. Then Hardesty Maratta died in 1924 and his pigments were no longer available commercially. As time went on Sloan became more interested in plastic and formal challenges rather than those of the colors in a landscape or a woman's complexion, and he drifted away from a palette pre-selected for a subject.

He may also have come to suspect that harmony in color tones could not be ordered by scientific application of a color wheel, or triangle. As far back as the 18th century critics had been arguing that the comparison between color and music was flawed. They said you can blend two colors together, yellow and blue for example, to make an intermediate color, green. But combining two musical notes does not create another note between them. Furthermore, they said the emotions aroused by a musical chord were in no way similar to the feelings generated by corresponding colors. At an even further subjective extreme, they asserted that a sequence of colors could never be remembered like the sequence of notes in a catchy tune.

The Fauvist Raoul Dufy had misgivings that might have been persuasive to a fellow artist like Sloan. Dufy observed that, to the eye, certain colors do not belong together, contrary to the law of complementary colors. Michel Eugene Chevreul, who supervised the production of dyes for Gobelin Tapestries, pointed out another optical illusion: to the eye, strong colors tend to bleed over adjacent weaker colors, and are seen as an intermediate tone.

Psychologists further muddied the waters through studies indicating that one person sees colors very differently from another, depending upon the viewer's age, sex and frame of mind. And then there were variables such as saturation, luster, luminosity, iridescence and hue – as to the latter, it was discovered that humans can perceive more than 2.8 million different hues. Could any theory of color combinations be entirely trusted? Or was Sloan wiser to trust his own eye, as he said he did ultimately for each painting?

John Sloan must have become aware of the dizzying range of ambiguities an artist would encounter when probing deeply into color perception. Perhaps the Maratta system was not a painter's technological panacea after all.

Chapter Ten
ALLEGIANCES

~~

Citizen Jacobs / Villager Sloan

Citizen Jacobs

PERSONS OF note are usually best remembered for what they achieved in their primary pursuits. This was true of both John Sloan and Solomon Jacobs. Sloan was a consummate artist, and everything else in his life pales by comparison with what he created on canvas. Sol Jacobs was first and foremost a fishing captain, and his international squabbles are insignificant compared to his success in advancing fishing methods in his time. Those were the career highlights. But there were other dimensions to each man's life. Looking at Sloan and Capt. Jacobs off-duty gives a fuller picture of who they really were.

When Capt. Solomon Jacobs stepped ashore, he became a different man. At sea he had all the respect and responsibility of command. Men jumped at his word. He made every decision as to where to fish, when to fish, when to dodge a storm or keep going, whether or not to risk the ire of some Canadian customs agent.

But once in his stocking feet in the comfort of his own parlor on Prospect Street, surrounded by Sarah and the children, he shed all that. This was his safe haven, where he could enjoy occasional respites from the sea, and become simply Solomon Jacobs, citizen of Gloucester. Citizenship was important to Sol. Unlike native-born sons and daughters who took their nationality for granted, for Sol it had been a matter of conviction and decision. He had been a foreigner, an alien until that day in January 1873 when he swore his allegiance to the United States. Thereafter he would take his obligations and rights in his adopted country very seriously.

Over the years Sol accumulated the credentials that set a man apart as a substantial and fiscally responsible member of the community – and so he would remain, except for one dark episode that we will look into later. As we have seen, he had been made a Director of the Gloucester National Bank, and was regularly consulted by newspaper reporters and by government committees on fisheries matters. And, his friends would add, he was a man of compassion in an era when the needy depended upon private acts of charity. Soon after his arrival in the town Sol Jacobs would discover that Gloucester had a tradition of gathering around to protect its own. As, for example, after Capt. Ezekiel Call was lost in the schooner *William Murray* in that year so devastating to the fleet, 1871, the year before Sol arrived in town. Capt. Call left a widow and five small children. A fund was got up and the contributions funded the purchase of a house lot in the Riverdale section of the town. The subscription also paid for the lumber used for building the house. But money was only the beginning. Men from around Cape Ann turned up to volunteer their labor. They dug out a basement, did all the carpentry and painting, and presented Mrs. Call with her new home in the spring of 1873. If Gloucester was a rough seafaring town, it was also one with a heart. Over his many subsequent years in Gloucester Capt. Solomon Jacobs could be counted on to be as generous as any in helping out those who had fallen upon hard times.

In 19th century America much charity was performed through benevolent orders. Men joined fraternal lodges not only for sociability but for higher purposes as well. To raise money for charitable organizations – and for special causes – they circulated subscription lists, sponsored musical and literary entertainments, organized benefit balls. After severe losses of men at sea again in February 1879, $30,000 was raised to benefit the families left behind.

Ship owners and seamen contributed equally to the Gloucester Fishermen's and Seamen's Widows and Orphans Society. This concept of drawing charitable support from a broad base was not adopted nationwide until passage of the Social Security Act in 1935. Also, beginning just before Sol Jacobs arrived in Gloucester, a Tenement Association for Widows and Orphans maintained a building in which fishermen's widows and their children were housed in apartments at token rents. Beginning in 1877 the Gloucester Relief Association provided poor relief for victims of fishing disasters. And the Gloucester Female Charitable Association distributed food and clothing to the poor, many of whom were fishermen's widows. Capt. Jacobs did his part as an active member of both the Tyrian lodge of Masons and Ocean Lodge of Odd Fellows. In his family papers was a Certificate from the Tyrian Lodge dated May, 1916, exempting "Our Brother Solomon Jacobs" from further dues "having paid dues for 35 years." During the Civil War the Masonic lodges had been refuges for soldiers away from home, and in the decades after the war Freemasonry was seen as a patriotic order devoted to good works in the community. A large number of the Gloucester fishing community were Freemasons; most were Christians as well, and saw no contradiction between the two.

In addition to contributing to worthy causes, Capt. Jacobs was known for looking after his friends, and was open-handed when it came to neighborhood appeals. He was particularly generous to the Methodist church on Prospect Street, but when he heard that the Bethany Chapel on Eastern Avenue needed a new flag, he bought them one on the spot. The grateful chapel organized a formal acceptance, at which the boys' and girls' choir sang the national anthem. The new flag was raised, and someone spoke in gratitude to the captain, absent at sea. After the formalities there was ice cream, strawberries and cake for all. Said the *Boston Globe*, "Capt. Jacobs is a man of marked social traits, and an appeal to him for funds from any source is almost invariably met with a generous response."

On June 2, 1879, a year and a half after she and Sol were married, Sarah gave birth to their first child, Ethel. They were living at 49 Warner Street, and Sol's occupation was listed as "mariner." Two and half years later, on December 5, 1881, Sol purchased from Orlando Garland a lot of land and residence on "Prospect Street and west from Taylor Street" for $5,500. Witnesses to the transaction were Garland's wife Mary and Sol's brother, Bill Hodder. The purchase price of $5,500 represented about $111,000 in today's dollars.

In the nine years from Sol's arrival in Gloucester as a downeaster seaman, he had so prospered as a fisherman that he now qualified as a substantial property owner. This was the house, at 150 Prospect Street, that Sol and Sarah would share for the rest of their lives together. It was on a good street in a residential neighborhood, yet only a short walk from the wharves. The house was a rambling structure, of substantial size, with a good-sized back yard that could incorporate a vegetable garden along with plenty of space for children's games. The family also had a summer cottage at Brier Neck, on the east-facing shore of Cape Ann, where Sol and Sarah could look out on Salt Island and open ocean beyond, and their youngsters could splash in the waves.

By the time their second child and first son Albert was born, on August 1, 1883, Sol was listed as "master mariner," reflecting his status as captain and vessel owner. The next child was also a boy, Arthur, born June 25, 1885. Sarah gave birth to the final addition to the family, Alice Maude Jacobs, on October 11, 1887. As in many middle-class Gloucester households at the time, Sarah had a live-in domestic helper; in 1900 it was a 29-year-old French-Canadian woman, Frances Comeau.

The two daughters would eventually marry, although under very different circumstances. Ethel wed Arthur Dodge, an architect who was an army major in World War I. During that war Ethel was a traveling representative of the American Red Cross; she had graduated from nursing school in Boston, after attending Wilbraham Academy. Later she was active in the Cape Ann Scientific, Literary and Historical Society (today's Cape Ann Museum), and the Methodist church, until her death at seventy-seven.

In July, 1908 Sol's wife rushed to the Gloucester depot and boarded a train to Boston. She was hoping to intercept her husband when he arrived at T-wharf from a trip in the last schooner he owned, the *A.M. Nicholson*. Sarah wanted to be the one to break the news to Sol. Their youngest child, Alice, had eloped to Providence to marry Peter J. Cox the day after her father set sail. Sarah arrived too late: Sol had already received word of Alice's clandestine nuptials as soon as he docked. The *Boston Globe* reported that "Capt. Jacobs received the news philosophically."

We do not know what prompted Alice to marry apart from her parents, and presumably without their consent. But Alice remained fiercely loyal to her father. When someone writing to a newspaper spoke of the captain's "anger," Alice responded directly to the individual with the challenge, "I would be interested to know what prompted you to write of his 'anger,' such anger was reserved for ship use, for I can truthfully say that it was never displayed in the house." While Capt. Sol could be a terror at sea when challenged, on shore he was modestly self-assured. A man of his ease of command and proven accomplishments had no need for bluster.

Alice and Peter Cox lived in Providence and then Rockport. There one of their two children, also Alice, lived out her life, which ended in 2006, in a house surrounded by photos of her grandfather's vessels.

As to his sons, the captain was determined that they have a better start in life than he – and not follow in his footsteps into the harsh and dangerous life of a fisherman. Arthur was sent to college, to Cornell, and in 1913, a year after he graduated, he was seen at the wheel of his brother-in-law's Stanley Steamer on Prospect Street. His father, no stranger to steam propulsion, must have been intrigued by this automobile powered by a steam boiler. In October of 1937, a "mild-mannered gentleman" climbed the stairs to the Master Mariners' Society rooms on Main Street and introduced himself as Arthur Jacobs, a son of Capt. Solomon Jacobs. He was warmly welcomed by old captains who had known Arthur's father well. They recited epic achievements of the legendary Capt. Sol, and were eager to show the fifty-two-year-old son artifacts and photos of the schooner age displayed about the society's assembly room. Arthur lingered to study a photo of his father's fishing steamer, the *Alice M. Jacobs*. Little is known of the other son, Albert, who moved to Minneapolis.

Although politics was not of first concern for him, Sol felt that he had a responsibility as a franchised voter to get involved. His first recorded effort at participation landed him in a hornet's nest of partisanship, perhaps due to unfamiliarity with American street-level politics. It was in November, 1886 that a public caucus was convened in Rogers Hall in Gloucester to sound out popular opinion on a choice for mayor in an upcoming election. The hall was filled with men (men only – it would be many years before women won the right to vote). They were of "all political persuasions," and Capt. Jacobs agreed to be one of five who would count the votes. There were cheers for speakers supporting William Pew, Jr., a popular young schooner captain. Nevertheless, a Dr. George Morse had the most votes on the first ballot.

Consternation erupted when Capt. Jacobs announced that he had seen several unauthorized ballots added to Dr. Morse's total by a member of the vote-counting committee whom Sol would leave unnamed. Sol called for adjournment of the whole travesty, but he was shouted down. Another vote was taken and, during the deliberations of the counting committee, Capt. Jacobs called for adding the ballots for Capt. Pew that had been left in the hat which had served as a ballot box from the first count. Otherwise, Sol insisted, Pew would be deprived of a fair count.

The committee concurred, and the second vote showed Pew ahead. But, in a minority report from members of the voting committee to whom the captain had not endeared himself by his charge of ballot-stuffing, Sol was accused of stuffing the ballot hat himself. Disgusted, Capt. Jacobs firmly tugged on his own hat, left the hall and went home.

Having noted Sol's departure, supporters of Dr. Morse demanded that Capt. Jacobs rise to defend himself. Another vote was taken and Dr. Morse was declared the popular choice. The contentious straw poll at Rogers Hall was reported in the *Cape Ann Advertiser* of November 25th, together with Capt. Jacobs' response in which he asserted that the only reason he was at the meeting in the first place was to cast ballots pledged to David Robinson, no one else. He added that, had he known that he was to be charged with a misdeed, he would have remained in the hall and stood his ground no matter what the consequences. No one who knew Capt. Jacobs doubted that he meant what he said. In the subsequent election the Republican candidate, David Robinson, handily defeated Dr. Morse and became Gloucester's mayor. Robinson was a successful fish dealer who had served in campaigns in the West during the Civil War and was mustered out as a first lieutenant. "Dr." Morse was a homeopathic faith healer.

This was Sol's only recorded venture into popular democracy. Thereafter he confined his political activism to support of the Republican Party, specifically the McKinley wing of that party. William McKinley came to be associated with the expansionist sentiments shared by large segments of 19th century Americans in what came to seem "manifest destiny" as the nation expanded its borders across the continent to the Pacific. That the captain shared this viewpoint should not be surprising. Sol had had his run-ins with British crown authorities on both the east and west coasts of North America, and with the Irish on the other side of the Atlantic. How much more convenient it would be if the stars & stripes flew over as much of the land and seas as possible. Of course, Sol had had his misunderstandings with American authorities, too, especially off the coast of Alaska. By and large, though, he no doubt felt that it would be advantageous to men of initiative like himself to be pleading their case before authorities of their own nationality.

Sol not only agreed with McKinley's expansionism but admired him as a man who, in the Civil War, had enlisted as a private in the Union Army and risen to the rank of captain through battlefield promotions. He was the last president to have served in that war.

From what Capt. Jacobs heard about McKinley, he liked the cut of his jib. The president was for tariffs to protect fledgling American industries (such as the fisheries), and he sang hymns and patriotic songs. He was devoted to his invalid wife. And he enjoyed sitting with his cronies for a game of cards, with a spittoon within sharpshooter range. McKinley was seldom if ever accused of reading a book, and spoke in platitudes. He was genial with a magnetic personality but, more important to Capt. Jacobs, he was known to be incorruptible in that age of political machines, graft and bribery. McKinley was a man of modest means; he had not, like many, acquired mysterious wealth during his years in politics. "His public career had been as honest as his personal life was upright."

In the captain's language, McKinley was an "A-1 article." He had Capt. Jacobs' support in his successful run for the presidency in 1896. During the campaign Sol reportedly paid the president a high compliment by sending him a half-barrel of fresh mackerel. That was not the most unusual of tributes McKinley received; the crowds of devoted pilgrims who journeyed to Canton, Ohio to take part in McKinley's "front-porch" campaign brought gifts of every description: a gavel made, it was said, of wood from Lincoln's log cabin, miniature railroad rails, a marble bust of McKinley, and four live eagles.

The Spanish-American War confirmed Sol's support for McKinley. The President had held out against public demands that America declare war against Spain after the mysterious explosion that blew up the battleship *The Maine*, even as William Randolph Hearst's *New York Journal* and Joseph Pulitzer's *New York World* vied for readership by clamoring for retaliation. The newspapers asserted the claim, never confirmed, that the Spaniards had attached a bomb to the hull of the man-of-war. Under Secretary of the Navy Theodore Roosevelt, also agitating for war, said that McKinley had "no more backbone than a chocolate éclair." McKinley, though, who had been at the blood bath at Antietam, said "I shall never get into a war until I am sure that God and man approve. I have been through one war. I have seen the dead piled up, and I do not want to see another."

McKinley made every attempt to bring Spain to terms through diplomacy, but eventually war it was. It was a brief war, won in four months after decisive U.S. naval victories at Manila Bay and Santiago. The successes at sea overshadowed poor performance on land of American troops led by inept commanders. Reports gradually surfaced of a heavy toll of American lives in battle and atrocious conditions in fever-ridden army camps, such as the one in which artist Bill Glackens was embedded.

With victory, the U.S. inherited responsibility for the former Spanish possessions of Cuba, Puerto Rico, Guam and The Philippines. The Philippines presented a special dilemma. An archipelago half way around the world, inhabited by restive peoples, it offered little attraction to the United States – except that other nations had their eyes on the islands. Germany, Japan, Russia and Great Britain, all competing to acquire new territories, were eager to establish a presence in the Philippines. McKinley concluded that it was inevitable that the entire group of islands would fall into the hands of either the United States or Spain. Spanish rule could not be tolerated, so America annexed the Philippines.

The Hawaiian Islands were equally vulnerable in the sweepstakes of nations competing to colonize the Pacific. In 1893 American sugar planters had overthrown Queen Liliuokalani and set up a puppet republic, anticipating that the United States would annex those islands and confirm the planters in their dominance over the economy.

For McKinley, a willing, pro-American government on the ground was too inviting to ignore, particularly as Japanese immigrants were being sent to Hawaii in large numbers and threatening to establish a *de facto* occupation of the islands by that nation. McKinley said "we need Hawaii just as much as we did California," and the process of annexation moved forward. Later generations, with a retroactive sense of guilt, may sometimes overlook the geopolitical complexities their predecessors had to deal with: on November 23, 1992, President Bill Clinton signed a resolution apologizing "to Native Hawaiians on behalf of the people of the United States for the overthrow of the Kingdom of Hawaii ... and the deprivation of the rights of Native Hawaiians to self-determination."

McKinley had become an expansionist almost in spite of himself, first for the strategic purpose of protecting America's flanks, and second tor the economic opportunities those annexations promised. In speeches in western states in 1899 he thrilled audiences with the words, "What we want is new markets, and as trade follows the flag it looks very much as if we were going to have new markets." He called on Americans to have "the courage of destiny," as the country now, with dizzying rapidity, found its flag flying not only coast to coast but over lands in both hemispheres.

This vision of national expansionism, putting America right up there with the European powers in the building of empires, was something that Capt. Jacobs could endorse wholeheartedly. Did not America, with its doctrines of individual liberty and free enterprise, owe it to these misruled territories to annex them before they fell anew into the clutches of one or another of the corrupt powers of the Old World? Was not the U.S. best able to arrange equitable trading (and fishing) arrangements with these territories? The reasoning might have been simplistic, but it had its appeal to a man of action like Sol.

In 1900, when McKinley ran for reelection, Capt. Jacobs, recently returned from the Northwest, took an active role in the campaign. He offered his name as a candidate to be alternate delegate for the Massachusetts Sixth Congressional District to the Republican National Convention that would convene in Philadelphia in June. Sol was then fifty-three, but his campaign photo showed a slick-haired man in his early forties – probably a photo that the captain had gone to a studio to have taken years before. He would not be the first candidate for office to project himself as younger and presumably more vital than an up-to-date likeness would suggest.

Sol won the contest, and the 926 Republican delegates to the convention re-nominated McKinley by acclamation. He won re-election to a second term as president, trouncing Democrat William Jennings Bryan. It would have been a moment of great satisfaction for McKinley's steadfast Gloucester supporters, including Capt. Solomon Jacobs.

In September of the following year President McKinley attended the Pan-American Exposition in Buffalo where he was shot and mortally wounded by Leon Frank Czolgosz. The assassin called himself an Anarchist, and in his papers were found pamphlets by impassioned Anarchist Emma Goldman who had been a house guest of John and Dolly Sloan during the Lawrence strike. Czolgosz had sought a meeting with Goldman, but was turned down; nobody took this ill-informed fringe radical seriously.

Capt. Jacobs would have been shocked and shaken at the murder of the president he so much admired. He might have had some reservations about the firebrand vice-president who now succeeded McKinley, but Theodore Roosevelt was as dedicated to expanding America's influence globally as his predecessor had been. By initiating construction of the Panama Canal, Roosevelt set the wheels in motion for linking the Atlantic to the Pacific under American control, and he sent the Great White Fleet of the U.S. Navy around the world to assert America's emergence as a global power.

What's more, Roosevelt was an outdoorsman who thrived on adventures in the wild. Sol could applaud that in the man, and also agree with much of Roosevelt's Progressivism, which Richard Hofstadter summed up as an "effort to restore a type of economic individualism and political democracy that was widely believed to have existed earlier in America ..." If any man in Gloucester was an economic individualist, it was Sol Jacobs – so it is likely he would support Teddy Roosevelt, bravado and all.

Sol simply tried to use good judgment in all of his civic roles – as voter, supporter of worthy charities, taxpayer, husband and father.

Occasionally he may have been tripped up by misjudgment, but no one could fault him for lack of good intentions. Capt. Solomon Jacobs, with the aid of Sarah, was able to give his children the advantages of a respectable middle-class background and education. He thus broke the chain of poverty and hardscrabble existence that his forebears had known generation after generation on the Newfoundland shore. Sol had fared well in his adopted country, and had proved himself a worthy (if occasionally rambunctious) citizen.

Villager Sloan

UNLIKE SOL JACOBS, John Sloan was not a man with family responsibilities, except for an obligation to provide for Dolly – a task at which he barely succeeded over the years. In his excursion into Socialism he thought he was acting for the betterment of mankind, but that was all very abstract. It was when, after his third summer in Gloucester in 1916, he took on art instruction at the New York Art Students League as his primary occupation that John Sloan began to feel that he had a real stake in the lives of other individuals, that he could contribute to their self-realization. His students became his community.

Sloan discovered that, in teaching, he was in his natural element. He always liked a good argument, and now he could express his opinions on art to a more-or-less captive audience. Not that Sloan was didactic: with an honesty that seemed brutal to some he sought to guide his students toward finding their own voices, discovering their best talents. He especially liked teaching young people; their potential was precious. "Teaching has made me dig into my own work; I want to say something worthwhile to the fresh young minds with which I come in contact." His teaching style might seem brusque because he expected that those who decided to study with him came fully motivated. As Jacques Barzun said, "In art one can teach only those who already know – those who instinctively feel – how words or paint or sounds can be handled. ... The true teachers give goals, not rules ..."

Sloan would teach for most of a quarter century, primarily at the Art Students League but also at other schools, and with private students. His students at the Art Students League included Peggy Bacon, Alexander Calder, David Smith, Anita "Angna" Enters, Reginald Marsh, Aaron Bohrod, Lee Gatch, John Graham, Adolph Gottlieb and Barnett Newman. (Jackson Pollock, marching to his own beat, left after a month.)

Some of Sloan's students had vivid recollections of their teacher. Adolph Dehn studied under him and wrote of Sloan's hatred of commercial art – of making anything to sell. (Sloan must not have been including illustration, the trade by which he had paid his bills for twenty years.) Dehn described John Sloan as "a man of about 40, black hair with some grey … Glasses and a good tan about his face. Oh, how he rails against institutions, how he rails at commercial artists, portrait painters, etc.! … He can swear real handy too."

Another student, Adolph Gottlieb, found Sloan's openness to modern art liberating. "… John Sloan had the most valuable influence on me because Sloan was a very liberal guy for his time. For any time. He was interested in Cubism, for example. … as a result of Sloan's interest in everything that was happening in modern art, I became, in New York before I went to Europe, interested and read every book that I could on the subject, went to see whatever was available in New York."

Aaron Bohrod said that, of all his instructors, Sloan exerted the most profound influence, teaching him to value both the old masters and the vibrant realities of the American urban scene. Bohrod returned to Chicago "determined to do for Chicago in [his] own way what Sloan had done for New York."

One young woman student in Sloan's Art Students League classes was particularly attentive. Helen Farr was infatuated with everything about Sloan, his words and his art. She took down much of what he said and, years later in 1939, she showed Sloan those notes and gained his cooperation in publishing them as *John Sloan on Drawing and Painting (Gist of Art)*. They included many of his words of advice to his students, expressed as epigrams, such as "Don't think of sea as color. Make it a solid that can support a boat. Think of 'wetness' as color-texture."

Sloan explained to his classes what he found in artists that he most admired. He would talk, as with his Gloucester students, about how Rembrandt, Renoir, Titian and Delacroix orchestrated their palettes, and he would bring in the Dudeen triangle and the Maratta system. But he would talk motivation as well.

Daumier was one of his favorite examples – Daumier who was never condescending in his portrayals of common people and found much to admire in them as individuals. Sloan, like Daumier, never drew or painted his rooftop or street scene subjects as simply types. They were always persons. He advised his students to "draw with human kindness, with appreciation for the marvel of existence."

Sloan always credited Robert Henri with making a serious artist of him, but he was clear with his own students that there were differences between his point of view and that of Henri's. He remembered that when he was a newspaper artist in Philadelphia, "there was a great deal of emphasis on inspiration, self-expression, wit, and pictorial beauty. Robert Henri was the great teacher of this school." Of his own teaching style, Sloan said "I have tried to go on from the inspirational teaching of Henri to give my students more technical information about how to think and do."

Although John Sloan was regarded as radical, he did not lead a rebellion as Robert Henri had done. Henri, with his anti-academic fervor, led a revolt against the vapid Romantic style that prevailed in American art in the late 19th century. That battle had been won by the time Sloan became a full-time instructor. What Sloan could teach his students was to be open-minded to new movements. He told them they could learn much from those he called the "ultra-modernists," Cézanne, van Gogh, Gauguin. But he scorned any abstract art that he felt left out the human dimension, and in which the artist's underlying mastery of painterly skills was suspect. "Pure abstraction isn't art," he said "… it escapes from life. … The human mind cannot grasp an idea unless it has texture, the texture of living existence."

Sloan found himself ironically in the position of defending technique against untrained inspiration. He insisted that artists must learn the skills of working with paint, and learn empathetic skills, too – be sensitive to all the complexities of the life around them. It was an emphasis on acquiring the basics that many artists-in-training would resist, infatuated as they were with Modernism in all of its intellectually appealing guises.

Although Sloan was becoming an influential art instructor, few of his paintings were selling. This lack of recognition by galleries and collectors somehow added to the mystique that became attached to Sloan. He was regarded in some awe as one of the Urban Realist pioneers of the early years of the century. He would say later, "It is a sort of escape, a kind of refuge, not to have too much recognition while one is alive. You can go along doing your own work without being bothered too much by what people think." The Sloan brand was gaining credibility though, after his one-man show at the Whitney Studio Club, and with representation by the Kraushaar Gallery.

He was beginning to get better press, too. The *New York Times*, which had earlier been lukewarm toward Sloan's paintings, gave a sympathetic appraisal of his work displayed at the Kraushaar: "Sloan never forgets that he is an illustrator born and made. He gives you full measure of human expressiveness … But up his sleeve he keeps a painter who works for him gayly whatever his subject." Despite Sloan's assertions that he was ignored by the art establishment, it was clear that he was gaining professional respect, and those credentials would have been reassuring to those who signed on for his classes at the Art Students League.

Sloan made a significant change in his New York surroundings. After living in the Tenderloin district for more than a decade, he and Dolly regretfully left the neighborhood. As far back as 1910 he had complained "there is building going on all about us now on 23rd, 24th, 25th Sts. Big buildings are taking the place of the old … dwellings of the neighborhood." They were going one by one, the tenements that had spilled humanity into the streets, inspiring so many of Sloan's vibrant etchings and paintings. John and Dolly now took an apartment farther downtown, at 88 Washington Place, on Washington Square. It was at the edge of Greenwich Village which was fast becoming thronged with real and would-be artists.

In this bohemian milieu John and Dolly's circle of acquaintances expanded. Sloan, now in his forties, had become something of a distinguished elder in the eyes of the idealistic youths – most of them recent arrivals – who were caught up in the contagion of hopeful creativity that pervaded the neighborhood. Greenwich Village was rapidly becoming the nerve center of ideological dissent and creative ferment in America. Kenneth Burke, associate editor of *The Dial*, saw T.S. Eliot's *The Waste Land* into print for the first time, and rendered valued critical assistance to Thomas Mann, e.e. cummings and Ezra Pound.

The American theatre found new life in the Village too. The Provincetown Players were staging Eugene O'Neil's disquieting one-act plays both in Provincetown and in the first-floor apartment on MacDougal Street converted into a theatre. Some of those plays, notably *The Long Voyage Home*, would move uptown to Broadway.

Edna St. Vincent Millay was a standard-bearer for the liberated New Women who populated the Village. Noted for her brilliant poetry and sexual versatility, she bedded countless partners of both sexes. The males included Edmund Wilson and Floyd Dell. At 23 Fifth Avenue, bored socialite Mabel Dodge indulged her intellectual aspirations by conducting a salon that attracted the likes of music critic and portrait photographer Carl Van Vechten, muckraking author Lincoln Steffens, and birth-control advocate Margaret Sanger.

The bohemian intelligentsia frequented Romany Marie's cafés. Marie had arrived from Romanian Moldavia in 1901 at the age of sixteen and eventually opened a series of taverns that were more like Parisian salons. Over the years Marie moved her café fifteen times; from 1915 through 1923 it was in a tiny house at 20 Christopher Street. Pretty, vivacious Romany Marie was warm-hearted, tearing up the tab when a deserving artist was temporarily out of funds. She was Buckminster Fuller's confidante during the most difficult years of his life, and kept Eugene O'Neil alive by forcing food into him when the only nourishment he took otherwise was alcohol. Politically she had been, like so many at the time, an Emma Goldman Anarchist, but later distanced herself from that ideology. Sloan and Dolly were among the regular customers at Marie's cafés, and in 1920 John painted a portrait of her that is now in the Whitney Museum collection. Two years later he made an etching, *Romany Marye in Christopher Street*.

John and Dolly had become confirmed Villagers, and in 1917 Sloan symbolically asserted his solidarity with the artistic insurgents. On a cold, snowy January night he was atop the Washington

Square Arch. He, together with artist Marcel Duchamp (who would forever be remembered for *Nude Climbing a Staircase* at the Armory Show), poet Gertrude Drick, and three Provincetown Playhouse actors had discovered an unlocked door and climbed a spiral staircase to the roof of the monument.

They spread out blankets, hung red balloons and Chinese lanterns, and discussed the universe over tea until morning. Gertrude Drick read a manifesto that pronounced the "Free and Independent Republic of Washington Square." Sloan would celebrate the event in a print he titled *Arch Conspirators* (ever the incorrigible punster, this was the John Sloan who, in *Hairdresser's Window*, named the hairdresser "Madame Malcomb," she of the bad comb).

The Washington Square area was inhabited by persons of diverse ethnicity, predilections and preferences. One element of a normal population was in short supply, however. There were few children. Many of the Sloans' friends and acquaintances were childless artist and writer couples like themselves. It was during their Gloucester summers that John and Dolly reveled in borrowed domesticity. Sloan painted the neighborhood children who were drawn by curiosity to these peculiar strangers occupying the red cottage. Sloan often painted a young boy, "Reddy." Sloan saw him as all-boy – clambering over ledges, perching in trees – and described him as "a happy little boy from Gloucester town … who said he would be tough like his brother in about a year!" Sloan said that Reddy "was glad to earn a little money by sitting for the 'artist.' Several studies record his sun-pink face and carroty hair."

Sloan painted little girls of the neighborhood, too, notably Sally Stanton. She was always in action in his paintings, turning somersaults in the grass or climbing an apple tree. Sally adored Sloan and wrote him years later about those years. "Do you remember the frogs we caught and the snakes you caught – and the baby owl you found and named 'Minerva'?" Another of the neighborhood children, summer resident Elizabeth Oakes, remembered Sloan as a good-natured man who amused them with practical jokes. Elizabeth and her sisters "roamed the moors with our governess." When one of the neighborhood children had a birthday, Dolly baked a cake and the little ones would be invited to a party on the lawn.

It was all make-believe. John and Dolly entered and departed the children's summer world with no commitments. After the summer was done they would return to the adult world of Greenwich Village, leaving with warm feelings on all sides this vicarious experiencing of family life.

Greenwich Village became his home for the rest of his life, and within that home neighborhood John Sloan's offspring were his students. His community was defined by shared commitment to the rigors of art.

Chapter Eleven

ANECDOTAL CASUALTIES

~~~

Deadly Inconvenience / A Fallen Regiment

Deadly Inconvenience

THE WAR that had broken out in Europe would seem, at the outset, inconsequential both to Capt. Sol and to John Sloan. The captain, gradually withdrawing into retirement from the sea, was not planning any more fishing excursions to the Irish coast, which was uncomfortably close to the conflict.

To Sloan's New York art world the war in Europe that began on August 4, 1914 was emphatically something "over there," a dreadful mistake but of remote concern to Americans. To the artists in particular, Europe was a place of largely professional interest, centered around the academies of Paris, Munich and Rome, as well as shrines like Giverny, Pont-Aven and – more recently – the Provence of Cézanne and van Gogh.

The annoyance of the war did strike home when one of The Eight, Maurice Prendergast, was forced to return early from a trip to Europe. It would be, as it turned out, the fifty-six-year-old artist's final trip abroad. The hostilities spreading across Europe intensified John Sloan's anti-war convictions. "Ever since the Great War broke out in 1914 this world has been a crazy place to live in. I hate war ..." Like the only politician he admired, Eugene Debs, John Sloan was intensely opposed to any American involvement in the European fray.

When one after another of the major powers issued declarations of war, reports began to drift in of 3,000 Americans stranded in France. Express companies would not honor their checks or letters of credit, and the agencies of American banks abroad had no funds to lend; they could barely meet the demands of their depositors. American tourists who did have cash discovered that the westward-bound transatlantic steamers were booked solid. One man was overjoyed when he was able to buy a ticket in steerage for $1,000. Even travelers who had tickets for their passage might be out of luck if they were vacationing at some distance from the coast. Space on trains to meet the boats at Le Havre was at a premium. Two of the most luxurious Paris hotels closed, driving formerly pampered guests into the streets to scramble for accommodations. They had to go in person – telephone service was badly disrupted.

Ambassador Herrick formed a committee of prominent fellow Americans in Paris who sought to reassure their countrymen that they would be safe in the city until means of departure became available. The stranded tourists and expatriates were not convinced – they besieged the American Embassy, begging that transport ships be sent by the U.S. government to take them home. They snatched up the latest copies of James Gordon Bennett's Paris *Herald* for the latest war news in English. For even fresher news, they gathered in the *Herald*'s reading room at 49 avenue de l'Opera hoping for some shred of advice that would help them escape a once beguiling Europe where all of the governments seemed suddenly to be at one another's throats.

As the war progressed there was for John Sloan in New York the second-hand immediacy of death that was striking near to his friends. Old John Butler Yeats spoke of the loss, when the *Lusitania* was sunk in 1915, of Hugh Lane. He was the beloved nephew of that close friend of William Butler Yeats, Lady Gregory, who with him founded the Abbey Theatre in Dublin. An even greater tragedy would befall Lady Gregory when her son Robert was killed when his plane was shot down on the Italian front in 1918. John Butler Yeats was an Irish Protestant and a strong supporter of the British cause. Friction arose between him and Sloan when Yeats protested that Sloan's anti-war position was indefensible with civilization at stake.

While many artists were pacifists as he was, Sloan would hear reports of others who were risking their lives for the cause they believed in. A French sculptor, Henri Gaudier-Brzeska, was decorated for bravery in action, then killed in the trenches at Neuville-St.-Vaast in 1915 at the age of twenty-four. His distraught widow went mad. Gaudier-Brzeska would be posthumously admired as a founder of modern sculpture. "All the young art and intellect of France is being killed in the trenches," said Maud Gonne, the actress and Irish nationalist whom William Butler Yeats had pursued in a long and one-sided love affair. The war was squandering the talent of the rest of Europe as well. T. E. Hulme, British critic for the *New Age* whose modernist thinking influenced Wyndham Lewis, T. S. Eliot and Robert Frost had survived one serious wound but was sent back to the Front, and this time did not survive.

The American poet Alan Seeger, one of the group at the dinner table in Sloan's painting, *Yeats at Petitpas*, was killed in the trenches at Belloy-en-Santerre. Seeger, uncle of the folk singer of later years, Pete Seeger, had been living in the Latin Quarter in Paris when the war broke out. He joined the Foreign Legion, impatient to fight even if his own country was not yet ready to enter the war. Famously he cheered on his comrades as he lay mortally wounded. His prophetic poem, *I Have a Rendezvous with Death*, was published after he was killed.

Many went to their deaths wondering why they were fighting. From the Front came grisly accounts of men huddled in the mud in rat-infested trenches until ordered over the top and into barbed wire to their deaths by machine guns, artillery fire or poison gas — the "mustard gas" that blinded or left its victims in such blistered agony they had to be tied to their cots for the four or five weeks it took them to die. The scale of the casualties was incomprehensible: 19,000 British casualties in the first day of the Battle of the Somme on July 1, 1915.

The ordered life of Victorian and Edwardian England, and of a fragilely balanced Europe, had been shattered. To John Sloan it was confirmation of his conviction that Seeger and Hulme and Gaudier-Brzeska and the others were dupes of the munitions interests and war profiteers. Let Europe keep its madness. For Sloan the expanding war was all a mindless mistake.

A Fallen Regiment

WHEN THE two men walked on Gloucester's Main Street that summer day in 1916, there was the shadowy unease over that unthinkable war in Europe. It had now gone on much longer than anyone had expected, the newspapers reporting small advances and retreats, but no indication of a decisive breakthrough by either side. The carnage had come to seem commonplace, the war news boring. Gloucester's summer visitors wanted diversion, not battle bulletins, and the town's tourist business was flourishing. Recreational sails dotted the waters off Eastern Point and Annisquam. The guests in the Hawthorne Inn & Cottages were tip-toeing into the chilly waters for a dip, or striding all in whites to a tennis court, or catching up on light reading under a beach umbrella. The scenes were duplicated at other popular summer hotels in East Gloucester and at Bass Rocks, and in the evenings there were orchestras and dancing.

It was, then, the pattern of seasonal *dolce far niente* that took over large swaths of Cape Ann for July and August every year. The locals were complacent, too. America was prospering as a neutral, supplying the war needs particularly of the English and French. The demand for fish to be shipped overseas was strong.

Sol Jacobs would think his fellow residents of the town, and those visiting, were living in a fool's paradise. The war was approaching America, as Sol had good reason to know. He would have heard, relayed through friends and relatives from his home island, reports of the tragic fate of the Newfoundland Regiment earlier that summer. The bravest young men of Newfoundland had volunteered at the outset of the war. On July 1 1916, the first day of butchery in the Battle of the Somme, 753 men of the Newfoundland Regiment were sent into action in the Beaumont-Hamel section. Only sixty-eight of them answered roll call the following day. Overall, of the nearly 7,000 men who served in the regiment, roughly 1,300 were killed and over 2,300 wounded. These were the strong Newfoundland men who were the backbone of the island's fisheries. It was a blow from which Newfoundland would not soon recover.

By a paradox of war, Newfoundland experienced an unprecedented, if short-lived, economic boom while its resources of prime humanity were being squandered in battle. The demand for fish was great, especially in the countries on the southern rim of the Mediterranean to which shipments from the Scandinavian fisheries had been cut off by the hostilities. The price of fish soared, and

Newfoundland fisheries companies invested heavily in equipment and boats to meet the demand. They fully expected the value of the island's fish trade – which accounted for 80% of Newfoundland's exports – to reach $18 million in the 1918 season. With their sudden prosperity the Newfoundlanders had money to buy the best boats available, and came shopping on the Gloucester waterfront. Soon many of the finest of the Gloucester schooners were sailing from Newfoundland under the British flag. Many of these fell victim to German raiders. The *Monitor*, one of the handsomest in the Gloucester fleet, was bought by Philip Templemen of Bonavista, Newfoundland in 1916 for $14,000. The following year, after discharging a cargo of salt fish in Italy, *Monitor* sailed for Cádiz to take on a cargo of salt for Newfoundland. She was shelled by a German submarine on April 25 and sank as the crew scrambled to get the dories over. (Because many fishing vessels flying the British flag were armed, they were deemed by the Germans to be fair game to shell without warning.) *Monitor's* crew arrived safely at Monte Carlo.

Campbell & McKay of St. John's was a big purchaser of Gloucester schooners too, including such prime vessels as the *Tattler* and *Clintonia*. The company bought the *Rose Dorothea*, too, for $14,000. Five months later, in February 1917, she was sunk by Germans when on a voyage from Oporto, Portugal to St. John's with a cargo of salt. The crew took to the boats and landed at Lisbon.

The handsome *John Hays Hammond*, designed by the renowned Thomas McManus of Boston and built at the Tarr & James yard in Essex, was one of the most successful halibut boats after the turn of the century. She was sold in 1916 to David W. Simpson, a shipbroker in Boston, who in turn sold her to a Newfoundland buyer. Bound from Iceland to Ireland with a cargo of salt fish she was intercepted by a U-boat and destroyed. A British destroyer picked up the crew, all of them Newfoundlanders.

The talk of the Gloucester waterfront would have been the sad fate of these noble vessels that had once sailed from the port, as well as of the destruction by U-boats of other vessels close to the American shore. Feelings ran strong against the Central Powers. Capt. Jacobs had not been partial to the German military ever since, that time in 1871, when he was mate aboard the down-easter *J. S. Winslow*, calling at Antwerp at the close of the Franco-Prussian war. From his conversations with Belgians, presumably met along the waterfront, he concluded that their hatred of the Germans "knew no bounds."

With war raging so close by, it must have been frustrating to Sol that America continued to ignore the warning signals, and that petty self-interest even ruled the Gloucester waterfront. In a development unthinkable in his day as a fishing captain, the crew members on the haddock boats had gone on strike. On March 1, 1917 the New England Coast Fishermen's Union called its members out on picket lines in Boston and Gloucester. At issue were the compensation practices that had been imposed by the large fleet-owning companies.

The company typically leased the schooner to a captain who rounded up a crew to make a trip. When the fish were sold, the company received a fifth of the proceeds, and the remaining four-fifths were divided in shares among the crewmen. Fair enough. But the company also charged each crewman 10% of his share toward food, fishing gear and the oil for the auxiliary motor that was now standard on every vessel. Each crewman was charged, too, for hauling out and repairing those engines as needed.

In the grievance filed by the union, the crewmen demanded that gear and engine expenses be assessed against all parties to the trip, including the company that owned the boat. The owners refused, and the captains sided with them (as had been the case in Sol's day, many of the masters owned a percentage of the vessel they commanded).

Fish landings at the port of Gloucester dried up, except for the Portuguese boats which had come to a separate understanding with their union. The gillnetters were also exempt from the strike, as were the large beam trawlers that worked out of Boston. Negotiations remained deadlocked throughout the month, and the fishermen's families suffered in what was normally the richest fishing season of the year. The union paid no benefits because it defined the action as a company lockout, not a labor strike.

If it had all happened a few months later in the summer, Dolly Sloan would without doubt have been on the scene to cook for hungry families and rally support for the walkout, as she had done for the Lawrence strikers. By March 21, tensions had escalated and striking fishermen began standing guard on the docks around the clock to prevent the owners from hiring scab crewmen. The police department decided it would be prudent to place a night patrol on the scene. Sol Jacobs must have been dumbfounded. This was not the brave, simple world he had known in which a man knew where he stood with his crew, and with the "lumpers" who off-loaded his catch at the pier, and the dealers who quoted him a price. To be sure, much had changed for Capt. Jacobs since the days when he was the epitome of the enterprising, innovative Gloucester sea captain. After the costly loss of the *Alice M. Jacobs*, he returned to fishing by conventional means. In September of 1904 he purchased the Bucksport, Maine schooner *A.M. Nicholson*, and immediately demonstrated that his legendary prowess in harvesting mackerel had not forsaken him. He was first to sail south for the 1906 and 1907 seasons, was highline then and again in 1908. In 1909, after Sol sold the *Nicholson* to Capt. Howard Smith of New Bedford, the vessel was converted for hunting whales. She operated as a whaler in the North Atlantic and Indian Oceans until after the First World War.

With his continuing success in landing the most profitable catches year after year, it was assumed that Capt. Sol Jacobs was once again prosperous. Consequently the headline in the *Gloucester Daily Times* of September 9, 1911 was especially shocking: "Capt. Sol Jacobs in Bankruptcy."

Disbelief spread beyond the fisheries. Said the *Boston Globe*, "Down and out at 65 might be written of many men, but not of Solomon Jacobs, who filed a petition in bankruptcy today... Of all the 'Captains Courageous' of Gloucester, Capt. Jacobs may be accounted one of the elect. ... Of indomitable spirit and pluck, it would be a rash man who would venture to say that Capt. Sol is down and out for good and will not come back. ... The news of his embarrassment was received everywhere with regret. The hope is expressed that he will come back strong and duplicate his former successes."

The Gloucester paper expressed sad regret over the news. He was, it said, "in Gloucester's long list of fishing skippers, the most famous." It spoke of "this indomitable man ... around whom could be woven sea tales so full of dash and dare, of luck, pluck and chance, as to almost pass belief. … Wherever he has been he has made history, so that from the coast of Ireland to the Bering Sea his name has been one with which to conjure …" Sol's friends were quoted as asserting that the next season would see the aging captain, now seining in the little steamer *Quartette*, "once more on his feet and on the road to another snug competence …"

In the feverish business world of 19th and early 20th century America, it was not unusual for men of consequence to become insolvent. William McKinley had been declared bankrupt while governor of Ohio when he co-signed notes for a friend. The notes proved to be worthless and McKinley was temporarily wiped out. But he went on to become president.

Capt. Jacobs was no stranger to financial peaks and valleys, but how had he fallen so deep into difficulty? Perhaps it was by risking capital in ventures over which he had no direct control. These sometimes required substantial up-front investment: two years earlier he had sent a schooner sailing under British papers to Connaigre Bay, Newfoundland to pick up 1,500 barrels of herring, destined for sale to the Gloucester fleet as bait. If there were buyers, fine – otherwise Sol would have an expensive load of herring on his hands.

In his petition for bankruptcy Sol set his liabilities at $6,669, of which $1,600 were secured, as against assets of $2,500. On December 19 he was discharged from his outstanding debts which consisted mainly of small amounts for rigging, ships stores and provisions to maritime suppliers in Gloucester and Nova Scotia. By far the largest item was a $2,000 claim from Bartelson & Nicholson, the East Boston company that had supplied the steam power plant for the *Alice M. Jacobs*. Sol issued a counter-claim against the company, but it was deemed to be "of doubtful value."

Perhaps Sol was not satisfied with the way the Bartelson & Nicholson steam equipment had performed. With the *Alice M.* no longer afloat and earning, this may have been the claim that pushed him against the wall. Back in the '80s, when he was found liable for over $4,000 due the seal merchant Baxter in Victoria, Sol preferred doing jail time to paying an amount he insisted he did not owe. Now, in his mid 60s, the captain may have decided that bankruptcy was a better alternative for getting clear of another sizeable debt that he contested.

Did Sol also wish to default on his obligations to the ship outfitters and suppliers? All debts had to be included in the petition for bankruptcy, but Capt. Jacobs might have quietly made good on those small invoices, or otherwise squared things with the merchants he had dealt with honorably for many years. Otherwise he would not have continued to enjoy the credit a captain needed in order to outfit and provision his vessel for a trip. And Sol did continue going in command of other men's boats – auxiliaries, steamers and gas boats – for another four years. He seined for herring and pollock close inshore in the schooner *Pythian* and a converted steam yacht, the *Bethulia*. Apparently his suppliers were happy to do business with Capt. Jacobs again.

When he finally came ashore in 1915 at age sixty-eight, Solomon Jacobs appeared, by all accounts, to be once again enjoying a "snug competence." And it was a good time to quit. By then the Gloucester fleet had become even more consolidated. In 1906 the Slade Gorton, John Pew and David B. Smith companies had merged, creating a dominant fish business that owned the largest fleet of fishing vessels anywhere along the Atlantic seaboard. The new company also had marketing muscle. Billboards along rail lines across America proclaimed the virtues of the little wooden boxes packed with Gorton's boneless salt cod, said to require only some soaking in water to become a delectable seafood dish, no matter how far removed from the ocean.

Gorton's diversified their product lines, offering ready-to-fry codfish cakes, smoked halibut, pickled fish – and Gorton's Cod Liver Oil Cough Candy. With the consolidation of the fleet, and the high-powered marketing of fishery products, there was little room for an independent fishing captain who owned his own boat. It was no longer the world of a go-it-alone sea adventurer like Capt. Solomon Jacobs.

Walking on Main Street in 1916, Sol was now a man with time on his hands. After a lifetime of action, leisure was perhaps the last thing he wanted. At the same time he was dissatisfied with what had become of his proud little world of Gloucester. Men who should have been off fishing were idled by the labor dispute. People were wasting time and money on picture shows and vaudeville, while a menacing foreign power had already reached its tentacles into America's territorial waters.

Sol Jacobs refused to remain becalmed. There had to be some way he could serve in the war he was certain was on its way to Gloucester.

Chapter Twelve

Naked Coast

~~

The Septuagenarian Ensign / The Embattled Pacifist

The Septuagenarian Ensign

AMERICA DID not rush into war in 1917, but instead sidled in. President Woodrow Wilson had long been ambivalent as to which side, if either, the United States should be on. He had been furious with the British for intercepting ships flying under U.S. and other neutral flags and herding those vessels into British ports. There they were inspected even if they were bound for other neutral countries, and all contraband was seized. The American shipping companies complained that the British definition of "contraband" included everything that might be useful to the Allied cause.

On the other hand, there was irrefutable evidence of German acts of espionage and sabotage within the United States. In 1915 it was revealed that Paul Koenig, head of security for the Hamburg-American shipping line, not only had his paid spies on every steamship pier in America served by the line, he oversaw a vast network of informants who were clerking in hotels and banks, cleaning windows, operating telephone switchboards.

From the information gathered by these moles, German saboteurs were planting bombs in American vessels at dockside, timed to explode after the vessels were at sea. The subversives were suspected, accurately as it turned out, of blowing up the Black Tom munitions depot in New Jersey. The explosion at 2:08 AM on July 30, 1916 was spectacular, equivalent to a 5.5 earthquake on the Richter scale. It blew out windows in Times Square, damaged the Statue of Liberty, and was felt as far away as Philadelphia.

Agents from both sides of the conflict in Europe were pitted against one another, sometimes colliding like characters in a Mack Sennett comedy across an unsuspecting America. The Czech nationalist patriot Emanuel Voska built his own counterespionage organization in the United States to counter the German agents. Voska had spies everywhere. One of them, a restaurant waiter, overheard reporter James F.J. Archibald say he was on his way to Europe carrying secret information he meant to convey to Berlin. When Archibald was preparing to leave the Austro-Hungarian consulate in New York, he was blissfully unaware that the valet packing his bags was another of Voska's agents. As soon as Archibald's ship arrived in England he was arrested by British authorities, who knew exactly where to look for the incriminating papers.

While weighing the merits of both sides, Woodrow Wilson found the German ambassador to Washington, Count Johann von Bernstorff, engagingly congenial. Not so his British counterpart, Sir Cecil Spring-Rice, who struck Wilson as being insufferably supercilious and arrogant. But Count von Bernstorff's suave charm ceased to endear him to the President after he was implicated in a German plan to put both Mexico and Japan at war with the United States. It was part of a coordinated effort by the Central Powers to achieve a quick victory.

In 1917 Germany had cause for optimism. Revolution had swept Russia, Czar Nicholas II and his son Alexei abdicated, and the Bolsheviks sued for peace with the Central Powers. German troops that had been tied down in Russia could now be shifted to bolster battered divisions on the Western Front. General Ludendorff was about to launch a spring offensive that would carry his forces to within seventy-five miles of Paris, spreading panic throughout the City of Lights.

As another key chess move in their master strategy, the German high command resolved to announce, effective February 1, resumption of unrestricted U-boat attacks upon neutral vessels (a policy they had suspended following American protests over the sinking of the *Lusitania*). The Germans knew the action would almost certainly bring America into the war on the side of the Allies, but believed they had time on their side.

Count von Bernstorff's role was to forward a telegram from German Foreign Secretary Arthur Zimmerman to the German ambassador in Mexico City, Heinrich von Eckardt. That remarkably indiscrete communication promised the return to Mexico of all territories "stolen" by America from its neighbor (a goodly portion of the American Southwest), in exchange for Mexico's support for Germany upon America's entry into the war. The Germans were convinced that the U.S. would not be able to mobilize rapidly and that meantime, as Zimmerman put it, "ruthless deployment of our submarines will compel Britain to make peace." Mexico was also to invite Japan to join on the side of the Central Powers to further complicate an American response to the European war.

When the Zimmerman telegram was made public (by British Intelligence) the American public was outraged. Germany had gone one provocation too far, and in effect had made up the President's mind for him. On April 2 Wilson formally requested Congress to issue a declaration of war. Two days later it was official: the United States had joined in the conflict.

It is unlikely that Solomon Jacobs ever felt the urge to ship a barrel of mackerel as a gift to President Woodrow Wilson. He would not have had the same fellow-feeling toward the self-righteous Wilson as toward William McKinley. But Woodrow Wilson was President, and that was all Capt. Jacobs needed to know. Probably the captain's one criticism of Wilson would be that the President was slow to act. How could the President not have seen the need to resist German domination of the Atlantic, and the increasing threat posed to American shores?

Wilson might have agonized over entering the war, but Sol Jacobs did not. He saw his opportunity a month before the American declaration of war. In March, 1917 Sol learned that two U.S. Navy officers, together with representatives of the Massachusetts Committee on Public Safety, were on their way to Gloucester to seek recruits for coast patrol service.

Earlier in the year a Committee on Naval Forces had been formed within the state's Committee on Public Safety to "arrange for the more effective protection of our coast defenses." The need was seen as urgent. As a history of the Committee on Public Safety later stated, "Massachusetts ... with war declared, had no defense, naval or military, State or national, on which she could properly rely. Naked of equipment and man power, she was helpless to oppose the Hun, who might land anywhere on our coast ... and eventually march up and down [Boston's] State Street to his heart's content." A first priority was recruitment of men for the Coast Defense Reserve, who would serve by patrolling the waters of the First Naval District that stretched from Chatham on Cape Cod to Eastport, Maine. When the recruiters arrived in Gloucester on March 11 they found the hall filled with "rough clad fishermen." That a tall, lean figure was first in line surprised no one, but merited an Associated Press release the following day: "Perhaps the oldest in years and from point of service in the fisheries was Capt. Sol Jacobs who for years had the title of 'mackerel killer' among the seining fleet." Capt. Jacobs was interviewed, given a physical and enrolled as an ensign in the Coast Defense Reserve. He was then seventy years of age (the bulletin gave his age as seventy-nine, another instance of the captain's tailoring his birth date to suit the circumstances). The Navy Department was establishing a school to train new ensigns at the Corinthian Yacht Club in Marblehead, but highline captain Sol Jacobs had no need for maritime training, least of all at some yacht club.

Less than a month after he was sworn into the Coast Defense Reserve, Ensign Solomon Jacobs found himself in the service of his country now officially at war. A goodly percentage of Gloucester's population of 25,000 joined in the war effort one way or another. Many, including the Jacobs' daughter Ethel, were active in relief organizations such as the Red Cross. In the course of America's nineteen-month involvement in the conflict, 1,686 men from the city served in the military, and another close to 3,000 crewed on the vessels that harvested essential food from the sea.

It was widely believed that, with the U.S. now committed, the war would soon be brought to an end. Gloucester's Roger Babson, "acclaimed authority on international matters," hedged his prediction. "The big war will be over in three months," he confidently asserted – then less confidently added, "... or it will last three years longer [in which case] the submarine would be the controlling factor in the imbroglio." Babson's recognition of the important role U-boats would play proved to be spot on.

There is no record of the patrol vessels, if any, on which Ensign

Jacobs served, but there are many possibilities. The Committee on Naval Forces surveyed vessels in civilian hands that could be used for coast patrol, and determined that over 100 yachts and motor boats were "ready for service in case of war." Ketches, yawls, sloops and motor launches of every description qualified. Forty-one vessels were identified in Gloucester "that might be taken for government use," although the Navy promised no weaponry other than machine guns to arm the boats pressed into service. A typical Coast Defense Reserve boat was the *Lynx*, an armed motorboat that operated as a patrol vessel and aviation support craft from 1917 to 1919. Her owner, Nathaniel Ayers, had the boat built privately in 1915 at Neponset, Massachusetts, but specifically for the Coast Defense Reserve. The *Lynx* participated in Coast Defense Reserve exercises while still in civilian hands. With the onset of war she was purchased by the Navy, armed, and commissioned as the *U.S.S. Lynx (SP-2)*.

Other vessels available to the Coast Defense Reserve were three small power boats. In 1916 the Britt Brothers in Lynn, Massachusetts had been awarded a contract to build five motorboats of five tons each that would be sold to private parties with the understanding that the vessels could be requisitioned by the Navy in the event of war. When America did enter the war, the Navy called up four of these vessels into active duty in 1917, and three of these were assigned to patrol New England waters. They were manned by two to five men. For firepower each motorboat was armed with one machine gun.

Ensign Jacobs probably greeted with amused equanimity the news that some of his coast patrol shipmates would be women. At about the time he signed up, the Bureau of Navigation notified the commanders of the Naval Districts that they were now authorized to recruit women into the Naval Coast Defense Reserve. The expectation was that these "yeomen (F)" would serve in such support capacities as stenographers and messengers. As time passed, though, the young women proved that they could hold their own in more roughneck assignments, serving as mechanics, truck drivers and munitions workers.

With war now a reality in America, the East Coast was considered particularly vulnerable to the infiltration of German spies and even armed attack. In that first American spring of the war, the thirty-five-year-old Assistant Secretary of the Navy, Franklin D. Roosevelt, wrote from Washington to his wife Eleanor at their family compound on Canada's Campobello Island, just off the Maine coast: "I meant to tell you that if by any perfectly wild chance a German submarine should come into the bay and start to shell Eastport or the Pool, I want you to grab the children and beat it into the woods. Don't stay to see what is going on. I am not joking about this, for though it is 500 to 1 against the possibility, still there is just that one chance."

Despite the Zimmerman telegram there were many voices raised in opposition to America's entry into the war. Many resented the German skullduggery, but not all were convinced it was worth going to war over. Capt. Jacobs' eagerness to serve was shared widely, but not universally, in 1917 America. In the first month after the declaration of war only 3,500 men, nationwide, volunteered for the armed services.

Opposition to America's involvement came from unexpected quarters. On April 11 the Gloucester paper carried an opinion ad by isolationist carmaker Henry Ford that, ironically, sounded much like the Socialist positions proclaimed in *The Masses*. "Militarism is a menace to industrialism and a promoter of warfare," it read. Ford called upon nations to "put down their arms and abandon warfare. … A battle between nations is a war between the exploiters and humanity, which has suffered long under exploitation."

The waterfront was slow to take the war seriously. At the time of America's entry Gloucester was, judging from the local headlines, more concerned with the long-unsettled fishermen's strike than with the war. On April 9th a train from Boston brought in forty-one strikebreakers hired by the fleet owners. By the time they reached the wharves the striking fishermen were waiting and rounded them up. A riot call was sounded that brought out the entire police force. The out-of-town scabs were herded into the police station lockup; five were charged with carrying revolvers, the others escorted back to the railroad station and corralled, with the encouragement of nightsticks, onto the morning train back to Boston. The Gloucester authorities were congratulated for steering a sensible middle course that averted violence.

At the national level Capt. Sol Jacobs might question just how prepared the country was to fight a war at sea when its Secretary of the Navy was a certified landlubber. Josephus Daniels had been a newspaper editor in Raleigh, North Carolina. When he found himself at the head of the nation's ocean armada, he conducted a thorough review of the Naval Department, and became convinced that streamlining was in order. These maritime fellows were awash in archaisms that no one else, notably he, could understand. Daniels called in his admirals and asked them why they were confusing him and others by using words like "port" and "starboard." Get rid of that jargon, he said, and say "left" and "right" instead, words that any sensible person could understand. The admirals humored the Secretary and, eventually, Daniels came to see the futility of his attempt to reverse hundreds of years of naval tradition. (Prohibitionist Daniels did succeed in eliminating forever one cherished naval institution, the dispensing of alcohol in the officers' mess.) Eventually Daniels became somewhat salty himself. In his book *Our Navy at War* of 1922, he wrote of torpedoes passing harmlessly to *port* and *starboard* of fighting ships. It had taken a war to educate the new Secretary of the Navy to the usages of seamen, but he was finally on board. Daniels, a confirmed pacifist, was the only member of Wilson's cabinet who had opposed America's entry into the war.

An American of more authentic naval stripe, Admiral William S. Sims, was dispatched to Europe as Naval Force Commander. Strongly pro-British, Sims did not endear himself to the Gloucester fleet when he persuaded the Navy and the government that the best way to protect the American coast was to send all available U.S. fighting vessels to serve in the North Sea off the British coast. America's sparse peacetime fleet was only just beginning to be built out, and such American destroyers as were fit to put to sea were placed under British command – leaving the New England coast to be defended only by the Coast Defense patrol boats with their insignificant firepower.

At the end of that summer of 1917, when it still seemed that America's involvement in the war would continue to be at arm's length, Gloucester had a surprise visitor: the Commander-in-Chief. President Wilson's trusted personal advisor, Colonel Edward M. House, noted in his diary that "around seven o'clock [on September 9], the Navy Yard of Boston called me over the telephone to say they had a wireless stating that the *Mayflower* would be in Gloucester Harbor at two o'clock." House and Mrs. House went to greet the President and Mrs. Wilson aboard the presidential yacht in Gloucester, and they "motored along the shore for two hours or more."

They then stopped at the Houses' summer cottage in Magnolia where the Wilsons would be staying. Then they all went over to Mrs. T. Jefferson Coolidge's substantial place on the coast in Manchester to look at her prints, china and other heirlooms inherited through her family from another U.S. President from the South, Thomas Jefferson. The neighborhood was popular with foreign diplomats, most notably the less-than-congenial (in Wilson's opinion) British Ambassador Spring-Rice who summered nearby at Prides Crossing.

Next morning Wilson and House played a round of golf, and later in the day the President and Mrs. Wilson were back on board the *Mayflower*. They steamed down through the Cape Cod canal where Wilson waved back to "great groups of people gathered along the banks to cheer him." Wilson was then riding the crest of his popularity as a wartime president.

At the end of the year came news of disaster at Halifax. Early in the war Britain, recognizing the strategic importance of the chief port of Nova Scotia, had transformed its once-rudimentary harbor facilities into a world-class naval facility, and it became Britain's key marshaling point for men and supplies shipped from North America. War matériel manufactured in Canadian factories traveled east via the Intercolonial Railway to Halifax for transshipment overseas. Troop trains arrived with recruits drawn from Canadian provinces across the continent. They boarded troopships in the sheltering harbor, where convoys were assembled to set sail for England.

Halifax harbor was continually crowded with vessels arriving and departing on the business of war. On December 6, 1917, a Norwegian relief ship, *Imo*, drifted into the path of the *Mont Blanc*, a freighter chartered by the French government. The *Mont Blanc* was a munitions ship, but carried no pennants to identify itself as such – the captain wished to remain anonymous to avoid detection by German spies.

The *Mont Blanc* caught fire in the collision, and its French crew attempted to warn off vessels that approached to render assistance. But Halifax was in English Canada and those in the boats did not understand what the French where trying to tell them. After twenty-five minutes the fire reached the cargo of munitions and the *Mont Blanc* blew in what was the most cataclysmic man-made explosion prior to Hiroshima. (The blast was equivalent to 3 kilotons of TNT, while the Hiroshima atomic bomb explosion equaled 15 kilotons.) The blast drained the harbor almost dry, and a subsequent man-made tsunami swept over the wharves and warehouses along the waterfront. The blast leveled the north end of Halifax, killed 2,000 of the population and injured 9,000 more. The following day a blizzard moved in that paralyzed relief efforts, aggravating the distress of the tens of thousands of survivors left without shelter.

The neighboring provinces organized relief efforts, and donations arrived from around the world. Halifax was grateful for the aid rushed from Massachusetts, and every year since then has donated the Christmas tree decorated on Boston Common. The calamity would deal a heavy blow to the large Nova Scotian population in Gloucester, many of whom had family and friends in Halifax.

America was not yet deeply committed to the war. But clouds of anxiety were blowing in from the Atlantic, and menace seemed to build with each tide. Sol Jacobs had spotted trouble on the horizon early on. Now, as Ensign Jacobs, he was at the ready for wherever duty called him.

The Embattled Pacifist

CERTAIN OF John and Dolly Sloan's friends, among them John Butler Yeats, were elated that the United States was now officially in the war, and bolstering the Allied cause. Many, like the Sloans, held to the pacifist position that America had no business becoming involved. Two months before America declared war, Dolly was an active member of a Keep Out of the War Committee that staged a mass meeting of labor unions and pacifist organizations to demand a referendum on U.S.

entry into the hostilities.

Among both the pro and con groups, it was generally assumed that American participation would be limited to funneling food and ammunition to the Allies, and beefing up Britain's naval flotillas with a contribution of our antiquated fighting vessels. Even President Wilson, in an appeal to the nation on April 16, made no mention of sending troops to France. He merely called for intensified efforts to raise food for war (and implicitly to harvest more of it from the sea). He spoke, too, of putting the Navy on a war footing, and expanding the Army. No mention, though, of where he might plan to send that army. The public was lulled into sharing Wilson's early conviction that the United States would play only a supporting role in what was broadly considered to be a war among foreigners an ocean away.

Settling in for that summer of 1917 in Gloucester, Sloan could shrug off politics and concentrate on his painting. When he wrote to Robert Henri on June 17 he made no mention of war. "We have settled into our little red cottage now. It's quite like our 'summer home' … I have not yet got to work painting." But he did get to work, and painted forty-six canvases that summer, including seascapes like *Red Rock and Quiet Sea*. His favorite subject continued to be Dolly, as in *Dolly by the Kitchen Door*.

Sloan returned to his signature subject of the human scene in *Main Street, Gloucester*. In his later note on this painting he said it was an effort "to paint life from the street." Here again – as he had never done before the Gloucester years and would never do thereafter – he took his painting gear onto the street to paint people living their lives. In this instance there is no anecdote, the street scene is story enough in itself. Its people are real and there is a dynamic between them and the setting, an interplay that faded from Sloan's later works as he became more interested in defining form.

Of *Main Street, Gloucester* he said, "this picture was painted on the spot with my easel set up in the main street. Apart from the unpleasantness of an encounter with an intoxicated man whose inquiry, 'What d'yer think yer doin'?' was a bit disconcerting …" Here was John Sloan, the previously invisible voyeur, caught in the act of painting his subjects.

An opportunity may have been lost here. It is likely that the drunk was a fisherman, perhaps celebrating with a drink or two his survival of a harrowing trip in a schooner. To be sure, by then most of the schooners sported auxiliary engines that provided some leverage against wind and tide. But it was still a chancy way to make a living (commercial fishing still is, when you look at the statistics). Twenty-three crewmen from the port had found graves of no certain address in the Atlantic in 1917. They joined the thousands of Gloucestermen who, over several centuries, had their luck run out at sea.

It was hardly surprising, then, that a crewman – especially if he had no family waiting for him in town – might, upon stepping ashore for a brief respite from the sea, toss down repeated drams of forgetfulness. It was often a matter of pent-up demand: under the sobriety strictly observed at sea, crewmen might go weeks or months without a drink – not to mention without a bath, or clean bedding, or a change of clothing.

The man had earned his right to a drink at least as legitimately as any of the patrons Sloan painted at McSorley's. And he might not have been as drunk as Sloan thought. He was perhaps more curious than belligerent. A reply from Sloan to the effect of, "I'm just plying my trade," could have earned an interested response from the other, who could appreciate a skilled craftsman. Many maritime crafts were still being practiced in Gloucester, even with the increasing mechanization of the fleet. After he had sobered up, Sloan's interrogator could tell him about the truly skilled artisans in the trades that supported the fisheries. Those able sailmakers in the Colby Sail Loft, for instance, at the head of the harbor, engaged in the demanding labor of cutting and sewing the mainsails, foresails, topsails and jibs for those schooners that still relied mainly upon their sails for locomotion.

The work at Thurston's spar yard in Harbor Cove might have interested John Sloan, too, descended from woodworkers as he was. Here tall pines from Oregon were shaped by hand into true, straight masts strong enough to carry heavy sail under unremitting stresses of wind and swinging booms. As a man skilled in wielding a paint brush, and in using a carpenter's tools to build cabinets for Dolly, John Sloan might have been impressed.

But it never happened. John Sloan packed up his paint box and resolved to make "no more attempts in that fisherman's town to paint life from the street." And his sidewalk critic would have set an unsteady course toward the next saloon.

Shortly after the Fourth of July that summer, word surely reached the Sloans and Winters and Stuart Davis that *The Masses* was in trouble with the government. President Wilson's Postmaster General, Albert S. Burleson, had requested Judge Learned Hand to enjoin the magazine from publishing its August issue on the grounds that it was in violation of the Espionage Act.

That law, passed in June, two months after the United States entered the war, cast a wide net. It was now unlawful to "Promote the success of [America's] enemies ... to attempt to cause insubordination, disloyalty or refusal of duty in the military or naval forces ... or willfully obstruct the recruiting or enlistment services of the United States." Judge Hand dismissed the case against *The Masses*, ruling that he had read the magazine and nowhere did he see that it advocated violence. The government appealed and, while waiting for a new trial, Postmaster Burleson continued to ban distribution of *The Masses*. He contended that "the general tenor ... of the paper [was] subversive to authority and seditious in effect."

By the time of the second trial, by which time Judge Hand's prudent ruling had been overturned, *The Masses* had already expired, unable to survive without mailing privileges. Burleson was given a free hand by the White House to impose the Espionage Act as broadly as he saw fit. Wielding that latitude energetically, Burleson also suppressed *The Public* and *The Nation* magazines on vague charges of disloyalty. Under his arbitrary definition of sedition he banned criticism of America's ally, the British Empire (even forbidding criticism of the actions of British troops attempting to put down the American Revolution). All in all, Burleson and his subordinates would block eighteen magazines from being sent through the mails. His zealous throttling of printed dissent was symptomatic of a climate of fear and distrust that had swept from Washington across the nation after the United States entered the war.

Safeguards of personal liberty that had been considered among the solid underpinnings of American democracy were abrogated.

It is paradoxical that this reversal of protections guaranteed by the Bill of Rights was endorsed by a president who, as an academic and president of Princeton University, was thought to be liberal and progressive. But in an address in 1890 as a young college professor, Woodrow Wilson had sounded positively Nietzschean, urging that unlimited power be granted to the man who answers the call of the public to be their leader.

John Butler Yeats had long been suspicious of Wilson, calling him "a timid man of the sort common everywhere, hiding his poltroonery under the well-chosen words of a second-class literary professor." Yeats was equally caustic regarding Wilson's writing style, saying he "writes like an archbishop and as all archbishops have always written – slumberous, sonorous sentences all permeated with official dignity, but no life anywhere."

Wilson had been well aware that war would pose a threat to human liberties. In an interview with a newsman in New York prior to U.S. involvement, he had predicted that war would let loose uncontrollable passions and prejudices. "War," he said, "would mean that we should lose our heads along with the rest and stop weighing right and wrong... Once lead this people into war and they'll forget there ever was such a thing as tolerance."

Ironically, it was Wilson himself who took the lead in creating a climate of suspicion and persecution. Ernest Sutherland Bates wrote in *The Story of Congress* that "the first result of the war 'to make the world safe for democracy' was to eliminate democracy from the United States." Wilson took the position that the normal protections of democratic government must be suspended for the duration, and demanded that Congress grant him whatever powers he deemed necessary to win the war. There was grumbling in Congress as Wilson's demands for authority escalated, but the lawmakers went along. What Wilson believed, he insisted, reflected the will of the people.

The dilemma he faced was the same as that which led to the Alien and Sedition Acts passed by a Federalist Congress in 1798. To what extent does a citizen enjoy the right of freedom of expression in time of war? President Wilson and his officials came down hard on the side of censorship backed by prosecution, pointing to the multiple acts of espionage and sabotage by German agents.

Wilson also felt he had a mission to unite a fractured nation, one that seemed to many to have lost its identity and was struggling to digest a flood of recent immigrants. Between 1905 and 1914, nearly 10,500,000 new residents had entered the United States. By 1914, nearly a third of the population of the country had been born abroad, among them three million adults unable to speak English.

Nearly 10 million – 13 percent of the population – had been born in Germany. Many of the German-Americans, concentrated in Midwestern cities like Cleveland, Milwaukee and Cincinnati, and in Omaha where they constituted over half the population, were outspoken in their support of Germany when war broke out. When he ran for re-election in 1916, Wilson had openly questioned the patriotism of these "hyphenate" Americans, and warned that there was "a disloyalty active in the United States" that must be "absolutely crushed."

Old-stock Americans felt disenfranchised by what they saw as a dilution of their heritage, and they looked to Wilson for redress. John Sloan's New York City was a case in point. Midwestern author Hamlin Garland said, "Manhattan is a city of aliens – who know little and care less for American traditions. After a lecture trip in the interior I return each time to New York as to a foreign seaport." In 1910 the parents of fewer than a quarter of the people living in New York City had been born in America.

The war legitimized reprisals against all of the new seemingly quasi-Americans who had one foot planted back in some distant homeland. "Vigilance" and "public safety" committees sprang up in many communities, organized by superpatriots intent on ridding the streets of pro-German subversives, pacifists and radicals. Volunteers besieged the White House with proposals for promoting Americanism – and gained the president's ear. George Creel, a newspaperman most recently working for Colorado papers, won approval to form a special propaganda arm, the "Committee on Public Information," within the Department of Labor.

Gloucester's Roger Babson, who would come to be regarded as a financial oracle a dozen years later in the Great Depression, offered to contribute his expertise. Babson's company, Wellesley Associates, specialized in industrial relations projects for large employers. Babson joined the Committee on Public Information at a token salary of $65 a month plus expenses, and moved into office space at 16 Jackson Place in Washington. His most ingenious contribution to Creel's public relations offensive was "Pay Envelope Stories." Pamphlets bearing patriotic messages were stuffed into the pay envelopes of the nation's workers. Babson's team had posters made up with similar messages exhorting the labor force to work for victory, and greater plans were emerging from Babson's fertile patriotic imagination. After a month, though, George Creel perhaps decided that this tireless idea man was a threat to his own authority. The duties of Babson's office were summarily absorbed into the Labor Department.

Creel signed up writers, scholars, artists, and filmmakers by the thousands to spearhead America's first concerted propaganda offensive. Hollywood willingly joined in the campaign, churning out films that demonized the Germans with such provocative titles as *The Prussian Cur*, *To Hell with the Kaiser* and *The Claws of the Hun*. The large newspaper ad for the propaganda film *Pershing's Crusaders*, playing at Gloucester's North Shore Theatre, highlighted dramatic moments in the movie: "Our Boys Go Over the Top," and "German Prisoners Taken by the Yanks." As an additional incentive to pull in patrons, the ad shouted "You may see your boy or your neighbor's boy."

An energetic branch of the Committee on Public Information bore the patriotic title of "The Four-Minute Men," harking back to the Minute Men of the Revolution. A volunteer group of 75,000 speakers made over 750,000 speeches to more than 314 million people to drum up support for American participation in the war. The speeches were mostly made in movie theatres, and limited to four minutes each – the time it took to change reels.

With the suppression of *The Masses*, and in this pervasive environment of intolerance, John Sloan must have been concerned about his activist left-wing friends in New York and how they were faring. John Reed had left *The Masses* and traveled to Russia where he was in on the ground floor of the Communist Revolution. It was, Reed excitedly reported back, the first step in the inexorable march toward worldwide Socialism. Robert Henri's friend, the unrepentant Anarchist and feminist Emma Goldman, was under indictment for opposing the draft. In September she would be sentenced to two years in prison. Emma Goldman was just the kind of person most alarming to nativist Americans: she had emigrated from Russia, was seen as an unassimilated Orthodox Jew, and one who had brought with her the radical political fanaticism that bred revolution in Europe.

But John Sloan did not sound worried. In one passing reference to America's entry into the war he wrote to Henri from Gloucester, "Stuart Davis 'registered' [for the draft] up here ... his father is keen for the war. ... I should say if asked that this town is not for the war very enthusiastically." Stuart Davis was drafted, and was assigned to less-than-hazardous duty in U.S. Army Intelligence in New York City. He reported up to Walter Lippmann, onetime contributor to the Socialist periodicals *The Coming Nation* and *The Masses*. Nevertheless, in 1917 Lippmann was appointed assistant to Newton Baker, Woodrow Wilson's Secretary of War.

Whoever gave John Sloan the impression that Gloucester was "not for the war very enthusiastically," it was certainly not Ensign Solomon Jacobs of the U.S. Navy Volunteer Coast Patrol.

Chapter Thirteen

SUMMER OF THE PERISCOPES

~~

Toll of the U-156 / *Cows and Conspirators*

Toll of the U-156

W HEN SUMMER made its welcome return to Gloucester in 1918, following one of the coldest winters on record, there was a sense of the unreal in the contrasts between war and diversion. An appeal went out to the Massachusetts public to go without sugar for the next two to three months so that children and the sick would be sufficiently provided for. Newspapers were slimmer because the War Industries Board had ordered a reduction of 15% to save paper. Yet in an article entitled "The Height of the Season," the Gloucester paper reported that "While other shore and mountain resorts are not so well filled, Cape Ann has every appearance of having as many guests here as usual. Our streets are filled with strangers and never has there been such a display of pleasure cars ... [although] the gaiety of the season is not up to the usual pace."

The war effort took peculiar turns. In Gloucester women and children were recruited to make "good money" gathering sumac branches that summer. The tannin in sumac was needed for tanning and dyeing because the war had cut off shipments of commercial tannin imported from Sicily in peacetime. The waterfront was now on a wartime footing. The fishermen's strike had finally been settled, and the Gloucester fleet's 225 fishing vessels were returning with great hauls and earning high prices. By the beginning of July their catch was 15 million pounds ahead of the year before. The *Gloucester Daily Times* trumpeted "Local Fishermen Hustle for Hoover," reflecting Herbert Hoover's challenge to supply the nation with fish so that more meat could be shipped to America's troops overseas.

Mining engineer Hoover had worked tirelessly for Belgian relief efforts up to 1917, and when the U.S. entered the war Wilson appointed him head of the Food Administration. Proclaiming that "food will win the war," Hoover issued one challenge after another from his new post, calling for meatless Mondays, wheatless Wednesdays and sugarless candy every day. Hoover's campaign was publicized with posters that carried catchy messages like "If U fast U beat U boats. If U feast U boats beat U."

The fishermen were fulfilling a commitment to serve their country, while incidentally filling their own pockets. But their efforts, and their very lives, would soon be under a very real gun. In June the U-boats made their presence felt in U.S. waters, although the first targets were not the fishing boats. Two coastal cargo carriers, the three-masted *Hattie Dunn* and the four-masted *Hauppauge*, were captured off Winterport, Maine by the German submarine *U-151* and sunk by time bombs after the crews were allowed to get away in lifeboats. The masters of the two vessels, Capt. C. F. Holbrook from the *Hattie Dunn* and Capt. Sweeney from the *Hauppauge*, were taken aboard the submarine and enjoyed a reunion. They had been boyhood chums in St. George, Maine and their wives were friends in that little village, but the two men had spent their lives at sea and had not seen one another for years. It was a fine, if bizarre, opportunity to catch up on old times. After their release both men spoke highly of the hospitality they received during their stay aboard the *U-151*. It would not be unusual for a U-boat captain to play the gracious host to captains of American vessels he had just sent to the bottom. Many ashore saw this as an attempt to undermine anti-German sentiment.

Less than two months later, down the coast on Cape Cod, Germans launched an attack that was anything but chivalrous. It was a quiet Sunday in July and vacationers were basking on the beach at Orleans. Offshore they could see a tug pulling a row of three barges, two of them empty and one loaded with stone. The *Perth Amboy* had left Gloucester that morning and was on its way to New York, with forty-one people aboard, three of them women and five children. It was the lazy sort of scene one could expect on a Cape Cod summer day.

Then, to the disbelief of the beachgoers, a submarine surfaced. It was later identified as the German *U-156*, under the command of

Korvetten Kapitän Richard Feldt. The U-boat shelled the tug and its row of barges for more than an hour and a half. Over that time 147 rounds splashed around and pounded into the slow-moving tow, wounding three men and sinking the tug. Four shells hit the shore. It was the first time enemy shells had struck the U.S. mainland since the War of 1812.

An emergency call went out to the naval air station at nearby Chatham, where a baseball game was in progress. Four pilots and their one-man crews dropped mitts and bats and ran to their aircraft. The pilot of one was Ensign Eric Lingard from Annisquam. Lingard circled slowly over the sub at 400 feet in his seaplane, H.S.L. 1695. His bombardier took careful aim and dropped their single bomb. It missed the sub, falling harmlessly into the sea. Bombs from the other planes also failed to hit the *U-156* or did not explode. One pilot was so frustrated he dropped a monkey wrench upon the sub, without discernible effect. The seaplanes returned to their base for more bombs, but by the time they returned the *U-156* had submerged and gone its way. When the attack was reported, the public was outraged that the submarine had attacked a blameless row of barges, rather than the airbase which was a legitimate military target.

That Ensign Lingard was a brave pilot was tragically confirmed three months later. A South American steamer radioed the Chatham base that it was under attack by a U-boat. Lingard volunteered to go as gunner aboard an aircraft dispatched to defend the steamer. The plane was forced down in a gale, and broke apart when it crash landed. Lingard clung to a wing, holding up his unconscious flying partner. He kept the two of them afloat for twenty-seven hours in rough seas until they were rescued. The long exposure proved fatal to Lingard, though. He died of pneumonia in the hospital.

After attacking the barges off Orleans, the *U-156* cruised east with orders to attack the fishing fleet. On July 22nd the Gloucester schooner *Robert and Richard* was intercepted by the *U-156* on Cashes Bank, sixty miles south of Cape Porpoise in Maine. Fishermen expect the unexpected from the deep, but the sight of the steel-hulled German submarine bursting to the surface, sloughing seawater as it rose, must have caused a few jaws to drop. The *U-156*, 195 feet long, was twice the length of a typical Gloucester schooner. Black-clad submariners swarmed topside, manning the two 105mm guns, mounted fore and aft, that discouraged any thought of resistance.

The Germans boarded the *Robert and Richard* and their first officer said he had owned a summer home in Maine since 1896. He took the vessel's American flag, which he said he would fly over his house after Germany won the war. The schooner's crew was ordered to abandon ship. The Germans placed mines aboard, then returned to the sub as the *Robert and Richard* shuddered under the explosions and swiftly sank. The crewmen rowed away in five dories. Some were eventually picked up by other fishing vessels, others made shore a day later. The men lost all of their personal belongings in the sinking, but Capt. Wharton and the other owners of the *Robert and Richard* dug into their own pockets to recompense the crew for their losses.

This would be the pattern the U-boat commanders followed. Rather than waste torpedoes on the schooners, they captured the vessels after sending shots over their bows, then sank them with mines. The crews were allowed to row away because they would have further cramped the limited space in the subs. They could hope to be picked up or make their way to shore. Sometimes after a schooner was destroyed the crew members would be taken aboard the submarine and lined up on deck for photos with their captors before being cast off in their dories. A German officer might tell, in flawless English, of slipping ashore and bellying up to the bar in a waterfront tavern for an evening of beers. The American crewmen were quick to repeat these stories to the newspapers when they were rescued, and that was probably what the Germans intended – to create confusion in coastal communities. How could a townsman be sure a neighbor or a drinking companion was who he said he was?

The schooners posed no threat to the Germans as long as they remained unarmed. A Congressman, James Galvin, advocated arming the fishing vessels, but the fishermen were dead set against the suggestion. They said that if the schooners were armed, U-boats would have every excuse, under international law, for sinking them without warning. An officer on the U-boat *U-117* made a further threat of retaliation: submarines would approach major American seaports and release tanks of poison gas into an on-shore wind.

When word of this intimidation reached the coast, residents, fearful of being subjected to the mustard gas attacks that were the scourge of the trenches, petitioned for gas masks. The *U-117*, incidentally, failed in what should have been a routine sinking of one of its prey. The sub's crew boarded the three-masted Canadian schooner *Bianca* southeast of Sable Island and placed bombs aboard. The bombs exploded according to plan, and the U-boat continued on its way. However, contrary to the certain expectations of the Germans, the *Bianca* did not sink. She was carrying a cargo of tobacco and, after the bombs blew holes in her hull, the inrushing water swelled the bales of the fragrant weed, plugging the leaks. Three days later a fishing schooner from Boston came across the *Bianca*, bloated but still afloat, and towed her into Halifax.

After sinking the *Robert and Richard*, the *U-156* continued on its campaign of destruction. On August 5th the submarine fired a torpedo into the tanker *Luz Blanca* fifty miles south of Halifax. The sub surfaced to finish the kill by gunfire, but the tanker fired back in a battle that lasted an hour. The *Luz Blanca* finally succumbed to the mortal wound it had suffered from the torpedo and sank. When attacked, the tanker had telegraphed distress messages, but no American or Canadian naval vessels arrived on the scene for nine hours. Still, it was a lesson for Kapitän Feldt to shun vessels that could fight back. Thereafter he confined his depredations to the undefended fishing fleet.

And he was soon at it again. During that same week the *U-156* dispatched to the bottom the schooners *Rob Roy* and *Muriel* of Gloucester, and the *Annie Perry* of Boston. Survivors of the *Perry* said the U-boat commander and his crew all spoke perfect English, were in good spirits and said they had sunk six schooners that afternoon. The U-boat, the American crewmen said, remained on the surface all night, displaying a brilliant light. Kapitän Feldt flaunted his conviction that there was little likelihood the U.S. Navy or Coast Guard would appear on the scene.

The *Rob Roy*, built at Essex in 1900 and owned by the Gorton-Pew Vessels Company, had just taken on bait in Nova Scotia and was headed out for a week of mackerel seining. Her fate was sealed when the U-boat fired a shell over her bow and four German sailors came aboard with sticks of dynamite. They demanded no supplies, only the ship's papers, before they ordered the crew off in dories, to watch as the charges exploded and the *Rob Roy* settled under the waves. The men in the dories rowed in the direction of Nova Scotia shore all night, and next day were picked up by a steamer and landed ashore. They made their way to Digby, then across the Bay of Fundy to New Brunswick, and returned by train to Gloucester (service on the Yarmouth-to-Portland ferry had been suspended because of the submarine menace).

One of the crewmen on the *Rob Roy* was Michael Clark, later a captain. In the 1970s he would narrate his recollections for an oral history project conducted for Gloucester's Sawyer Free Library. Speaking with a disarming chuckle, Clark made his encounters with perils at sea sound like a walk in the park. A Newfoundlander like Capt. Jacobs, Clark was the kind of seaman who would have been welcome as one of Sol's crew members. He was an able schooner-man of the age before radio and phonographs, when men aboard amused one another by playing a harmonica or guitar, or displayed their talents in some other form of amateur entertainment.

Clark came to Gloucester in 1916 where he met up with many he had known along the Newfoundland shore. The fishermen's strike was still in progress, though, so he moved on to New York to look up an uncle. He learned his kinsman had died in a fishermen's bethel, so Clark hopped a train to California and landed a berth on a fishing boat out of San Francisco. His shipmates took the unsuspecting young sailor to a red light district in that brawling port, but the police stopped them with a warning that the area was going to be raided. The report proved to be accurate, as the police picked up 1,500 "sporting ladies" the following night. Clark fished in the Bering Sea for two seasons before making his way back to Gloucester after the strikers had gone back to their boats.

Michael Clark's specialty in shipboard entertainment was to re-cite ballads. He knew by heart the many verses of favorites like *The Shooting of Dan McGrew* that he recited in a casual, conversational tone, shunning any theatrical bombast. The boys in the focsle sooner or later would ask Mike Clark to recite *Toledo Slim*. *Toledo Slim* was one of those folk ballads that were known to both black and white audiences, but it was the white version that Clark and his fellow fishermen were familiar with. So Mike Clark would oblige them with …

> We were seated in a pool room on a cold December day,
> Telling jokes and funny stories just to pass the time away,
> When the door was softly opened and a form walked slowly in,
> All the boys soon stopped their kidding when they saw Toledo Slim.
>
> But a different man was he and they hardly knew the guy.
> He no longer wore the glad rags he had worn in days gone by.
> He took a look around him as he crept into the place,
> And we saw a look of hunger on his dirty, grimy face.
>
> "Hello Slim, old boy!" said Boston Red, "you're looking on the pork,
> Why you used to be the swellest guy of any in New York.
> Come, tell us, Slim, what happened that you are on the bum?"

Slim says he used to be well-off, "my roll was always there." But that was before he dropped in at Kid McCoy's for a drink one night and met a woman. One thing led to another and "Next day we saw the parson and paid a month's rent down." Wedded bliss suited Slim, but then things went wrong. He burgled a house with his friend Jackie Brown, and as they were fleeing Jackie escaped but a patrolman shot Slim in the leg. Slim was sent to jail and when he emerged years later, he discovered his girl had run off with Jackie Brown.

In search of the pair, Slim eventually met someone who told him Jackie was living well in 'Frisco, but had left Slim's woman penniless in Denver where she died of consumption. Slim followed the trail to San Francisco, tracked down Jackie, and killed him in a shoot-out. Then Slim hopped an eastbound train …

> "That's all there is to tell, boys, I'm like the other bums,
> I've lost all my ambition and don't care what becomes –"
> And as he finished talking, from his hip he drew a gun,
> In a moment came a sharp report – his grafting days were done.

The end of the ballad would bring appreciative applause, Mike Clark modestly tapping and refilling his pipe. His shipmates most likely had never dabbled in crime, but they could well sympathize with Slim in such matters as a treacherous chum who made off with a faithless girlfriend. It had happened to more than one of them. Throughout the summer the headlines in the *Gloucester Daily Times* were more often than not of U-boat attacks. On August 12 the news was that a U-boat had been attacking at will on Georges Bank, and had sunk nine swordfishing vessels. By late August the *U-156* had made its way to the Grand Banks off Newfoundland, and there Kapitän Feldt employed an ingenious stratagem. To avoid alarming and thereby scattering the fishermen, he first captured the 129-ton Canadian steam trawler *Triumph*, put aboard a prize crew, and armed the vessel as a surface raider. The original crewmembers of the *Triumph* were taken aboard the *U-156* in a great show of hospitality that included the passing around of a bottle of brandy. While this conviviality was taking place within the submarine, the *Triumph* steamed innocently in upon the fishing schooners working fifty-some miles south of Canso.

The *Triumph* was flying the Canadian flag as it approached the *A. Piatt Andrew*. Capt. Wallace Bruce of the *Andrew* was caught totally by surprise when German sailors suddenly appeared on the deck of the *Triumph*, brandishing machine guns. While the *A. Piatt Andrew* was being boarded, Capt. Joe Mesquita in another Gloucester schooner nearby, the *Francis J. O'Hara, Jr.*, was equally unsuspecting when he sailed over to see what was going on. The *O'Hara*, too, was captured, and both vessels were sent to the bottom by time bombs. (Another schooner that Capt. Mesquita had owned, the *Frances P. Mesquita*, was also sunk by a U-boat, but that was after Mesquita had sold her to Newfoundland interests.)

When Capt. Mesquita was summarily ordered off the *O'Hara* by the Germans, there was no time to collect any of his gear. What he was forced to leave behind would have been typical of the effects lost by other masters of schooners destroyed by German submarines. He lost his sextant, log books, binoculars, barometer, compasses, nautical charts and books, oil clothes, rubber boots, woolen socks and shirts, a shaving outfit, street clothes for going ashore (including a gold watch and chain), and $200 locked in a closet (a substantial sum of cash which might be needed if a crew member became ill or was injured and had to be taken ashore and perhaps sent home). It was one thing to be stripped of these items of value and convenience when a vessel fell prey to the forces of nature, but to forfeit possessions by armed foreign attack was infuriating.

The Gloucester schooner *Sylvania* was also sunk by the *U-156*, aided by its decoy the *Triumph*, on August 21, ninety-five miles off Canso. Capt. Jeffrey Thomas and his crew took to the boats and rowed to land. With the sinking of the *A. Piatt Andrew*, the *Francis J. O'Hara, Jr.* and the *Sylvania*, the *U-156* had destroyed three of the most productive fishing schooners in the Gloucester fleet. After the fishermen learned to be wary of the *Triumph*, the Germans had no further use for their decoy and scuttled it too.

Although the Germans said they meant to sink the boats but spare the men, many of the crews had an arduous time rowing their dories hundreds of miles to shore with only the supplies they were allowed to hastily gather up before abandoning ship. The loss of life among crewmen of all of the fishing vessels attacked was substantial. Twenty-two died, mainly in dories that failed to make it to shore.

Compounding the impact of the submarine war against the fishing fleet was the newspaper reportage. After a schooner was reported sunk by a U-boat, days might pass, or a week or more, before the press would report that the crew had been picked up by a passing steamer, or had rowed to shore and found a telegraph office. (Few fleet owners had followed Capt. Jacobs' lead and installed telegraph sets in their vessels. Only the Bay State Fishing Company of Boston responded to the U-boat attacks by equipping its steam trawlers with wireless transmitters.)

Loved ones ashore were made more apprehensive when accounts of U-boat attacks were distorted by panic. On August 13 the Gloucester paper reported the arrival in Gloucester of three of the seven crewmen from the little (27-ton) motorized schooner *Mary E. Sennett* of Rockport. They were still in their oilskins, having fled the doomed *Sennett* under U-boat attack. According to one of the crewmen, the Germans fired deck guns at them in their lifeboat, missing by "about two feet." There were also reports that the Germans had shelled two other schooners, which disappeared, presumably with the loss of all aboard. This was alarming news. Were the Germans now shelling fishing schooners, as well as their fleeing crews? After crewmen from the supposedly sunken vessels arrived safely ashore, the facts of the matter were put together. The U-boat (later determined to be the *U-117* under Kapitänleutnant Drescher) had, sheepdog-fashion, herded together the nine small motor schooners fishing for swordfish on Georges Bank. One of the schooners attempted to flee, but her skipper quickly changed his mind when geysers of foam burst ahead of and behind his vessel from shells fired from the sub's deck guns (those were the shots that alarmed the men from the *Sennett*). Then, in the usual fashion, the Germans placed time bombs aboard the schooners and warned the crews off in dories. The true version of the attack did not make the headlines, however, and the apprehension engendered by the first accounts could not be easily dispelled.

The population ashore would have been further unnerved by articles such as that in the paper on August 23 that included photos of the captain and a crewman of a British freighter who were the only two survivors when a U-boat lined the entire crew of the freighter on its deck, then closed the hatches and dove beneath the waters. Such barbarous acts on the part of the "Huns" alarmed schooner crewmen and townspeople alike in this port that was taking the brunt of attacks on American fishing vessels, a campaign the German U-boats were able to pursue with impunity.

In an editorial on August 21 the Gloucester paper protested:

> Get After the Submarines. There is something very exasperating in the leisurely way in which the submarines which have of late sunk so many vessels off our coasts have gone about their work. … It is just as if they knew they were perfectly safe and could go about their dastardly work without fear of molestation. … The coast of the United States must be made a decidedly uncomfortable place for each and every one of the Hun pirates.

Food directors of the Massachusetts Public Safety Committee sent an urgent telegram to the Navy Department demanding protection for the fishing fleet against U-boats. In response, Admiral Benson, in what the fishermen saw as another hollow gesture, announced that one vessel had been delegated to regularly patrol

Georges Bank. The *Boston Transcript* decried the lack of action:

> There has been a great deal of talking around and about this submarine menace, but the U-boats appear to have found the American waters … empty of everything except the easy prey … a great public which is making great sacrifices to fight the war have a right to expect the maximum in energy and vigilance in guarding the necessary traffic, and particularly the food traffic, of our coast.

But protection of the homeland coast, and of those fishing vessels that were still willing to harvest the waters for the common good, remained a low government priority to the end of the war. The vessels assigned for Naval Coast Patrol service, and manned by reservists like Ensign Solomon Jacobs, were invaluable for spotting enemy vessels near the coast and sounding the alert. But bullets from their small machine guns would have bounced harmlessly off the steel plates of a submarine.

The fishing-for-food effort was further complicated by restrictions on fishermen who were technically aliens. As the need for heightened coastal security became palpable, new rules stated that admittance to any waterfront or dock could be obtained only by a pass issued by a United States marshal. What's more, the captain and every crew member of a coastal trading or fishing vessel was required to carry an Identification Card issued by the U.S. Customs Service. The authorities would not permit a vessel to sail unless every member could produce this ID card, which was issued only to U.S. citizens. The rule was particularly hard on crewmen from the Maritimes who considered themselves citizens of the Gulf of Maine, not of any specific nation bordering its waters.

The German submarine policy achieved its goals. As a result of the raids of the *U-156* and other U-boats, the entire Canadian Grand Banks fishing fleet was driven into port. The American fleet soon followed. With no protection forthcoming from the American government, crewmen shunned the risk of having to row for their lives. And with insurance rates soaring, Gloucester fleet owners prudently kept their schooners tied up at the dock.

Following his leading role in executing the plan of the German High Command to decimate and terrorize the New England fishing fleet, Kapitän Feldt turned east and set out back across the Atlantic. All in all during its summer cruise in American waters the *U-156* had destroyed thirty-four ships, eight of them Gloucester fishing schooners. Kapitän Feldt was not to enjoy a hero's welcome in Germany, however. Nor would he become a Hollywood star, which was rumored to be the post-war ambition of more than one U-boat commander whose treatment of his American prisoners was impeccably gallant. In late September, less than two months before the Armistice, the *U-156* was threading its way through the heavily mined North Sea, en route to the safety of its base at Kiel on the southwest shore of the Baltic Sea. It never made it. In all likelihood it did strike a mine, water rushed through the craft, and the *U-156* drifted lazily down to the ocean floor with its cargo of seventy-seven drowned crewmen.

The reinforced German forces on the Western Front were more than matched by the American troops who arrived to fight – and die - in great numbers in the trenches in 1918. Whereas there had been only 14,000 U.S. soldiers in France in June of 1917, by May of the next year the number had swelled to a million American troops, arriving in convoys of assorted vessels that included converted cruise ships and seized German freighters. General John J. Pershing had sought to keep the American Expeditionary Force separate from the French and British armies, but large numbers of American doughboys found themselves being sent in to replace Allied troops felled in the trenches. American combat deaths totaled 53,402, the greater part of whom were killed in nine months of 1918. That was far more than U.S. combat deaths in three years of the Korean War, or during the eleven years of the Vietnam War (but a fraction of the close to 300,000 U.S. combat fatalities in World War II). More than 200,000 American soldiers were wounded during America's brief participation in that First World War.

By September, support for the war was crumbling within Germany, dissent brought to a head by a revolt of German naval forces at Wilhelmshaven. In November, three months after the peak of U-boat attacks on America's East Coast, the Armistice was signed and the war ended. The Gloucester fleet returned to fishing, with only its traditional enemies to do battle with: the sea and the weather.

All in all, Ensign Solomon Jacobs could be proud. In the Naval Coast Patrol he may have only played a supporting role, but he had served his country – and his old comrades in the fishing fleet.

Cows and Conspirators

IN THAT same summer of 1918, John Sloan's thoughts and interests were entirely remote from what was happening on the offshore waters. It is unlikely that he was even aware that the fishermen he saw on the street in downtown Gloucester might be among those who would sail off in a schooner, run afoul of a U-boat, see their vessel blown out of the water, and be forced to row for their lives. On August 16, 1918 the Gloucester paper had noted that "John Sloan, the New York artist, is located at one of Mrs. Clara L. Harrington's cottage [sic] on East Main Street near Rocky Neck Avenue again this season." The lead stories on the front page were of transport ships crowded with American troops on their way to the Front, and of Herbert Hoover's austere food restrictions.

The John Sloan who arrived in Gloucester that summer was at last an artist getting on in the world. He was comfortable in his role as instructor at the Art Students League, and as president of the Society of Independent Artists. Finally, at age forty-seven, Sloan had sold the first of his New York "city" paintings: Gertrude Vanderbilt Whitney, she who had given Sloan his first one-man show, purchased his *Spring Rain*, painted in 1912.

It is a simply composed work in which a solitary young woman under an umbrella walks ahead of the viewer in a park, framed by bending trees and distant indistinct buildings. The foliage is light green but all else is dark, except for the girl's yellow hat. Sloan's later facetious comment was: "Memory tells me that my motive was to record this glimpse of an ankle (an ankle counted in those days) and the fresh green and the spring rain." He mentions, too, the special "chord of color" he used in the painting; he had been making use of Hardesty Maratta's system of tonal pigments well before his Gloucester years.

The young woman's lithe form is as youthful as the bending wet trees in their fresh spring yellow-green. There is no need to delve any deeper for symbols – the viewer supplies them as needed. Author and musician John Erskine said "great artists create more than they know – meanings they have not heard of, beauty they have not seen. … art is a constant collaboration between the artist and the audience."

True, but viewers can react indignantly to meanings they perceive in a painting, as Gertrude Whitney herself was to discover. She later acquired *Love on the Roof*, a New York drawing from 1914 in which Sloan depicted a young matron in the arms of a boy in his teens who has interrupted her as she hangs out her husband's washing on the roof. Her child plays nearby unattended. Sloan said of the scene, "I just saw it and etched it."

Gertrude hung the print in her apartment, and in 1934 it was cited in court as evidence that ten-year-old Gloria Vanderbilt would be brought up in an immoral environment if she were placed in the custody of her paternal Aunt Gertrude, where she would be exposed to such lewdness. Nevertheless, custody was granted to Gertrude Vanderbilt to protect Gloria and Gloria's millions from her mother's mismanagement. Whether or not Sloan's painting exerted a pernicious influence as predicted, Gloria's later life provided sensational copy for gossip columnists.

As he had in the previous four summers in Gloucester, Sloan in 1918 painted morning and afternoon. His lectures to his Gloucester students continued to be a mixture of painting theory and unsparing but stimulating critiques of their efforts. Sloan's output that summer would be the smallest of his five years in Gloucester. Just thirty-one of the forty-six canvases he painted that year were of Gloucester subjects. Of them, he commented later only on *Wayside Inn, Gloucester*, saying "A true sense of Gloucester sun, air, and sky pervades this one."

The day after the arrival of the Sloans, the *Gloucester Daily Times* announced that other visitors were in town: President and Mrs. Wilson, together with the ever-present Col. House, had motored down Gloucester's Main Street "practically unrecognized." (It seems odd that Gloucester residents, however preoccupied with their own affairs, did not notice the heavy wartime security detail that always accompanied Wilson.)

The party drove on to Bass Rocks and Eastern Point with "frequent stops for the better observance of scenes made famous by prominent artists." The President wore "an outing suit of white flannel, and a cap." Two days later, the paper carried a story brimming with local boosterism. The President, it said, was loath to leave the area, and had prolonged his visit to Colonel House in Magnolia.

After another drive through downtown Gloucester, the party "journeyed to Rafe's Chasm where [President Wilson] stood on the heights looking down on Norman's Woe and drank deep of the beauties of the North Shore." With America in the midst of a war, and its young men being shipped in unprecedented numbers to do battle overseas, astute readers of the newspaper could guess that the military and governmental leaders assembled with the President in Col. House's Magnolia residence were there to discuss matters other than the beauties of the North Shore.

The residents of Magnolia were generally blameless in their reception of President Wilson, with one shocking exception. On August 20 a Boston paper stated that "Summer residents of Magnolia are discussing with indignation today the ease with which men in the uniform of the United States who attended a fashionable hotel dance there on Saturday night obtained intoxicating liquor. They feel that with the President a guest not quite a mile away from the hotel such actions reflect discredit on the town and its distinguished guest." In a foreshadowing of the Prohibition Amendment that would darken the nation's taverns shortly after the war, efforts were underway nationwide to keep America's fighting men pure of heart by barring them from access to ardent spirits.

John Sloan may have hoped to distance himself from the daily drumbeat of war news by roaming with his easel and students through the moors and along the shores of Gloucester. But the summer world of Cape Ann was swept with patriotic fervor. In July, just down the road from the red cottage in East Gloucester, socialites were organizing a wax works evening at the Hawthorne Casino to benefit the war effort.

Sloan showed again that year at the third annual exhibition of the Gallery-on-the-Moors. The proceeds were pledged for the benefit of French artists wounded in battle, so Sloan here was at least

peripherally involved in a patriotic endeavor. If there was any interest in Sloan's entries, *Landscape with Cow* and *Landscape*, neither
found a buyer.

Meantime, the federal government's stepped-up activities in fer-
reting out dissent were not auspicious for an outspoken pacifist like
John Sloan. While Woodrow Wilson in Magnolia spun visions of
worldwide harmony following this war to end all wars, his Attorney
General and Postmaster General in Washington were busily pounc-
ing upon any word or act of supposed sedition. Attorney General
Thomas Watt Gregory complained that too many disloyal citizens
were slipping through the net of the Espionage Act. In May, with
the wholehearted support of the President, that law was reinforced
by passage of the Sedition Act. Drafted with intentionally vague
language subject to creative interpretations of all sorts, the Sedition Act made it a criminal offense to utter or publish any "disloyal,
profane, scurrilous, or abusive language" that could induce feelings
of "contempt, scorn, contumely, or disrepute" towards the nation's
constitution, political system, flag, or military uniform. An offender
could be fined $10,000 and/or be sentenced to prison for twenty
years.

The new law was promptly enforced to lodge a charge of sedition against Max Eastman, specifically with reference to utterances
in *The Masses*. Additionally, in July Floyd Dell, another stalwart of
The Masses, was thrown out of the army after failing to disclose that
he, Eastman and six other former *Masses* employees had been indicted under the Espionage Act. The case was brought to trial in
April, 1918. One of the defendants, illustrator Henry Glintenkamp
who had drawn covers for *The Masses*, did not appear – he had fled
to Mexico. Glintenkamp had studied under Henri, and for a time
shared a studio with Stuart Davis. Floyd Dell delivered a give-me-
liberty-or-give-me-death speech to the court: "There are some
laws that the individual feels he cannot obey, and he will suffer any punishment, even that of death, rather than recognize
them as having authority over him." The jury deliberated for
three days but failed to come to a verdict.

It would have to be unsettling that many of John Sloan's earlier
associates were either under indictment or at least suspicion. The

Sloans, the Winters and the Davises might well have concluded among themselves that the government was tightening the noose around everyone who ever had anything to do with *The Masses*. And there was a grim historical parallel: one of Sloan's idols, Honoré Daumier, had been imprisoned after his politically satirical drawings were published in a radical magazine.

The Espionage and Sedition Acts were enforced rigorously. Within the Justice Department, Chicago advertising executive Albert M. Briggs formed an "American Protective League" to aid, ostensibly, in monitoring the activities of enemy aliens. In time a quarter-million official "agents" were accredited to spy on neighbors, fellow workers, and in general anyone they might judge to be acting suspiciously. They flashed official-looking badges that read "American Protective League – Secret Service."

Attorney General Thomas W. Gregory announced that "several hundred thousand private citizens, most of them members of patriotic bodies," were volunteering, "keeping an eye on disloyal individuals, and making reports of disloyal utterances ..." The government deputized American Protective League patriots, together with stateside soldiers and sailors, into vigilante squads in many American cities. Their professed mission was to round up draft-dodgers and deserters, but they were keenly alert to any act or remark – especially if uttered in a foreign accent – that might be interpreted as a slur upon the flag.

All of this official scrutiny bore little fruit. Occasionally an incident of purported disloyalty would be reported in the newspapers. Daniel Sylvester, aged sixty-five, a resident of Gloucester's Annisquam area, was arrested by police at the request of the Department of Justice and held for $1,000 bond. Allegedly Sylvester had made "disloyal remarks" that were reported to the U.S. Assistant District Attorney Ward Dewey.

Later in the summer an artist from New York, William A. Levy, was picked up by police who charged that he had sent a "suspicious telegram" from East Gloucester's Wayside Inn. After the *Gloucester Daily Times* reported that Levy had been released but would be required to report his movements to the police, the artist complained to the editor that he was a "loyal American" and that he had been released without restrictions. Levy tactfully thanked the Gloucester police for their restrained treatment while he was in their custody.

In neighboring Manchester the former German consul-general in Boston, Oswald Kunhardt, was arrested as an enemy alien who had failed to register as such. Neighbors had often seen Kunhardt walking alone on the beach and, knowing that he was German, surmised that he had been communicating with unseen vessels offshore. The fact that he had been a summer resident of Manchester for sixteen years earned him no sympathy. Assistant District Attorney Dewey sprang into action again, and disclosed that a search of Kunhardt's rooms revealed a stick to which a white handkerchief had been attached. This mysterious contrivance was deemed by the authorities as suitable for use as a semaphore for signaling submarines. (It was later determined to have had no sinister intent.) When asked if the arrest had anything to do with recent U-boat activities off the coast, Mr. Dewey maintained an eloquent official silence.

Indeed, anyone venturing onto a beach was inviting scrutiny. Two men were apprehended as suspected spies on or adjacent to American beaches. One was changing a lightbulb in his hotel room. The other was waving to attract the attention of another beachgoer. In Provincetown thirty-year-old Eugene O'Neil, writing the plays for the Provincetown Players that would bring him fame, had taken his typewriter to the beach. When a sunbeam glanced off the metal, the flash was spotted by the alert chief of a government radio station across the dunes. The forces of national security responded swiftly and, when the suspect was dining in a hotel, federal agents descended, revolvers drawn. O'Neil was held incommunicado in the town hall lock-up, not allowed to call a lawyer.

All ethnic minorities were suspect. The Finns who had emigrated to work the granite quarries in the Gloucester village of Lanesville stirred unease because it was known that Finland was in sympathy with the Central Powers, probably because their arch-enemy Russians were in league with the Allies. The Gloucester paper suggested that it would be helpful if Gloucester's loyal Finnish-Americans were welcomed into American society, rather than being regarded as "slightly modified Eskimos."

Town vagrants were regarded as a subversive element as well.

Gloucester's City Marshal gave the order that "The police department is to round up all loafers and it will be one of three places for those who persist in loafing about the streets ... either to work, to war, or to jail." It was no idle threat. In July the following year two men in their thirties were arrested and sent to jail for "loafing."

In this environment of suspicion, might Neddy's parents, for example, be keeping an eye on goings on at the red cottage for the government? Not likely. Gloucester's population was patriotic but broad-minded about those they considered oddballs, so long as there was no clear threat to law and order. The port's mixed population bred tolerance, as did its long exposure to strangers arriving by sea who spoke, dressed and behaved in some peculiar manner .

Nevertheless, Sloan might think twice about venturing onto a Gloucester beach in 1918 to paint a seascape. A picture he had painted two years before and called *Signals* could easily be classified as disloyal under the elastic definitions of the Sedition Act. The painting gently pokes fun at the military: Pennants flying on a warship in Gloucester harbor, no doubt communicating some important naval message, are contrasted with washing on a line flapping in the breeze on Rocky Neck. Sloan speaks of the wash "gaily flapping in reply."

John and Dolly Sloan had decided that they would not be returning to Gloucester the following summer. Nowhere in the scant correspondence that survives from Sloan's Gloucester years does he mention the war as entering into his decision to terminate those summers at the red cottage. Sloan's much-quoted reason for leaving was that Gloucester had become overrun with artists, that there was an artist's shadow beside every cow in Gloucester and the cows were dying from eating paint-rags. It was something of a hypocritical remark inasmuch as some of the brush-wielding hopefuls who descended upon East Gloucester and Rocky Neck each summer to paint were there in response to ads he himself had placed. "Why did I stop going to Gloucester?" Helen Farr Sloan remembered him answering later: "It became over-run with artists. And Robert Henri encouraged me to consider New Mexico for new subject matter."

If the reasons for Sloan's departure from Gloucester were more complicated than that, he did not say so. But it is hard to believe that he was not aware of the submarine warfare that was decimating the Gloucester fishing fleet, and the state of alert along the coast with the resulting restrictions on access to the waterfront. Might authorities find it incriminating that Sloan, who had consorted with indicted disloyals, was frequenting beaches in a sensitive zone? Also, there was no telling how long the war would last – how long all the restrictions would remain in effect. Or how long the official hysteria would continue.

There is no doubt that Sloan liked Gloucester. He had come for five full summers in a row, sometimes from spring well into the fall. Stuart Davis said Sloan "used to rave" about Gloucester. He painted the harbor and moors and ledges on the scene, working outdoors as he almost never had before and never would again. Gloucester had provided the subject matter for a seismic shift in his creative development, when he painted with new confidence in his technique and exuberant expression in colors. He looked forward every year to returning to "our little red cottage" that he said had become "quite like our 'summer home.'" He was sentimental when he wrote to Dolly of an early spring trip to Gloucester when he "glimpsed the Red Cottage in the snow." He enjoyed all-night picnics on the beach, and dinner at the Savoy Hotel with friends and having too much to drink and ambling hilariously homeward through the dark streets of the town. He loved the "wistfully beautiful warmish days" of October with their "saddening chill in the evenings."

Nevertheless, John and Dolly had not put down roots in Gloucester, as the Davises and the Winters had. In their first years on Cape Ann, Stuart Davis' family rented in East Gloucester, then in 1925 they acquired a house on Mt. Pleasant Avenue. Helen Davis later had her sculpture studio on Reed's Wharf on Smith's Cove, where the North Shore Arts Association would establish its gallery. She became a nearly year-round Gloucester resident. Stuart kept a studio in the family house and each year until 1934 used it as his base for working Gloucester themes into his increasingly abstract compositions. In later years he frequently returned to paint in Gloucester and to photograph the waterfront.

Charles and Alice Winter became even more closely identified with Gloucester. In 1922 they too built on Mt. Pleasant Avenue. It was a studio house at No. 134 that they used summers until 1931 when they moved in full-time. They were pillars of the summer art colony, and in demand as painting instructors. During the Depression, which was felt severely in the East Gloucester art colony, Charles was fortunate to obtain WPA contracts to paint murals in Gloucester's city hall. Over the stage in the auditorium on the second floor he painted in 1934 a large allegorical work called *The Founding of Gloucester*. In it he celebrated the workers who built Gloucester, from the first fishermen in 1623 to later shipbuilders and stonecutters. Five years later, in a series that made use of every available space at the building's entrance adjacent to the mayor's office, he painted *City Government* and *Civic Virtues*, murals in which he portrayed Gloucester civic and political notables of the time. Shortly before his death in 1942, Charles Winter completed his final city hall mural, *Protection of Fishing*, in which men hauling fish into a dory are watched over by saints floating in clouds overhead. As might be expected, Winter eschewed Fauvism in his murals. He adhered instead to the American Scene style that romanticized small-town America, to which he added moralistic touches. Popular during the '20s and '30s, American Scene style had an anonymity that was deemed appropriate for government-funded art.

Alice Winter lived on until 1970, a kindly, talented artist best known for her paintings of children. By then few would remember, if they had ever known, that she, like her husband and others of their long-ago artist friends, was once considered a dangerous radical who had been a staff artist on *The Masses*.

But John and Dolly Sloan did not join their friends in any long-term commitment to Cape Ann. And if in 1918 there was an immediacy of war that made pacifist John Sloan uneasy, he could see an alternative in Robert Henri's ecstatic descriptions of the Southwest. Henri had spent the summers of 1916 and 1917 in Santa Fe, which was just beginning to attract artists, and his letters made much of the painterly subjects and settings. Randall Davey, too, was eager to give the Southwest a try. That last summer in Gloucester Sloan and Davey and their wives set about planning a trip to Santa Fe for the following summer. It would be about as distant culturally and politically as they could get from mainstream America without leaving the country.

John Sloan would have left Gloucester with no sense of guilt. He was opposed to the war because he was convinced that international bankers and munitions-makers were exploiting the worker-soldiers (and that would include the crewmen at war in Gloucester schooners). As to his left-wing sympathies, he pointed out years later that many of the causes taken up by *The Masses* that were denounced at the time as radical proposals – women's suffrage, the income tax, workmen's compensation, social security, regulation of interstate commerce – were eventually incorporated into the American social contract. Sloan never believed that he had been seditious; quite the contrary, he countered that he had been among those showing the way to a better America.

At the end of the season Sloan and Dolly packed up and handed the key to the red cottage to Mrs. Harrington. They would not see Gloucester again.

In the summer of 1918 Capt. Jacobs had reaffirmed his commitment to his adopted country and the defense of Gloucester. He would be remembered with respect, when he was remembered at all. John Sloan, the pacifist summer artist, was marginalized and somewhat suspect. His absence would not be regretted for some time.

Chapter Fourteen
VIEW FROM A DISTANT SHORE

~~

A Plaque in a Park / The Stamp of Recognition

A Plaque in a Park

A NEWSPAPER REPORTER who interviewed seventy-two-year-old Capt. Solomon Jacobs in 1919 described him as "tall, lean and swarthy," showing "scarcely a gray hair, [with an] active, springy walk [that] tells his long familiarity with decks." His manner of speech, the reporter said, was "abrupt and snappy," and he was "given to biting off the extreme letters of the words ... in the manner of the New England seamen of his day."

There was a proposal afoot to use airplanes to track schools of fish, and Capt. Jacobs was eager to take part. "I may be old and stiff, but if flying machines are going to be used this year to scout out mackerel schools, I am going to ride in one of them. I'd take a chance with my hope to play that game. It will be great." He added that "mackerel fishing is the greatest sport in the life of a fisherman." It was not as challenging as it had been, of course, back before fishing had been motorized. Again the captain was lamenting the loss of the purity of the old ways of fishing – after he, more than anyone else in Gloucester, had hastened the decline of wind-driven schooner fisheries through his introduction of the gasoline auxiliary and the steam seiner. Sol could be sentimental but, to the end, he could never resist the allure of innovation. Did this master of mackerel seining under sail conclude his fishing days by spotting schools of fish from the passenger seat of some bi-wing flying Jenny? Probably not. But, with the captain's boundless curiosity, he was certainly game for the challenge.

It was the next year, in October of 1920, that the *Boston Globe*'s man, George Nobel, interviewed Capt. Sol, "snugged in the parlor of his house on Prospect Street." Here it was that the reporter understood the captain to say that he had sailed in the Black Ball packets back in the '60s. But Nobel was more interested in Sol's opinions regarding the upcoming international fishermen's race. The *Halifax Herald* had offered a cup and a cash prize for the winner of a sailing match between a Gloucester fishing schooner and one from Nova Scotia. Benjamin A. Smith of Gorton-Pew Fisheries was quick to accept the challenge, and the town was a-buzz with debates as to which vessel and captain were best qualified to represent the Gloucester fleet. The man from the *Globe* quickly learned that opinion within the fishing community had settled upon three possible contenders: Capt. Marty Welch in the *Esperanto* (the only Gloucester boat ever named after an artificial language), Capt. Charles Harty who had commanded *Esperanto* in her initial voyage, and seventy-three-year old Capt. Solomon Jacobs who was the only one of them who had sailed in the celebrated 1892 race sailed in a fierce gale, remembered as "the race it blew."

Capt. Harty declined to go as a captain; he was now a fish broker on Cape Cod. Sol Jacobs, not too "old and stiff" to take himself out of contention, let it be known that he would be willing to command Fred A. Davis' schooner *Jaffre*. Some may have objected, not only because of his age but pointing out that Sol had lost the 1892 race when he allowed his fierce competitive spirit to overcome good judgment. Others would jump in as partisans of the captain, he who had proved himself the most canny and successful of any in the Gloucester fleet, and who had achieved astonishing speeds under sail in one vessel after another. But the issue was moot: the *Jaffre* was off fishing and would not return in time for the races.

That left the *Esperanto* as the leading contender, her claim solidified by the fact that she had been added to Ben Smith's Gorton-Pew fleet earlier in the year. The choice was generally endorsed by the town, but there were misgivings. The *Globe*'s George Nobel went to Howard Blackburn's tavern on Main Street, where he found Gloucester's legendary doryman in shirtsleeves behind the bar. It was difficult not to steal a glance at Blackburn's stubbed hands. He had lost all his fingers and some toes rowing bare-handed (mittens lost overboard) for five days with his partner frozen to death in the bottom of the dory, before he reached shore on Newfoundland.

Years later, with those fingerless hands, he somehow had twice sailed single-handed across the Atlantic.

As they each partook of a gin flip or some such libation, as Nobel recalled, Blackburn contended "It's not exactly fair. In the last dozen years almost no Gloucester fishermen have been built for speed under sail alone, but to have auxiliary power. That naturally results in cutting down the spread of canvas – the sail area – a whole lot. And their bowsprits are snubbed off." By contrast, Blackburn said, the Nova Scotia boats were still all-sail, and consequently carried much more canvas than the current generation of Gloucester schooners. And the crews were of necessity sailing men.

Sol Jacobs had no wish to contradict Howard Blackburn, but he did believe the *Esperanto* was up to the challenge. Built in 1906, she was of the old school of Gloucester schooners – good-sized at over 107 feet long, ninety-one tons, and presenting a large spread of canvas to the wind. She had been designed by Boston's famed Tom McManus. Sol's only reservation was that the donkey engine *Esperanto* carried for hoisting sail was inadequate as ballast. (Before the races that engine was removed and *Esperanto* was properly ballasted with pig iron.) Remembering the 1892 races, Sol insisted that "a whole cupful of wind was the thing necessary" to prove which boat was superior.

The contest was held off Lunenburg, Nova Scotia, and *Esperanto* took the first race easily in strong winds, a good "cupful of air." The second race, though, was run in light airs that favored the Canadian contender, *Delawana*. Marty Welch sailed *Esperanto* to victory by dint of maneuvers that would have been condemned as reckless had they not succeeded. At the victory banquet held at the Gloucester armory, Massachusetts governor Calvin Coolidge declared "The victory was a triumph for Americanism." Silent Cal was probably unaware that Capt. Welch was a native son of Digby, Nova Scotia.

Smarting from the defeat, Halifax interests were determined to build a racing schooner that would be a triumph for Nova Scotianism. The following year the *Bluenose* was launched, over 160 feet long, with a sail area of 11,150 square feet. Though she did some creditable fishing in her career, *Bluenose* was designed primarily for racing. She would never be defeated in the half-dozen official international fishermen's races held between Nova Scotia and Gloucester over the next eighteen years, although some of the races were indecisive or contested.

Howard Blackburn was basically right, of course. By 1920, races between all-sail fishing schooners had become an anachronism. Sol Jacobs had the first auxiliary fisherman, the *Helen Miller Gould*, built to classic schooner proportions. But thereafter the designs of fishing vessels built in Essex and Gloucester reflected the diminishing role of sail. And while Gloucester crews would deny that they had lost any of their sail-handling skills, they were coming more and more to rely on that engine down below to get them onto the fish and power them out of trouble. The international fishermen's races had thus come to be an exercise in nostalgia – a tribute to the epic age of the all-sail schooner that was now in the past. In fact, that 250th anniversary race back in 1892 had been the final real contest between captains and men who fished under sail because they knew no other way. It had been, as the *Globe* man wrote, "the last really important race of fishermen, all rigged and equipped for the occasion."

In 1930, in an unofficial race sailed at Lunenburg, *Bluenose* was defeated by Gloucester's *Gertrude L. Thebaud*, a yacht-designed racing/working schooner like *Bluenose*, although somewhat smaller. The two vessels met one-on-one in an official competition in 1938. *Bluenose* took home the trophy cup by winning the rubber race. All parties agreed that the race marked the end of the fishing schooner era.

This was well after Sol Jacobs' time. On the night of February 12, 1922 Capt. Jacobs went down to the basement to tend the furnace. When he was slow to return, Sarah decided to investigate. She found her seventy-five-year-old husband dead on the cellar floor. The cause of death was listed as "apoplexy," which was then still a catchall term used to describe either a heart attack or stroke. The funeral was held at home, and was "largely attended" by Sol's mariner friends, members of the business community, others of the many friends he had made around town, and of course brothers from the Tyrian Lodge of Masons and the Ocean Lodge of Odd Fellows.

Two ministers eulogized, Thomas Hancock of the Methodist-Episcopal church and William Rider, retired pastor of the Independent (Unitarian/Universalist) church. If the presence of clergymen of two denominations was Sol's idea, it suggests he was hoisting a spare sail for his cruise to the hereafter. Actually, Sol and Bill Rider had been close friends from way back. Rev. Rider could speak personally of Sol's credentials for a passport to a better place, notwithstanding a few smudges on his dossier. Rev. Hancock could attest to one munificent donation Sol made to the Prospect Street Methodist church: the marble clock manufactured by the Howard Clock company in Boston that Sol donated in 1883 and that had hung on the balcony of the church from that time forward. It was identical to one donated to the city at the same time by Nathaniel Webster, proprietor of the Webster House where Sol would be feted by his fellow captains prior to his departure for the West in 1888.

The list of pallbearers read like a roster of celebrated Gloucester fishing schooner captains: George H. Peoples, Augustus G. Hall, Frank H. Hill, Reuben Cameron, William H. Thomas, Edward A. Proctor. The cortege wound its way along the streets of Gloucester and through the gates of Oak Grove cemetery to the family plot. Sarah would join Sol there in 1940 when she was 82. While she lived, Sarah supported her husband's memory by conscientiously responding to queries, mainly about his vessels.

Sol's obituary in the *Gloucester Daily Times* spoke of him as "the most daring and intrepid mariner of the Gloucester fishing fleet." But as the fishing schooner became a relic of the past, the glory of the fabled captains faded to a dim glow in the memories of the men who had sailed with them, and those shipmates were dying out. Then in 1952 the Cape Ann Savings Bank sponsored the publication of *Builders of Gloucester's Prosperity* by Gordon Thomas, dedicated historian of the fleet. In it Thomas told the stories of the *Helen Miller Gould* and the *Alice M. Jacobs*, and saluted Capt. Jacobs as a man of "great courage, determination, fearlessness, judgment and ability." Thomas would elaborate upon the captain's career in subsequent editions of the book, re- titled *Fast & Able: Life Stories of Great Gloucester Fishing Vessels*.

Still, there was no public reminder of what Capt. Sol had meant to Gloucester, and Mary Favazza often told her husband Salvatore that was a shame. Mary died, but Sal was Executive Secretary of the Gloucester Fisheries Commission in 1974, when Massachusetts was offering state money for worthy initiatives to celebrate the upcoming national Bicentennial. Sal led the drive to have the little park next to the Coast Guard station named in honor of Capt. Jacobs. In his presentation to the city council, Sal pointed out that artist Fitz H. Lane had been honored by the restoration of the granite house Lane built near the harbor, and a traffic circle bore the name of doryman Howard Blackburn. The creation of a Solomon Jacobs park, he said, would "further enrich our conscious heritage by bringing back from near extinction another son of Gloucester." One who, he said, was a "pioneer fisherman, considered by many in his day as the greatest of the Gloucester fishermen."

The park was dedicated on June 17, 1975, with an unveiling of a plaque with a compass rose radiating in the direction of Gloucester landmarks. The sculptor was Adio diBiccari, an immigrant from Italy known for religious statues he executed for churches in the Boston area. In the center of the plaque diBiccari placed an image of the *Helen Miller Gould*, and the words "Fisherman – Pioneer – Adventurer." The inscription on the plaque touched on the captain's achievements, and concluded with a tribute from Gordon Thomas: "This man had no superior. … This tall, strong, raw-boned man was smart, capable, determined and had great vision – and he had guts." Among the honored guests at the dedication was Alice Cox, the captain's granddaughter.

Despite the memorial, Capt. Sol today is scarcely remembered by his fellow townsmen. And it is doubtful that many visitors notice the plaque at the little park, or much care. Capt. Solomon Jacobs was an energetic, achieving, transformative figure in his day. He was a man of late 19th century America, the Gilded Age, the time of raw industrial might and mechanical invention. It was a period of heedless, devil-take-the-hindmost expansion westward with slapdash cobbling of unplanned towns that burgeoned into urban ugliness. It was the age, too, of the myth-makers of the American West, of Buffalo Bill Cody, self-promoting Indian-fighter and showman who helped rationalize the driving of the tribes from their lands and onto reservations to make room for homesteaders swarming in from the eastern third of the continent or directly from Europe. The headlong expansion and crass materialism depressed writers like William

Dean Howells; Henry James, too, who eventually fled permanently to Europe.

But Sol Jacobs reveled in the challenges of an untapped continent. Like many immigrants in those times he eagerly adopted the values of a new America that placed high priority on ambition and "spunk." He was a man of the frontier when that frontier meant fishing and seal-hunting in the far northern reaches of both the eastern and western shores of North America.

He was a visionary more than a businessman, a romantic rather than an empire builder. He was the dreamer who imagined a great trade in halibut traveling over the rails east from the waters of Puget Sound, and he would prove the enterprise feasible. But other men, in powerful combines, would profit from his concept.

He would be first to prove that a gasoline auxiliary engine could be a great boon to fishermen, once the kinks in the technology were worked out. After his trailblazing efforts, the dozen schooners on order in the yards of Gloucester and Essex were all to be equipped with auxiliaries. Capt. Jacobs did not profit a nickel from his foresight in that direction either – he was busy proving that steam, which had long been the standard motive power for tugs and ferries, could be used just a successfully for harvesting mackerel. Steam proved to be less efficient for fishing than oil-fueled internal combustion engines, but the concept of power to supplement, and eventually replace, the wind-driven sailing schooners was irreversibly on its way. Sol, the pioneer, saw his only gains in satisfaction that he had been right all along.

His was a competitive spirit, relishing a contest and sometimes going over the boundaries of legality to gain an advantage. But he acted with courage and skill and basic regard for fairness that earned the respect of his fellow mariners as one of their own breed.

It was entirely within Capt. Jacobs' character that later, on the eve of America's entry into the First World War, he would be quick to sign up for coastal patrol duty in his 70's, to serve America against the German submarine threat in New England.

Little of what Sol Jacobs accomplished survived him. The technology of fishing in the port changed drastically, far outstripping his early innovations. Partly as a result of electronic devices taught to outwit the fish, the stocks of cod and haddock became so depleted that the right of a fisherman to put down a hook or a net became a battle between hard-pressed boat owners and heavy-handed government bureaucrats.

Over time, too, the fishermen changed. The Gloucester fleet became largely the fleet of Sicilian fishermen, who arrived in strength during the 1920s and following World War II. Along with the strong presence of the Italians, there continues a representation in the fleet of men from the Maritimes, along with Azoreans, old-line Yankees, Scandinavians and Irish. Many include in their bloodlines all of the above.

Gloucester was resistant to innovation after Sol Jacobs' time, and gradually fell behind other American fishing ports in the size and value of fish landed. But as of 2011 the port still remains in the top 10 in the quantity of seafood landed. Men with the same love of the sea and the outdoor life and competition for the catch chug into Gloucester's broad harbor in all seasons with their hauls of haddock, cod, scallops, lobsters – and peculiar creatures such as slime eels of which the less said the better, except that they are considered a delicacy in Korea. Like Sol, many of the commercial fishermen aim to make enough to educate their sons – and daughters – so that, unlike the old man, they will not have to fish for a living.

Capt. Solomon Jacobs, while he continues to be honored by way of his park, is seen as a figure from a Gloucester fishing era now far in the past. Sol would not have been disappointed that his name, in the long run, did not loom large in the American saga. He was content to earn a place high in the ranks of those who, like him, gloried in a heroic age of going to sea after fish.

The Stamp of Recognition

In the summer of 1919 John Sloan and Dolly and the Randall Daveys struck out upon the primitive road system of the day in Davey's chain-driven Simplex touring car. Said Sloan, "there was not a decent road west of Buffalo." Between breakdowns and other delays it took them six weeks to reach Santa Fe. The seven-year-old Simplex had an insatiable thirst, consuming a quart of oil a day and getting barely four miles to a gallon of gasoline. Nevertheless, a Simplex was a prestige automobile, and nothing was too good for Davey. Somehow on an art teacher's salary he had maintained a string of polo ponies. He was an avid player in, and painter of, polo matches. When the Sloan-Davey party reached Santa Fe, Davey and his wife bought an old mill and settled in year-round.

The mountainous landscape of the Southwest where every feature was etched in sharp relief was something entirely new to Sloan, a fresh challenge. George Bellows and Leon Kroll had also been persuaded by Robert Henri to come to Santa Fe, so Sloan was in familiar company. He painted the mountains and the barren valleys and the native people dancing in the church plazas. Contrary to his practice in the Gloucester years, he made no paintings outdoors. As in his earlier New York city scenes he stored images in his head, then did the painting in his studio. Some of his plaza scenes approach the humanism of his earlier work, but generally lack the spontaneity and the emotion. Some of them suggest the American Scene style.

Each winter Sloan would return to teaching in New York. Paradoxically, as he became a better instructor, he was becoming less the humanist painter he had been. He was still telling students to "draw with human kindness." But in the city subjects that he did sketch and paint, the old warmth and joy in depicting the human scene came to be replaced with a coarser strain. In *Subway Stairs* of 1924 a man on the way up the stairs of a subway station takes note of what is revealed by the wind-uplifted skirt of a young woman descending above him, who clearly welcomes his interest.

Under *Reading in the Subway* of the same period, Sloan added lines from 17th century Cavalier poet Sir John Suckling, "Her feet beneath her petticoat/ Like little mice peeped in and out,/ As if they feared the light." Sloan's subway rider reading intently shows a good deal more than her peeping feet. The advertising card behind her makes sly reference to a popular ointment with the line "Rub with Sloan's Liniment." This was not John Sloan's earlier preference for "the wholesome kind of humor that comes out in ribaldry," as in his *Connoisseurs of Prints*. In *Subway Stairs* and *Reading in the Subway*, a lone woman is singled out for suggestive attention. There is a more prurient tone here than in Sloan's earlier joyous studies of femininity.

In any case, these were the increasingly rare efforts of Sloan the illustrator-artist. He had become more interested in finding the innate reality of objects by exploring their plastic forms. With this new absorption Sloan painted female nudes that were formal studies, not images of breathing, vital women. Their flesh he often suggested by cross-hatching. The human warmth of his earlier work was distorted at times into cruel mockery, as in a nude painting bereft of any sensuality in which the young woman holds a banner that reads "Miss Boston" covering her private parts. The public indifference to the later work was a matter of some satisfaction to Sloan. He said "If what I am doing now were selling I would think there was something the matter with it." When, near the end of his life, he was awarded the Gold Medal for painting by the American Academy of Arts and Letters, he said "It is a bad sign for a man of my kind to achieve recognition in his lifetime."

Sloan and Dolly would return to Santa Fe every year until Dolly's unexpected death in 1943 (both had fully believed that an ailing Sloan would go first). He then heard from Helen Farr who had been his devoted student when she was in her twenties, and had later collaborated with him in publishing his lecture notes. She was forty-one years younger than Sloan, but he was lonely and they were married a year later. John and Helen lived comfortably in the then-residential Chelsea Hotel in Greenwich Village in the winter, and in Santa Fe in the summer. Shuttling between pueblos and bohemia, they had little contact with Main Street America.

The pattern with Helen continued for seven years until 1951. By an odd twist, death came to John Sloan in New England, although far from Gloucester. He had developed a heart condition and that summer his doctors in New York convinced him that it would be dangerous to return to the high altitude of Santa Fe. He and Helen took a house in Hanover, New Hampshire. He had a cousin at Dartmouth, and eventually was enjoying a full social life, and doing some painting. But shortly after his eightieth birthday Sloan entered the local hospital to have an early-stage malignancy removed from his colon. It was a relatively minor operation, but following the surgery his health failed rapidly and he died within a few days.

Helen Farr Sloan devoted the remainder of her long life to perpetuating the artistic significance, not only of John Sloan but of all the Urban Realist painters who flourished in New York just after the turn of the century. Her advocacy first bore fruit with her encouragement of a young graduate student, Bennard Perlman, who spearheaded the reevaluation of these overlooked pioneers of a seminal American art movement with books such as his *Painters of the Ashcan School: The Immortal Eight.*

In 1960 Bruce St. John, director of the Delaware Art Museum in Wilmington, wrote to Helen that he was organizing a 50th anniversary tribute to the "Exhibition of Independent Artists" held in New York in 1910, and asked for her advice. Helen pitched in enthusiastically. She was also a willing resource when St. John edited the diaries that Sloan kept between 1906 and 1913. They were published by Harper & Row in 1965 as *John Sloan's New York Scene.* Helen decided that the Delaware Art Museum was the suitable place to concentrate her husband's work, and donated to the museum works by Sloan and his contemporaries, along with much archival material. A shrewd investor, she would enrich the museum with a gift of $4 million for the support of the 30,000-volume Helen Farr Sloan Library and Archives.

With the insistent efforts of Helen Farr Sloan, and the books and articles by the art historians she encouraged and assisted, John Sloan came gradually to be recognized as an American master. He would have been grateful to Helen, but not particularly interested in what the buying public or the artistic establishment thought about his work. The satisfaction John Sloan had found in life came from the exercise of his creative impulses. "My life has not been very eventful but my work has made it utterly worthwhile."

If Solomon Jacobs was whole cloth of the 19th century, John Sloan was a man of the 20th century when it was still new. Sloan was of a generation in revolt, reacting against the capitalism gone wild of the post-Civil War period. He was a product of the Progressive Era, liberal in his political and social views, opting out of the scramble for success in business and choosing, as did many of his contemporaries from the middle-class, a life in art at the fringe of capitalist society.

As the pre-eminent artist of urban humanism in the new era, Sloan earned a position as a marker along the highway of art history in America. He would later dismiss his earlier work as lacking in solidness. He wanted to move on to what he considered more significant formal art. But the history had already been written. Decades later Americans would rediscover and revalue this native artistic movement that had thrived in the cities and the beaches and the picnic grounds of the nation as it felt its way into the 20th century. In time John Sloan's lyrically earthy New York city paintings and drawings would be recognized as a special contribution to American art that caught the spirit of a representative corner of urban life in an era of transition.

When he came to Gloucester for those five summers that bracketed World War I, Sloan was middle-aged and his most characteristic work was behind him. Nevertheless, on the Gloucester shore he painted splendid works of an artist exploring himself and his art anew. He was no longer the young virtuoso inspired by the human comedy, but the mature master who responded more to light and tints and form in his distinctive interpretations of shore and sea, and portrayals of Dolly against the rocks, and neighborhood children in trees, and Gloucester street scenes.

Of the dozens of paintings Sloan completed during his five summers in the red cottage, about a half dozen have been recognized as top-drawer works: *Gloucester Trolley*; *Hill, Main Street, Gloucester*; *Main Street, Gloucester*; *Signals*; *Sunflowers, Rocky Neck*; *Glare on the Bay*; and *Old Cone*. (A personal favorite is *Evening, Rocky Neck* of 1916, now at the Hirshhorn Museum. Here a young woman leads two frolicking children by the hand toward fishermen's cottages at the end of Rocky Neck, the afterglow from a Wagnerian sunset seen between the houses and reflected off the boats moored in the choppy outer harbor. The figures are diminished in size, subordinate to the beauty of the setting and the magical spell of a breezy summer evening by the sea.)

Of the more familiar works, *Old Cone* is a figure study. *Sunflowers* and *Glare on the Bay* are seascapes that owe much to the Post-Impressionists, particularly van Gogh, in color and technique. (The alternative title for *Glare on the Bay* is the more accurate *Glare on Gloucester Harbor*.) The remainder of the paintings are in Sloan's signature style as illustrator-artist. *Gloucester Trolley*, the most frequently reproduced of Sloan's Gloucester works, is clearly anecdotal, incorporating Dolly. In *Hill, Main Street, Gloucester* there is the clattering career of the speeding roadster contrasted with the languid street scene. In *Main Street, Gloucester* there is the general hubbub of a small city shopping district. *Signals* is all pun: the dead-serious communication flags on the warship answered by the colorful garments strung on a line.

Typically of Sloan's early- to mid-period works, these are *audible* paintings. You hear the trolley clanging impatiently to get moving, and the old Mercedes backfiring as it tears down the hill, and the buzz of the street crowd, and even the flapping of the clothes on the line. John Sloan was moving away from anecdote toward challenges of color and form, but here still was the work of the illustrator-artist that would appeal across the generations. During his half-decade in Gloucester Sloan ranged over all of Cape Ann, painting the moors of East Gloucester up behind his cottage, the working harbor, the ledges against the sea, the dunes seen from Annisquam, the unpeopled inland of Dogtown Common where there were only red cedars (actually junipers), boulders and berry bushes.

Homer, Hopper and Sloan were probably the three best-known out-of-town artists who painted at one time or another in Gloucester. As it happened, not one of the three did his most representative work on Cape Ann – but that was no fault of the area. Homer produced some of his finest studies of youth on the Gloucester waterfront and up among the blueberry bushes on the Common, but he would be remembered best for the seascapes of his late years when he probed the primordial forces of nature at Prout's Neck. Hopper painted evocative character studies of houses when in Gloucester, but it was not until later that he would invest similar scenes with haunting atmosphere that critics are still attempting to interpret. By 1914 Sloan had already completed the works with which his name is most closely associated, the paintings and sketches of the achingly human life of a burgeoning New York City. Still, Sloan – like Homer and Hopper – did much important work in Gloucester. With maturing command of color and composition, Sloan achieved, in Gloucester in his 40s, works that claim an individual distinction in American art. "Five ... happy summers were spent in Gloucester,"

Sloan wrote later. "Each year we moved into our little red and white cottage and each day was passed in painting the dunes, the sky, the rocks, the bay, and sea."

A former Socialist, Sloan was a pacifist who railed, to anyone who would listen, against America's entry into World War I. But he was not anti-American. On the contrary, by opposing the war-mongers, decrying the economic evils in American society of his time, and arguing for a more equitable distribution of wealth, he saw himself as championing a return to traditional American values, setting the nation on the path to social justice. He said, "Patriotism, love of country, is very different from love for the government. I love the country in Pennsylvania, New England and in the Southwest. I love the streets of New York. But I am suspicious of all government because government is violence. ... It is not necessary to paint the American flag to be an American painter."

Ultimately, for Sloan, social and political issues were secondary. Painting was its own justification. "Art makes living worthwhile," he said. "Art brings life to life." Henry James, an artist in a different métier, had said the same thing in different words: "Art makes life, makes interest, makes importance."

Death often confers respectability, and in its obituary the *New York Times* called Sloan the "dean of American painters." Today most major American public and academic art museums include Sloan paintings and prints in their collections. In 2002 Sotheby's auctioned *Gray and Brass*, Sloan's 1907 oil of haughty persons of privilege being driven in an open car through Central Park. The auction house predicted the work would fetch between $2 ½ and $3½ million. Sloan's paintings are highly valued holdings of the Canajoharie Art Museum near Albany, the Delaware Art Museum, the Bowdoin College art museum and the Cape Ann Museum.

In 1971, twenty years after Sloan's death, America honored him with a commemorative stamp bearing the image of his painting, *Wake of the Ferry*. The issue was first placed on sale at Sloan's home town, Lock Haven. It was a distinct national honor for a man who had been at the fringes of a group considered subversive by the government during the First World War. The irony is that the honest American patriot, Capt. Solomon Jacobs, is nearly forgotten, while the pacifist John Sloan – whom the captain would probably have shunned as a slacker – is assured of enduring fame in the annals of American art.

They were two very different men, at the antipodes of human nature. Sloan with his admitted "Tabasco temper" and reputation as an artistic and ideological rebel was a social outcast most of his life. "Rebel with a paintbrush," Charles Poore called him, and said "no other great artist in our history has ever given the American people more outright pleasure or outraged pain than John Sloan." Capt. Solomon Jacobs confronted officials and business interests of various nations, deployed every advantage of skill and ingenuity to outfish his fellow captains, yet earned their admiration and friendship by excelling in the professional and human values they all valued most.

In pursuing their chosen professions mariner Jacobs and painter Sloan lived lives of almost baffling dissimilarity. And yet ... each shunned the calm, sheltered coves of a safe career and chanced deeper waters. Each manned the wheel of his career with gusto, flair, exuberance and truculent independence for that splinter of time allotted him.

There were other parallels between the sagas of these two. Sol and Sloan when young lost the reassurance of a strong, trusted father at their shoulders.

Sol and Sloan underwent an apprenticeship at a trade that was pulled from under them by obsolescence, but from which they salvaged useful skills.

They both remarried after the death of a first wife. In the case of Sol, that was scarcely a year later. For Sloan it was after forty years.

Each man achieved resounding success after he got started in his true career. For Sol, recognition and acclaim was immediate. For Sloan, appreciation of youthful accomplishments came much later.

Neither man would follow a steady upward career path. Sol was laid low by overconfidence. Sloan lost ground after being seduced by an ideology.

Each recovered his equilibrium, and in doing so produced mature results comparable to, although different from, the early triumphs.

Both men depended on their own skills to gain a livelihood. After their apprentice years neither wore another man's collar. (Sloan was paid regularly for the classes he taught at the Art Students League and elsewhere, but he was a very independent instructor.)

Both men ran for a political position. Sol was elected to a presidential nominating committee. Sloan was defeated for a judgeship.

Each man responded to the siren song of technology that promised great advances for mankind. Sol transformed an industry, though at no profit to himself. Sloan sought to apply a science of color harmonies to painting, but few followed his lead.

Each man felt a responsibility for others. For Sol this took the form of charitable giving and serving his community. Sloan strived to pass along to a new generation of artists the insights he had gained through long struggles.

Both men, vigorous and independent innovators in their time and in their separate worlds, contributed to the fabric of American society in the years between the 1880s and the 1920s. Solomon Jacobs as the adventurer seeking new frontiers; John Sloan the artist who absorbed the spirit of the era into his brush. America in their day needed both kinds.

NOTES

~~~

Chapter One : Launchings

Of Icebergs and Seal Oil

1 – **Toulinquet, the name given the place by French fishermen:** *Frommer's Nova Scotia, New Brunswick & Prince Edward Island* (2006), p. 257.

3 – **The English joined them in the 1570s:** Brian Fagan, *Fish on Friday: Feasting, Fasting and the Discovery of the New World.* New York: Basic Books, 2006, p. 240.

The most prominent of these enterprises was Slade & Co.: *Slade papers, 1791-1852,* Maritime History Archive, Memorial University of Newfoundland in St. John's, Newfoundland and Labrador.

Irish Quakers of the Jacobs, Penrose and Harvey families: Hans Rollmann, *Anglicans, Puritans, and Quakers in Sixteenth- and Seventeenth-Century Newfoundland.*

4 – **their son Simon baptized:** *Baptisms Solemnized in the Parish of Twillingate in the Island of Newfoundland 1816 through 1823.*

"a happy English parson": Mary M. Price, "Missionary Life in Newfoundland," *American Church Review,* Jan. 1891.

Simon Jacobs executed his will in 1852: *Will of Simon Jacobs* from Newfoundland Will Books, Vol. 2, pages 100-101, probate year 1852.

5 – **Mary Ann did promptly remarry:** *Twillingate Methodist Marriages,* from Parish Records, Box 2, PANL, 1853-1870, in NFGenWeb Parish and Church Records, Notre Dame Region. The archives of the *Twillingate Sun* are a mine of genealogical and historical information. It was the hometown newspaper of the Twillingate district from the 1880s to the 1950s.

There is a Jacobs family Methodist cemetery at Northern Bay: *Newfoundland's Grand Banks* website.

6 – **Newfoundland trap skiff:** *Duck Trap Woodworking* website.

he must begin to learn the trade at as young an age as possible: George Brown Goode, *The Fisheries and Fish Industries of the United States.* Washington, D.C.: Government Printing Office, 1887, Vol. IV (co-authored by Capt. Joseph W. Collins), p. 51.

"lay his hand on any rope in the dark": *The Fisheries and Fish Industries of the United States,* p. 51.

7 – **It was really a matter of interpreting signs:** *The Fisheries and Fish Industries of the United States.* p. 51.

Of Log Runs and Joinery

11 – **cabinetmakers for generations:** John Sloan, *John Sloan on Drawing and Painting (Gist of Art)*. Mineola, NY: Dover Publications, 1944, p. xi.

12 – **John's mother, who taught English at a "young ladies' academy":** David Scott, *John Sloan*. New York: Watson-Guptill Publications, 1975, p. 14. Helen Barr Sloan in *American Art Nouveau: The Poster Period of John Sloan* (unpaginated). Hammermill Paper Company, 1967.

James Sloan took a job as a traveling salesman: *American Art Nouveau: The Poster Period of John Sloan*.

13 – **"My great uncle Alexander Priestley had a wonderful library":** *John Sloan on Drawing and Painting (Gist of Art)*, p. xi.

14 – **John took a job as assistant cashier at Porter & Coates:** *John Sloan on Drawing and Painting (Gist of Art)*, p. xii.

15 – **"I was fortunate in having been brought up on books illustrated by Walter Crane":** *American Art Nouveau: The Poster Period of John Sloan*.

met a Japanese artist, Beizen Zubota: *American Art Nouveau: The Poster Period of John Sloan*. No results for Zubota were found in an online search for artists.

steadiest client was the Bradley Coal Company: *John Sloan on Drawing and Painting (Gist of Art)*, p. xiii.

"to protect some kind of talent": *John Sloan on Drawing and Painting (Gist of Art)*, p. xxvi.

art department of the *Philadelphia Inquirer:* *John Sloan on Drawing and Painting (Gist of Art)*, p. xiii.

Chapter Two : Apprentices to Obsolescence

Education Aloft

16 – **Black Ball line in the '60s:** *Boston Daily Globe*, Oct. 24, 1920.

17 – **"the dread of a belaying pin … kept them in submission":** Robert Greenhalgh Albion, *Square-Riggers on Schedule*. Princeton: Princeton University Press, 1938, p. 150.

one of the crew of the American ship *General Berry*: Obituary of Solomon Jacobs in *Gloucester Daily Times*, Feb. 9, 1922; also thomaston.mainememory.net (Thomaston, Maine website).

18 – **in his 60s in 1909, he was at his ease standing masthead watch:** Capt. Jacobs was master of the *Benjamin A. Smith* in the summer and fall of 1909 (Gordon Thomas, *Fast & Able: Life Stories of Great*

Gloucester Fishing Vessels. Beverly MA: Commonwealth Editions, fiftieth anniversary edition, 2002, p. 195). Sol was then sixty-two.

19 – **the ship *Western Empire*:** "Abner Stetson's Clipper Ship *Western Empire*, 1852" by Marjorie and Calvin Dodge, Sep. 3, 2008. Damariscotta Historical Society, in *Lincoln County News* archives online; also cited in interview with Solomon Jacobs by newspaper reporter in *Boston Daily Globe*, Oct. 24, 1920.

20 – **"I got my early training from 'down east' skippers":** 1919 newspaper clipping, probably *Gloucester Daily Times*, Box #1, Solomon Jacobs papers, Cape Ann Museum library.

most sailing vessels of other nationalities carried dingy-looking flax sails: "Life aboard Down Easters," *Fishermen's Voice*, Gouldsboro, Maine, Mar. 2005.

second mate on the *J. S. Winslow*: Obituary of Solomon Jacobs in *Gloucester Daily Times*, Feb. 9, 1922; Gordon Thomas, "The Invincible Sol Jacobs" in *North Shore* supplement, Jan. 25, 1975. For information on the *J.S. Winslow*, see American Lloyd, *Register of American and Foreign Shipping*, 1870-83; The *Commercial & Financial Chronicle* and *Hunt's Merchants' Magazine*, Vol. 44, May 6, 1871.

21 – **The *Winslow* sailed south from Savannah:** The voyages of the *J.S. Winslow* from 1869 to 1872 were researched by David Dearborn, Research Assistant at the Maine Maritime Museum, Bath, Maine, making use of the superb resources of the museum's archives.

23 – **one forty-eighth share of a full-rigged ship at Castine was priced at $895:** Wayne O'Leary, *Maine Sea Fisheries*. Boston: Northeastern University Press, 1966, p. 25.

College of the Artist Reporters

25 – **"Work out abstract problems of design":** *John Sloan on Drawing and Painting (Gist of Art)*, p. xiii.

"I made illustrations for serialized stories": *American Art Nouveau: The Poster Period of John Sloan.*

"I prefer the wholesome kind of humor": *American Art Nouveau: The Poster Period of John Sloan.*

"used to go out on Sundays": St. John, Bruce, ed. *John Sloan's New York Scene.* New York: Harper & Row, 1965. Jun. 14, 1908, p. 226. The body text of *John Sloan's New York Scene* consists mainly of Sloan's diaries 1906-13. In subsequent citations from the diaries I will give only the date of the diary entry.

26 – **Sloan first met Robert Henri:** *John Sloan on Drawing and Painting (Gist of Art)*, p. xiii. Also Annie Cohen Cohen-Solal, *Painting*

American: The Rise of American Artists. New York: Alfred A. Knopf, 2001, p. 165.

27 – **"we became painters because Robert Henri had that magic ability"**: William Inness Homer, *Robert Henri and His Circle*, Ithaca, NY, Cornell University Press, 1969, p. 76.

28 – **"I rate Hogarth as the greatest English artist"**: *John Sloan on Drawing and Painting (Gist of Art)*, p. 2.

Espoused the agnosticism of Robert G. Ingersoll: *Robert Henri and His Circle*, p. 78.

Chapter Three : Redirected Lives
A Born Fisherman

31 – **Now the harbor teemed with vessels**: George Procter, *The Fishermen's Memorial & Record Book*. Gloucester: Procter Brothers, 1873, p. 97.

32 – **one of the most devastating for the Gloucester fleet**: *The Fishermen's Memorial & Record Book*, p. 53.

33 – **Quote from Fitz J. Babson, collector of customs at Gloucester**: *The Fisheries and Fish Industries of the United States*, Vol. IV, pp. 14-15.

34 – **went to Boston where he was naturalized**: *Gloucester Voters' List*, 1874, CC33, in Gloucester City Archives.

went as a "hand" in the schooner Nevada: Obituary, *Gloucester Daily Times*, Feb. 9, 1922; "The Invincible Sol Jacobs."

master of the schooner Sabine: Jacobs obituary, *Gloucester Daily Times*, Feb. 9, 1922; Pamphlet, *A Park Named for a Fisherman: Captain Solomon Jacobs*, in Box #1, Solomon Jacobs papers, Cape Ann Museum library.

Drawings for a "Light-Weight Dickens"

36 – **a job at the New York Herald**: *Revolutionaries of Realism: The Letters of John Sloan and Robert Henri*, ed. Bennard B. Perlman. Princeton, NJ: Princeton University Press, 1997, p. 28; *John Sloan on Drawing and Painting (Gist of Art)*, p. xvi.

French author Charles Paul de Kock: Peter Morse, introductory essay "John Sloan, Printmaker," in *John Sloan Etchings. A Selection of Etchings by John Sloan from the Philadelphia Museum of Art, exhibited at University of Missouri, March 3-24, 1967*. Columbia, MO: University of Missouri Press, 1967; *John Sloan on Drawing and Painting (Gist of Art)*, p. xvii.

"a sort of light-weight Dickens": *American Art Nouveau: The Poster Period of John Sloan.*

37 – **a syndicated Sunday supplement**: *American Art Nouveau: The Poster Period of John Sloan; John Sloan on Drawing and Painting (Gist of Art)*, p. xxi.

Chapter Four : Mating Calls
Eligible Widower

38 – **Elizabeth McCabe from Halifax**: *Vital Records, Marriages*, Vol. 1, p. 29 #15, Feb. 25, 1875, in Gloucester City Archives.
followed the child into the grave: *Vital Records, Deaths*, Vol. 1, p. 49, Sep. 1, 1876 and Vol. 1, p. 51, Oct. 18, 1876, in Gloucester City Archives.
twenty-two-year-old Sarah MacQuarrie: *History of Inverness County, Nova Scotia*, Chapter XI – Melville and Barberton; *Vital Records, Marriages*, Vol. 1, p. 89 #138, Nov. 1, 1877, in Gloucester City Archives. In marriage record Sarah's parental name was spelled as "McQuarrie," and her birthplace given erroneously as Gloucester.

39 – **Sarah would be comforted to have a sister living close by**: *History of Inverness County, Nova Scotia*; Chapter XI - Melville and Barberton, in *ElectricScotland.com*.

"Ludicrated" Lovers

40 – **"a common woman met up on the street"**: Letter from Henri to Sloan, Sep. 1898, quoted in *Revolutionaries of Realism*, p. 28.
Dolly and a friend joined them for drinks at a rathskeller: Letter from Sloan to Henri, Oct. 1, 1898, quoted in *Revolutionaries of Realism*, p. 28.
In 1901 Sloan married ... Dolly: *John Sloan on Drawing and Painting (Gist of Art)*, p. xvii.

41 – **neurosis she was seeing Dr. Collier Bower about**: *John Sloan's New York Scene*, p. xvi.

42 – **"She has a dear way of keeping me going"**: Sloan diaries, Aug. 28, 1906.

43 – **"Solomon Jacobs by S.M. Jacobs"**: Box #1, Solomon Jacobs papers, Cape Ann Museum library.

Chapter Five : Getting Under Way
Other Men's Boats

45 – **probably carried a quadrant, or a sextant**: *The Fisheries and Fish Industries of the United States*, p. 102.

typically the crew would make a set in the afternoon: The cycle of tub trawling I've given as an example is from Henry L. Osborne's account of a trip he made to the Grand Bank in the Gloucester schooner *Victor* in 1879, quoted in *The Fisheries and Fish Industries of the United States*, p, 75.

46 –   **in the *Sabine* he brought back 17,000 pounds of cod**: *A Park Named for a Fisherman: Captain Solomon Jacobs.*

Samuel Lane & Brothers signed him on: Wesley George Pierce, *Goin' Fishin': The Story of the Deep-Sea Fishermen of New England.* Salem: Marine Research Society, 1934, pp. 185-193; *Gloucester Daily Times*, Feb. 9, 1922.

hull down with 124,000 pounds of cod and halibut: George Procter, *The Fishermen's Own Book*. Gloucester: Procter Bros., 1882, p. 31.

47 –   **Sol's mackerel catches averaged a value of $14,000**: Clipping from unidentified Newfoundland newspaper, Jun. 1978, in vertical file for Solomon Jacobs, Sawyer Free Library.

A description of a "mackerel catcher": *Fishermen's Own Book*, "A Mackerel Catcher Dressing Her Fare by Moonlight," p. 215.

48 –   **"The Merry, Merry Mackerel Catchers" appeared**: *Fishermen's Own Book*, p. 169.

49 –   **what the Procter brothers called the "Fortune Bay Riot"**: *The Fishermen's Own Book*, pp. 109-112.

50 –   **It was a colorful, but fanciful, version of what really happened**: Depositions of witnesses in *House of Commons Papers*, Vol. 77, Session 5, Dec. 1878 – 15 Aug. 1879.

51 –   **perhaps the entire treaty should be revisited**: Letter from William M. Evarts, U.S. Secretary of State to John Welsh, U.S. Ambassador to London, Sep. 28, 1878, to be communicated to Marquis of Salisbury, British Foreign Secretary.

52 –   **Jim MacQuarrie had been lost overboard**: *History of Inverness County, Nova Scotia,* Chapter XI - Melville and Barberton; *Fishermen's Own Book*, p. 77 (where his name is spelled McQuarrie).

the *Moses Adams* was caught in a gale: *The Fishermen's Own Book*, p. 77.

Illustrator for Hire

53 –   **"I think all real art has an element of illustration in it"**: *American Art Nouveau: The Poster Period of John Sloan.*

56 –   **Henri's 2nd wife named Organ**: Sloan diaries Oct. 29, 1908, Nov. 26, 1908.

it is above all a personal document: By some accounts, Dr. Bower urged Sloan to keep a diary and enter favorable comments on Dolly, so that when Dolly sneaked a look she would see that her husband valued her. It is hard to believe that John Sloan would have entered into this devious approach to building his wife's self-esteem. In the years he kept the diary he carefully recorded his creative motivations and chronicled the stimulating milieu in which he and Dolly found themselves in turn-of-the-century New York.

"lives in a garret studio with me": Sloan diaries, Jul. 28, 1906.

"neither Dolly nor I have a whole regret": Sloan diaries, Aug. 5, 1911.

57 – **"I feel so rottenly ashamed of myself"**: Sloan diaries, Jun. 30, 1911. **Kent left to travel alone**: Sloan diaries, Oct. 13, 1910. Subsequent entries relate the discomforts the Sloans endured as friends and neighbors of the Kents.

58 – **a turkey that Sloan estimated "was about twice her size"**: Sloan diaries, Nov. 24, 1910. **"warm shower of reminiscences"**: Sloan diaries, Apr. 16, 1910. **presided over the outdoor boarding house dinners at Petitpas**: Sloan diaries, Aug. 11, 1910.

59 – **famous poet son William Butler Yeats joined the company**: Sloan diaries, Oct. 11, 1911.

Chapter Six : Early Triumphs
"King of the Mackerel Killers"

61 – **the *Sarah M. Jacobs* joined the Gloucester fleet**: Box #1, Solomon Jacobs papers, Cape Ann Museum library; Enrollment of Vessels, Custom House, Gloucester, Apr. 14, 1879. Records at National Archives, Northeast Branch, Waltham, MA. Includes notation that Jacobs confirmed that he was a U.S. citizen (and thus qualified to be master of a documented vessel).

only one fisherman in a hundred was able to move up: *Maine Sea Fisheries*, p. 209.

62 – **became half-owner ... of the *Edward E. Webster*:** *Enrollment of Vessels*, Custom House, Gloucester, Mar. 18, 1880.

first ... to arrive at the New York market with a trip of fish in 1879: "Early Catches of Mackerel in 1879," *Bulletin of the United States Fish Commission, 1883*.

In 1880 Sol in the *Webster* was again the first to land a trip in New York: In an undated letter to "The Lookout" in the *Gloucester Daily Times*, Billy Pierce wrote to say he remembered Capt. Sol sailing for the southern mackerel fishery in the *Webster* on March 3 one year. Pierce watched the *Webster* cast off from Samuel Lane's wharf flying "a red pennant and a yellow one."

250 barrels of mackerel: *Bulletin of the United States Fish Commission, 1883*, pp. 273-285.

63 – **A new seine cost $1,000 to $1,500**: *Maine Sea Fisheries*. p. 170.

marine insurance did not cover trawls: *Maine Sea Fisheries*, pp. 173-4.

He reasoned that the fish had learned to dive: *Twillingate Sun*, Mar. 11, 1922.

his big catch commanded a premium: *Twillingate Sun*, Mar. 11, 1922.

64 – **Forty-five boarding houses in Gloucester**: *Gloucester City Directory*, 1885.

twenty-two Gloucester vessels manned entirely by temperance men: *The Fisheries and Fish Industries of the United States*, Vol. IV, p. 71.

There were thirty-two saloons in town: *Gloucester City Directory*, 1885.

65 – **"no getting to windward of him"**: *The Fisheries and Fish Industries of the United States*, Vol. IV, p. 18. The details of the impromptu dance are based on the account in that section of Vol. IV.

66 – **you'll be caught up in a fishnet thrown over you both**: The Newfoundland marriage customs of the period are described in an article on Newfoundland fishermen in the *Cape Ann Advertiser*, Jan. 15, 1875, quoted on Vol. IV, pp. 17-18 of *The Fisheries and Fish Industries of the United States*.

The vessel was officially enrolled as the *Molly Adams*: *Enrollment of Vessels*, Custom House, Gloucester, Mar. 29, 1887.

67 – **entered Port Mulgrave ... in need of water**: *Compilation of Reports of Senate Committee on Foreign Relations, 1789-1901*, Item notes, Vol. 5; Affidavit of Solomon Jacobs in the Case of the *Molly Adams*.

He fed the rescued men for three days: Letter from T. F. Brayard, U.S. Secretary of State. Protest to Sir L. West, in which he encloses letter to him from Capt. Jacobs of Nov. 12, 1886. In *North Atlantic Coast Fisheries – By Permanent Court of Arbitration*, United States, Great Britain.

68 – **"the fishermen are at the mercy of a class of officials hostile to them"**: Letter from T. F. Brayard, U.S. Secretary of State. Protest to Sir L. West, in which he encloses letter to him from Capt. Jacobs of Nov. 12, 1886.

members of the Gloucester fishing community rallied to Sol's defense: *New York Times*, Sep. 1889.

69 – "we will make catches with a battleship alongside": *Detroit Tribune*, Dec. 23, 1902.

"Sloans"

"with a housekeeper mistress on the side": *American Art Nouveau; The Poster Period of John Sloan.*

70 – what Sloan called "eyesight painting": *Robert Henri and His Circle*, p. 83.

to the Durand-Ruel Gallery ... to see "Monet's several fine things": Sloan diaries, Jan. 29, 1907.

71 – "Don't imitate the color in nature": *John Sloan on Drawing and Painting (Gist of Art)*, pp. 162-163.

"We painted the life we knew as Balzac had drawn the French world he lived in.": *Robert Henri and His Circle*, p. 84.

"always fascinating, like a woman's smile": Avis Berman, "Artist as Rebel: John Sloan versus the Status Quo," *The Smithsonian*, Apr, 1988.

72 – "I liked their fine human animal spirits": Rebecca Zurier, *Art for The Masses*. Philadelphia: Temple University Press, 1988, p. 143.

"the poetic beauty of things seen when I moved about the city": *John Sloan: A Painter's Life*, p. 99.

73 – "bleached blond dresser bleaching the hair of a client": Sloan diaries, Jun. 5-10, 1907.

"bits of joy in human life": *John Sloan on Drawing and Painting (Gist of Art)*, p. xxviii.

76 – William Macbeth agreed to host the show: For details on the 1908 exhibition of The Eight at the Macbeth Gallery see William Inness Homer, "The Exhibition of The Eight: Its History and Significance," *American Art Journal*, Vol. 1, No. 1, Spring 1969, p. 60, and Victor G. Wexler, "Creating a Market in American Art: The Contribution of the Macbeth Gallery," *Journal of American Studies*, Vol. 25, No. 2, Aug. 1991, pp. 249-250.

"New York is having an art war": Cover page of Feb., 1908 issue of *World Magazine*, quoted in "Creating a Market in American Art: The Contribution of the Macbeth Gallery."

"apostles of ugliness": Biography of Henri in *Gale Encyclopedia of Biography*.

"The *Tribune* has a sermon for us": "Creating a Market in American Art: The Contribution of the Macbeth Gallery."

77 – **"We've made a success!"**: "The Exhibition of The Eight: Its History and Significance," p. 60.

"Is the exhibition game lost for me?": Sloan diaries, Apr. 17, 1912.

The insurgents would hold a non-juried show: See Robert Henri's account of the Exhibition of Independent Artists in *The Craftsman*, May 19, 1910.

In 1913 the American art world was turned on its ear: News and reviews of the Armory Show have been digitized and posted online as the "Walt Kuhn, Kuhn Family Papers, and Armory Show Records" at the *Archives of American Art*, Smithsonian Institution.

78 – **"I have not been so dry a reed"**: Letter from Sloan to John Quinn, Nov. 24, 1912, quoted in Grant Holcomb, *John Sloan: The Gloucester Years*, pp. 9-10.

79 – **Albert Barnes purchased *Nude, Green Scarf***: *John Sloan's New York Scene*, p. 11.

"I regret that the artist must *sell* his work": William M. Murphy, *Prodigal Father: The Life of John Butler Yeats*. Ithaca, NY: Cornell University Press, 1978, p. 370. Murphy quotes Sloan as saying this upon sale of a painting to Quinn, not to Barnes.

Camille Corot's mock dismay at finally selling his first painting: Sheldon Cheney, *The Story of Modern Art*. New York: Viking Press (Mid-Century Edition).

Chapter Seven : Straying Off Course

Northwest Passages

82 – **"We select ... the best located lots for investors"**: *Cape Ann Advertiser*, Apr. 20, 1888.

The *Northwest* published by the Northern Pacific Railroad: *History & Literature of the Pacific Northwest*, at www.washington.edu.

83 – **the town gave the *Adams* and *Webster* a glorious sendoff**: *Cape Ann Advertiser*, Oct. 28, 1887; *Twillingate Sun*, Nov. 27, 1887.

"all the vigor that has characterized his career": *Cape Ann Advertiser*, Oct. 28, 1887.

84 – **The *Adams* and the *Webster* carried Newfoundland sealing punts**: *Cape Ann Advertiser*, Oct. 28, 1887; Howard Chapelle, *American Small Sailing Craft*. New York: W.W. Norton, 1951, p. 90.

rugged fellows with solid sealing credentials: *Twillingate Sun*, Jan. 28, 1888.

His peers had organized the dinner: *Cape Ann Advertiser*, Feb. 10, 1888. The article describes the testimonial event, with highlights of the speeches. An invitation to the dinner is in Box #1, Solomon Jacobs papers, Cape Ann Museum library.

87 – **Sol and the other passengers would appreciate the steam heat**: Rudolph Daniels, *Trains Across the Continent*. Bloomington, Indiana: University of Indiana Press, 2000, p. 94.

It is possible that they were aboard one of the new vestibule trains: William F. Thompson and Norman L. Freeman, "History of the Pacific Halibut Fishery," in *Report of the International Fisheries Commission*, No. 5, 1930.

a dramatic climb over Stampede Pass: *Trains Across the Continent*, p. 55.

88 – **Mollie Adams already in the harbor**: Letter from F. Howard Bell, American Institute of Fishing Research Biologists to Salvatore Favazza, Executive Secretary, Gloucester Fisheries Commission, Dec. 24.1974. In Box #1, Solomon Jacobs papers, Cape Ann Museum library.

89 – **seals "as thick as they could swim"**: Letter to Senator Joseph N. Dolph of Oregon from James G. Swan, Assistant Collector, Port Townsend, Washington Territory, Mar. 7, 1888, "Relative to Fur Seals in the Waters of Alaska and the Behring's Sea." In *Fur Seal Arbitration*, by Bering Sea Tribunal of Arbitration, Appendix of Case of Great Britain, p. 213.

Four days after he arrived in Port Townsend, Sol took the *Adams* on a sealing voyage: Letter from F. Heward Bell to Salvatore Favazza.

it was entirely a tale of woe : *New York Times*, May 13, 1888.

90 – **The *Oscar and Hattie* had been built in Essex**: Salvatore Favazza quoting Gordon Thomas, in letter to Gloucester City Council, Mar. 3, 1975. In Solomon Jacobs vertical file, Sawyer Free Library.

91 – **a moment of triumph for the *Oscar and Hattie***: *History of the Pacific Halibut Fishery*, Report of the International Commission.

He gave glowing interviews to the California newspapers: *Daily Alta California*, San Francisco, Jul. 11, 1888, p. 5.

"recommend it to all as an A-1 article": Letter from Jacobs in Port Townsend Mar. 4, 1888 to James H. Tarr Company, in Box #1, Solomon Jacobs papers, Cape Ann Museum Library. The Tarr company quoted Jacobs' testimonial in an ad for their copper paint.

92 – **The captain had reason to suspect that the halibut trust**: *Science*, published by American Association for the Advancement of Science, Item notes, Vol.12, Jul-Dec 1888.

formally organized the Master Mariners' Association: "Master Mariners Organize," *Boston Daily Globe*, Mar. 20, 1888. The organization has been variously titled with or without apostrophe, and either as single or plural possessive.

On March 22 the members elected officers: *Cape Ann Advertiser*, Mar. 22, 1888.

an "elegant marble-top table" was donated by Mrs. Solomon Jacobs: *Cape Ann Advertiser*, Apr. 5, 1888.

93 — the wily skippers prevailed: *Boston Daily Globe*, Mar. 10, 1896.

the *Webster* would be seized forthwith: *Cape Ann Advertiser*, Aug. 9, 1889.

94 — waters controlled by the Alaska Commercial Company: For the dispute between the U.S. and Great Britain over sealing rights in the Bering Sea, see "Behring Sea Arbitration," Vol. 3, p. 777 of 1910 *Encyclopedia Britannica*.

95 — "What the fishermen want": Letter from Solomon Jacobs, Master of schooner *Mollie Adams*, May 24, 1889, in Vol. 1, *Senate Relations with Canada*, Senate Committee on Relations with Canada, by United States Congress.

96 — claiming that he owed Baxter nothing: *Boston Daily Globe*, Mar. 1, 1890. "Capt. Jacobs of Gloucester Locked Up – Sensation Created"; also Portland, Oregon *Oregonian*, Feb. 17, 1890, quoted in *Gloucester Daily Times*, Feb. 28, 1890, p. 1.

enjoyed the personal hospitality of Mayor Grant of Victoria: "The Invincible Sol Jacobs."

97 — reports of the demise of the *Webster* were greatly exaggerated: *Gloucester Daily Times*, Oct. 4, 1889.

The Masses

98 — "I'm not a Democrat. I'm of no party": Robert Hughes, *American Visions*. New York: Knopf, 1997, pp. 326-327.

Charles Wisner Barrell had been calling on Sloan: *Robert Henri and His Circle*, p. 181.

99 — joined Branch One of the Socialist Party: Van Wyck Brooks, *John Sloan: A Painter's Life*. New York; E. P. Dutton, 1955, p. 97.

100 — he ran for a judgeship and was defeated: Rebecca Zurier, *Art for The Masses*. Philadelphia: Temple University Press, 1988, p. 56.

Sloan also attempted to sway Bill Glackens: Ira Glackens, *William Glackens and the Ashcan Group*. New York: Crown Publishers, 1957, pp. 125-136.

felt he had "passed the feverish stage": Sloan Diaries, Dec. 19, 1909.

"offends so many people": *Prodigal Father: The Life of John Butler Yeats*, p. 476.

people relied on the printed word: Carl F. Kaestle, "Literacy and Diversity: Themes from a Social History of the American Reading Public," in *History of Education Quarterly*, Vol. 28, No. 4 (Winter 1988), p. 528.

101 — **"the sense of universal revolt and regeneration"**: Ross Wetzsteon, *Republic of Dreams: Greenwich Village, The American Bohemia, 1910-1960*. New York: Simon & Schuster, 2002, p. 54.

102 — **"tiny, vital, scrappy, devoted"**: Lloyd Goodrich, *John Sloan*. New York: MacMillan, 1952, p. 43.

Dolly helped to shelter the children: *Art for The Masses*, p. 32.

"mothering all 200 of them": Sloan diaries, Mar. 30, 1912.

John Sloan and Art Young contributed to *The Coming Nation*: For an account of this predecessor to *The Masses*, see "The Coming Nation: The Masses' Country Cousin," by Kent Kreuter & Gretchen Kreuter. *American Quarterly*, Vol. 19, No.3 (Autumn 1967), pp. 583-586.

103 — **Its credo was stated by Eastman**: John Sayer, "Art and Politics, Dissent and Repression: *The Masses* Magazine versus the Government, 1917-1918," in *The American Journal of Legal History*, Vol. 32, No. 1 (Jan. 1988), pp. 42-78.

Articles and poetry celebrated the liberated "New Woman": Stephen L. Vaughn, *Encyclopedia of American Journalism*, p. 295.

104 — **"had all saloons been conducted with the dignity and decorum of McSorley's"**: John Sloan, *Gist of Art*, American Artists Group, 1939, p. 305. This earlier edition of *Gist of Art*, dedicated by Sloan to "Dolly Sloan, the little woman who has been my right hand man," includes reproductions of a number of Sloan's paintings, with his comments on each.

105 — **"What I liked about *The Masses*"**: Cristina Bishop, excerpt from catalogue essay, *Drawing in the New York Scene: Sloan and Socialism in Greenwich Village*.

"I never allowed social propaganda to get into my paintings": *Art for The Masses*, p. 56.

"I put the hatred into cartoons in *The Masses*": *John Sloan on Drawing and Painting (Gist of Art)*, pp. 4-5.

106 — **"vigorous and combative personality"**: *Spartacus Educational* online.

"no longer was fun": *John Sloan: A Painter's Life*, p. 97.

Chapter Eight : Second Winds

The Ethel B. Jacobs

108 – **The *Ethel B. Jacobs* ... registered by Sol Jacobs as the sole owner**: *Enrollment of Vessels*, Custom House, Gloucester, May 9, 1891.

new look that Edward "Ned" Burgess was bringing to schooner design: W.M.P. Dunne, *Thomas F. McManus and the American Fishing Schooners: An Irish-American Success Story*. Mystic, CT: Mystic Seaport Museum, Inc., 1994, pp. 149, 151, 176.

109 – **agreed to take William Jordan's schooner *Brunhild***: "Capt. Jacobs Erred," *Boston Daily Globe*, Apr. 5, 1891; "The Invincible Sol Jacobs."

110 – **Each man had an enclosed berth**: Raymond McFarland in *A History of New England Fisheries*. Philadelphia: University of Pennsylvania, 1911 McFarland describes the amenities typical of a first-class mackerel schooner of the period.

111 – **the medicine chest in his cabin was replenished**: *The Fisheries and Fish Industries of the United States*, p. 91.

Sol "doctored him from his medicine chest": *Boston Daily Globe*, Dec. 22, 1902.

112 – **"a smother of canvas kites"**: *Boston Daily Globe*, Mar. 27,1897.

"*Ethel B.* was the best of them all": *Goin' Fishin': The Story of the Deep-Sea Fishermen of New England*, p. 187.

113 – **a man possessed of "pluck, push, energy, vigilance, character"**: Article in *The Fisherman*, 1895, in Box #1, Solomon Jacobs papers, Cape Ann Museum library.

"the most daring and intrepid mariner of the Gloucester fishing fleet": *Gloucester Daily Times*, Feb. 9, 1922.

Sol welcomed on board a Col. Russell: Undated newspaper clipping in Box #1, Solomon Jacobs papers, Cape Ann Museum library.

114 – **Some of the tackle hit Sol in the eye**: "Ship News," *Twillingate Sun*, Feb. 10, 1894.

Sol spread every inch of canvas: *Goin' Fishin': The Story of the Deep-Sea Fishermen of New England*, pp.185-193. In these pages Wesley Pierce gives a dramatic account of purse seining for mackerel in the *Ethel B.* under Capt. Sol.

115 – **It blew a gale all day**: Several authors of Gloucester maritime histories have written accounts of "the race it blew." See James B. Connolly, *The Book of the Gloucester Fishermen*. New York: John Day, 1930, pp, 85-101; Joseph E. Garland, *Down to the Sea*: Boston: David R. Godine, 1983, pp. 175-176; Dana Story, *Hail Columbia!* Gloucester: Ten Pound Island Book Co., 1985.

116 – **the captain-host of a birding expedition**: The Frank B. Webster company conducted a number of natural history expeditions in those years, including one in 1905-06 sponsored by the California Academy of Sciences to study "the gigantic land tortoises of the Galapagos Archipelago."

117 – **"having scoured the grounds for seals with his accustomed energy"**: *Boston Daily Globe*, Jul. 27, 1897.

"a flat little river, something like the Annisquam": *Boston Daily Globe*, Jul. 27, 1897.

118 – **"I know the country and how best to get there"**: *Boston Daily Globe*, Jul. 27, 1897.

arrived fourteen days later off the Irish coast: *Twillingate Sun* Mar. 11, 1922; John Leather, *The Gaff Rig Handbook: History, Design, Techniques, Developments*. Brooklin, ME: WoodenBoat Books, 2001, p. 797.

119 – **the patronage of an English noblewoman**: The *Twillingate Sun* said the benefactress was a countess, but it was very likely Baroness Angela Burdett-Coutts, "the richest heiress in England." Among her many charitable initiatives, Burdett-Coutts promoted the fishing industry in Ireland by "fitting out smacks and luggers" to compete with Billingsgate fishmongers and provide the common people with cheap fresh fish. *Boston Daily Globe*, Dec. 3, 1882, p. 12.

Ethel B. under the command of ... William Cluett: *Boston Daily Globe*, Oct. 27, 1899, p. 11; *Richfield Springs Daily*, Richfield Springs, NY, Jul. 24, 1900.

Seventeen men from the wrecked vessel were given shelter: With regard to compensation for rescue of the survivors, see *Questions before British House of Commons*, HC Deb, 11 May, 1900, Vol. 82, cc1368-9, Wreck of the American Schooner "Ethel B. Jacobs."

Capt. Jacobs for his part filed a claim of $25,000: undated newspaper clipping in Box #2, Solomon Jacobs papers, Cape Ann Museum library.

"A Good Outing"

121 – **"to have a vacation of several months in the country"**: Quoted by Helen Farr Sloan in Foreword to *The Red Cottage*, a booklet published in conjunction with exhibition at Cape Ann Historical Association (now Cape Ann Museum), May 29 – Sep. 26, 1992.

122 – **William Morris Hunt took his popular Boston art class ... to Annisquam**: "I have just returned from the usual sketching expedition which the Hunt class makes yearly. This time a little village called Annisquam beyond Gloucester was chosen and we spent ten days

there delightfully, sketching morning & afternoon, and the interval filled by many talks about this world & the next after the fashion of Boston women." Letter from Elizabeth (Lizzie) Boott, who would later marry Frank Duveneck, to Henry James, Jun. 13, 1874. From Cambridge ALS Houghton, bMS Am 1094 (32).

123 – **Others from the Pont-Aven crowd followed Picknell:** For American artists who migrated to Annisquam, and then Rocky Neck, from Pont-Aven for summer painting see William H. Gerdts, "John Twachtman and the Artistic Colony in Gloucester at the Turn of the Century," in exhibition catalogue, *Twachtman in Gloucester: His Last Years, 1900-1902.* New York: Spanierman Gallery, 1987; also *Painting American: The Rise of American Artists*, pp. 49-136; and Richard H. Love, *Carl W. Peters: American Scene Painter from Rochester to Rockport.* Rochester, NY; University of Rochester Press, 1999, pp. 251-252. Love gives as his authority David Sellin, *William Lamb Picknell, 1853-1897*, exhibition catalogue, Washington, D.C.: Taggart & Jorgensen Gallery, 1991.

125 – **Maxfield Parrish studied there under his father, Stephen:** *Maxfield Parris: A Retrospective*, by Laurence S. Cutler, Maxfield Parrish, Judy Goffman Cutler. ASaP of Holderness, 1995, p. 158. Maxfield was in Annisquam with his father, Stephen, in 1892. Stephen returned in 1893.

126 – **N.C. Wyeth ... studied under George L. Noyes at Annisquam in 1901:** David Michaelis, *N.C. Wyeth: A Biography.* New York: Perennial, 2003, p. 38; *Richard J. Boyle, "John Twachtman's Gloucester Years,"* in *Twachtman in Gloucester: His Last Years, 1900-1902.* New York: Spanierman Gallery exhibition, May 12 – Jun. 13, 1987, pp. 18-19.

painted in Annisquam while staying with the Williamses: Richard Wattenmaker, *Maurice Prendergast.* New York: Harry N. Abrams, Inc., 1994, pp. 74-5.

They had married after a long-delayed love affair: For an excellent account of the tragic history of Duveneck and Elizabeth Boott, see "Frank Duveneck & Elizabeth Boott Duveneck: An American Romance," by Carol M. Osborne, C*atalogue of Frank Duveneck & Elizabeth Boott Duveneck Exhibition*, Owen Gallery, New York, Feb. 12 – Mar. 23, 1996.

In Gloucester ... Twachtman's work was more forceful: For Twachtman in Gloucester, see articles by John Douglas Hale and Richard J. Boyle in catalogue, *Twachtman in Gloucester: His Last Years, 1900-1902.* Spanierman Gallery exhibition, May 12 – Jun. 13, 1987.

129 – **"no trouble with seasickness"**: Postcard from Sloan in Boston to Dolly in New York, Jun. 30, 1914. John Sloan Manuscript Collection, Delaware Art Museum.

arrived in Gloucester where the weather was cold: Postcard from Sloan in Gloucester to Dolly in New York, Jul. 1914. John Sloan Manuscript Collection, Delaware Art Museum.

"I can never tell you what it meant to me": Letter from Marianna ("Nattie") Sloan to John Sloan, summer 1914. John Sloan Manuscript Collection, Delaware Art Museum.

"Jack" would be overjoyed with the cake: Letter from Nattie to Dolly, Aug. 1914. John Sloan Manuscript Collection, Delaware Art Museum.

130 – **"And oh, do cherish her, for she is a frail little life"**: Letter from Nattie to John Sloan, summer 1914. John Sloan Manuscript Collection, Delaware Art Museum.

"smash moulds and declare liberty": Grant Holcomb, *John Sloan: The Gloucester Years*. Springfield, MA; Springfield Library and Museums Association for the Springfield Museum of Fine Arts, 1980, p. 11.

"one of the old corners of America": *John Sloan: The Gloucester Years*, p. 12.

"a good outing of works": *John Sloan: The Gloucester Years*, p. 11.

"the best means of advance in color and spontaneous design": *Gist of Art*, 1939 edition, p. 240.

131 – **"ambushed by a cop on horseback"**: Stuart Davis *Autobiography*, 1945, p. 106, quoted in Karen Wilkin, *Stuart Davis in Gloucester*. West Stockbridge, MA: Hard Press, Inc., 1999.

132 – **"We play at a game of cards called pounce"**: Letter from Stuart Davis to a cousin, Aug. 5, 1915. Quoted in *Stuart Davis in Gloucester*, p. 17.

his "Italian wife-beater music": Foreword to *The Red Cottage*.

133 – **Dolly thought it shocking**: *Prodigal Father: The Life of John Butler Yeats*, p. 415.

"you must work out your own salvation": *John Butler Yeats and John Sloan: The Records of a Friendship*, p. 20.

arrange for Yeats to give a lecture in Gloucester: *John Butler Yeats and John Sloan: The Records of a Friendship*, p. 16.

135 – **Sloan recommended that he include Glackens**: Letter postmarked Gloucester, Sep. 18, 1916, from John Sloan to Dr. John Weichsel. John Sloan Manuscript Collection, Delaware Art Museum.

"the prestige which my exhibition at 8 W. 8 established": Flora Miller Biddle, *The Whitney Women: A Family Memoir*. New York: Arcade Publishing, 1999.

136 –   **invited submissions from all and sundry**: For the 1910 exhibition of the American Society of Independent Artists, see "Robert Henri: The New York Exhibition of Independent Artists, 1910" in John W. McCoubrey, *American Art 1700-1960*. Englewood Cliffs, NJ: Prentice-Hall, 1965; also *The Story of Modern Art*. p. 366.

"glimpsed the Red Cottage in the snow": *Letter postmarked Boston, Apr. 10, 1916, from Sloan to Dolly in New York. John Sloan Manuscript Collection, Delaware Art Museum.*

137 –   **"the same little girl you left"**: Letter postmarked New York, Apr. 7, 1916 from Dolly to Sloan in Boston. John Sloan Manuscript Collection, Delaware Art Museum.

"My hardest working model": *Gist of Art* (1939 edition), p. 253.

"Why will a man take on all the agony of mind": Sloan diaries, Jan. 15, 1909.

"healthy types of the local population": *Gist of Art* (1939 edition), p. 250.

138 –   **"inanities of most of the art criticism in America"**: Letter postmarked May 11, 1916 from Sloan to E. (Albert Eugene) Gallatin, author of *Certain Contemporaries: Notes and Art Criticisms*. John Sloan Manuscript Collection, Delaware Art Museum.

the first exhibition of the Gallery-on-the-Moors: For an account of the gallery and its exhibitions, see James F. O'Gorman, "Parnassus on Ledge Road," in *The Red Cottage*.

140 –   **"These fall days are wistfully beautiful"**: James F. O'Gorman, *This Other Gloucester*. Gloucester: Ten Pound Island Book Company, 1976, p. 74.

also mentioned in the review, albeit cautiously: *Cape Ann Shore*, Aug. 11, 1917.

141 –   **"the rich, like some pest, have eaten off acres of granite rocks"**: Letter from Sloan in Gloucester to Henri, Jun. 17, 1917, quoted in *Revolutionaries of Realism: The Letters of John Sloan and Robert Henri*, pp. 232-233.

"seeing the lyric poetry of everyday reality": *John Sloan*, p. 50.

"a blue Mercedes, a few years old": *Gist of Art* (1939 edition), p. 249.

142 –   **"We have many parties and lots of liquor"**: Letter from Stewart Davis to cousin, Aug. 5, 1915, quoted in *Stuart Davis in Gloucester*, p. 17.

Sloan "chasing cats over the roofs": Letter from Stewart Davis to his mother, Sep. 26, 1915, quoted in *Stuart Davis in Gloucester*, p. 103.

Chapter Nine : Seductions of Technology
Power Fishing

145 –   **there were eight in service around the turn of the century**: John "Let" Sutherland, *Steamboats of Gloucester and the North Shore.* Charleston, SC: The History Press, 2004, p. 156.

146 –   **Mel McClain accepted the challenge**: Dana Story, *The Shipbuilders of Essex.* Gloucester: Ten Pound Island Book Co., 1995, p. 149.

 she was sending a set of flags for the boat: Newspaper clipping in Box #2, Solomon Jacobs papers, Cape Ann Museum library.

147 –   **more than 3,000 spectators lined the shores**: *New York Times*, Mar. 29, 1900; *Boston Daily Globe*, Mar. 29 & 30, 1900; *Gloucester Daily Times*, Mar. 29, 1900, pg. 1.

 there was a fluttering of handkerchiefs: *Boston Daily Globe*, Mar. 30, 1900.

148 –   **"that engine is the new fangle in mackerel fishing"**: "A Unique Fishing Craft – Captain Jacobs is Proud of the *Helen Miller Guild.*" Undated article, *Newark Evening News*, Newark, NJ.

 "the most daring and intrepid master mariner": *Boston Daily Globe*, Sep. 5, 1900, p. 2.

 The *Gould* broke all seining records that year: "The Invincible Sol Jacobs."

149 –   **Sol and the crew looked on in frustration**: *Boston Daily Globe*, Oct. 26, 1901, p. 5.

 the sole source for a story: James B. Connolly, *Seaborne: Thirty Years Avoyaging.* New York: Doubleday, Doran, 1944.

150 –   **specialists in this alien sphere of steam engineering**: Letter from Mrs. Peter J. (Alice M. Jacobs) Cox to Howard Chapelle, Sept. 30, 1960, in Box #1, Solomon Jacobs papers, Cape Ann Museum library.

 an honest wooden vessel: *Fast & Able: Life Stories of Great Gloucester Fishing Vessels*, p. 114; *Marine Engineering*, Vol. 7, May 1902, p. 250.

151 –   **The launching of the *Alice M.***: "The Invincible Sol Jacobs."

 Capt. Sol bought assorted steam engine supplies and parts from Stoddart: Invoices in Box #1, Solomon Jacobs papers, Cape Ann Museum library.

 "Mackerel by wireless": *Gloucester Daily Times*, May 20, 1902.

152 –   **Capt. Jacobs signaled his engineer to pour on the coal**: *Fast & Able: Life Stories of Great Gloucester Fishing Vessels*, p. 114.

153 –   **demonstrated her value in salvage**: *Boston Daily Globe*, Dec. 22, 1902, p. 14.

enhanced the occasion with gracious hospitality: Gordon Thomas in "Old Timers Corner," *Gloucester Daily Times* (undated clipping in Solomon Jacobs scrapbook, Cape Ann Museum library).

154 – **Capt. Jacobs protested indignantly to the U.S. consul:** Report from U.S. Consul in Halifax, Feb. 1902.

Hodder was at the wheel in a December gale: *Boston Daily Globe*, Dec. 17, 1903, p. 11; Dec. 18, p. 1; Dec. 23, p. 7; Dec. 25, p. 2.

rowed the dory to shore in the numbing cold, freezing his fingers and ears: *Fast & Able: Life Stories of Great Gloucester Fishing Vessels*, p. 116.

155 – **fighting the flames all the way in:** *Boston Herald*, Sep. 17, 1905; *Gloucester Daily Times*, Sep. 13, 14, 16, 18, 1905.

Refining the Rainbow

156 – **"attack of enthusiasm":** *John Sloan*, p. 190.

"full of a scheme of color": Sloan diaries, Jun. 13, 1909.

"Mr. Maratta ... called today": Sloan diaries, Jun. 28, 1909.

"The palette is an instrument": *John Sloan on Drawing and Painting (Gist of Art)*, p. 109.

157 – **"I wish ... that we had studied music harmony":** Sloan diaries, Oct. 31, 1911.

158 – **Winter introduced Sloan ... to the Dudeen color triangle:** *John Sloan*, p. 163.

159 – **"subject that had exciting plastic rhythms":** *The Red Cottage*.

"an arsenal of forty-eight tones": *John Sloan on Drawing and Painting (Gist of Art)*, p. 115.

"God Bless the Maratta Colors. I can think in these!": Letter from John Sloan to "Nannie," Jun. 1914. John Sloan Manuscript Collection, Delaware Art Museum.

wrote about calling in at John Sloan's studio: *Gloucester Daily Times*, Aug. 4, 1916.

160 – **"The palette is an instrument, like a piano or a violin":** *John Sloan on Drawing and Painting (Gist of Art)*, p. 117.

"I could always open the palette up": Sloan diaries, Jun. 13, 1909 (note added later).

"no two of them have the same color scheme": Sloan diaries, Jun. 13, 1909 (note added later).

Chapter Ten : Allegiances

Citizen Jacobs

163 – **after Capt. Ezekiel Call was lost**: *Fishermen's Memorial & Record Book*, p. 125.

severe losses . . . again in February, 1879: *The Fisheries and Fish Industries of the United States*, p. 127.

164 – **"having paid dues for 35 years"**: Box #1, Solomon Jacobs papers, Cape Ann Museum library.

he bought them one on the spot: *Gloucester Daily Times*, Jun. 23,1903.

"a man of marked social traits": *Boston Daily Globe*, Sep. 9, 1911.

Sarah gave birth to their first child: Birth records of Jacobs children from vital records, Gloucester city archives.

Sol purchased from Orlando Garland a lot of land and residence: Deed dated Dec. 5, 1881, Essex County Registry of Deeds, Salem, MA. Stephanie Buck, librarian/archivist of the Cape Ann Museum, provided a map from city records showing the location of this property.

165 – **also had a summer cottage at Brier Neck**: Jacobs family photos in Box #2, Solomon Jacobs papers, Cape Ann Museum library.

Sarah had a live-in domestic helper: *Gloucester City Directory*, 1900.

Ethel wed Arthur Dodge, an architect: *Gloucester Daily Times* (undated), obituary of Ethel (Jacobs) Dodge, in Box #1, Solomon Jacobs papers, Cape Ann Museum library.

"Capt. Jacobs received the news philosophically": *Boston Daily Globe*, Jul. 28,1908.

166 – **"such anger was reserved for ship use"**: Letter from Alice M. (Jacobs) Cox to Sydney H. Davis, Port Clyde, Maine (undated), in Box #1, Solomon Jacobs papers, Cape Ann Museum library.

seen at the wheel of his brother-in-law's Stanley Steamer: Jacobs family photos in Box #2, Solomon Jacobs papers, Cape Ann Museum library.

a "mild-mannered gentleman" climbed the stairs: *Gloucester Daily Times*, Oct. 23, 1937.

167 – **Capt. Jacobs firmly tugged on his own hat**: *Cape Ann Advertiser*, Nov. 25, 1886.

168 – **sending him a half-barrel of fresh mackerel**: "The Invincible Sol Jacobs."

169 – **"no more backbone than a chocolate éclair"**: Evan Thomas, *The War Lovers*. Little, Brown: New York & Boston, 2010, p. 224.

"I have been through one war": *The War Lovers*, p. 229.

170 – **alternate candidate for the Massachusetts Sixth Congressional District**: Certificate naming Jacobs as delegate, in Box #1, Solomon Jacobs papers, Cape Ann Museum library.

Villager Sloan

172 – **"say something worthwhile to the fresh young minds"**: *John Sloan on Drawing and Painting (Gist of Art)*, p. 192.

"true teachers give goals, not rules": Jacques Barzun, *Berlioz and the Romantic Century*. Boston: Little Brown & Co., 1950.

173 – **"Oh, how he rails against institutions"**: *Art for The Masses*, p. 189.

"John Sloan had the most valuable influence on me": *Abstract Expressionism* website.

"determined to do for Chicago ... what Sloan had done for New York": Spaightwood Galleries website.

"a solid that can support a boat": *John Sloan on Drawing and Painting (Gist of Art)*, p. 151.

174 – **"draw with human kindness"**: *Art for The Masses*, p. 129.

"tried to go on from the inspirational teaching of Henri": *John Sloan on Drawing and Painting (Gist of Art)*, p. 7.

"Pure abstraction isn't art": *John Sloan on Drawing and Painting (Gist of Art)*, p. 51.

175 – **"not to have too much recognition"**: *John Sloan on Drawing and Painting (Gist of Art)*, pp. 190-191.

"up his sleeve he keeps a painter": *New York Times*, Mar. 21, 1917.

"there is building going on all about us": Sloan diaries, May 5, 1910.

176 – **Marie had arrived from Romanian Moldavia**: Robert Schulman wrote of her as *Romany Marie: The Queen of Greenwich Village*. Louisville: Butler Books, 2006.

177 – **Gertrude Drick read a manifesto**: Ross Wetzsteon, author of *Republic of Dreams: Greenwich Village, The American Bohemia 1910-1960*, recounts the tale in "Arch Conspirators," an article in *The Village Voice*, Feb. 4, 1997.

"a happy little boy from Gloucester town": *Gist of Art* (1939 edition), p. 251.

"Do you remember the frogs we caught": Sally Stanton letter quoted in *John Sloan: The Gloucester Years*, p. 20.

remembered him as a good-humored man who amused them: Letter from Elizabeth Oakes Colford to James F. O'Gorman, Feb. 18, 1975. In John Sloan folder, Cape Ann Museum library.

Chapter Eleven : Anecdotal Casualties
Deadly Inconvenience
179 – **"this world has been a crazy place to live in"**: *John Sloan on Drawing and Painting (Gist of Art)*, pp. 4-5.

180 – **Yeats protested that Sloan's anti-war position was indefensible**: *Prodigal Father: The Life of John Butler Yeats*, p. 429.
Henri Gaudier-Brzeska ... killed in the trenches: *The Man from New York: John Quinn and His Friends*, p. 256.

181 – **His prophetic poem, *I Have A Rendezvous with Death***: The poem was one of President John F. Kennedy's favorites. His wife Jacqueline memorized it and would often recite it upon his request.

A Fallen Regiment
182 – **The tragic fate of the Newfoundland Regiment**: *Newfoundland in the First World War (1914-1918)*, website of Marianopolis College, Montreal.

183 – ***Monitor*, one of the handsomest in the Gloucester fleet**: Gordon Thomas recounts the noble but tragic career of *Monitor* on pp. 98-102 of *Fast & Able: Life Stories of Great Gloucester Fishing Vessels*.
The handsome *John Hays Hammond*: *Fast & Able: Life Stories of Great Gloucester Fishing Vessels*, pp. 200-205.
such prime vessels as the *Tattler* and *Clintonia*: Details of the destruction by U-boats of these Gloucester schooners, and of the *Rose Dorothea* and *John Hays Hammond*, are also in *Fast & Able: Life Stories of Great Gloucester Fishing Vessels*.

184 – **hatred of the Germans "knew no bounds"**: Undated article, probably in *Gloucester Daily Times*, reporting a 1919 interview with Capt. Jacobs, in Box #1, Solomon Jacobs papers, Cape Ann Museum library.
called its members out on picket lines: *Gloucester Daily Times*, Mar. 1, 1917.

185 – **striking fishermen began standing watch on the docks**: *Gloucester Daily Times*, Mar. 21, 1918.
purchased the Bucksport, Maine schooner *A.M. Nicholson*: "The Invincible Sol Jacobs."
Disbelief spread beyond the fisheries: *Gloucester Daily Times*, Sep. 9, 1911; *Boston Daily Globe*, Sep. 9, 1911.

186 – **"Wherever he has been he has made history"**: *Gloucester Daily Times*, Sep. 9, 1911.
"on the road to another snug competence": *Gloucester Daily Times*, Sep. 9, 1911.

sent a schooner sailing under British papers: *Gloucester Daily Times*, Jan. 15, 1909.

discharged from his outstanding debts: *Bankruptcy Case File for Solomon Jacobs*, filed at United States District Court for the District of Massachusetts, Sep. 8, 1911, National Archives and Records Administration, Northeast Region, Waltham, MA.

187 –   **the schooner *Pythian* and a converted steam yacht, the *Bethulia*.** "The Invincible Sol Jacobs."

Chapter Twelve : The Naked Coast

The Septuagenarian Ensign

191 –   **on their way to Gloucester to seek recruits**: Associated Press release printed in *Gloucester Daily Times*, Mar. 11, 1917.

"Massachusetts had no defense ... naval or military": George Hinckley Lyman documented the activities of the Committee on Naval Forces in *The Story of the Massachusetts Committee on Public Safety 1917-1918*. Boston: Massachusetts Committee on Public Safety, 1919, pp. 36-42.

192 –   **hall filled with "rough-clad fishermen"**: "Fishermen of Gloucester Rush to Enroll in Navy," Associated Press release printed in *Gloucester Daily Times*, Mar. 11, 1917.

Capt. Jacobs was interviewed, given a physical, and enrolled: Associated Press release printed in *Gloucester Daily Times*, Mar. 12, 1917.

Jacob's daughter Ethel ... active in ... the Red Cross: Obituary of Ethel (Jacobs) Dodge, in Box #1, Solomon Jacobs papers, Cape Ann Museum library.

"the submarine would be the controlling factor": *Gloucester Daily Times*, Apr. 14, 1917.

193 –   **A typical Coast Defense Reserve boat was the *Lynx***: Wikipedia.

awarded a contract to build five motorboats of five tons each: *The Rudder*, Vol. 32, 1916, p. 200.

authorized to recruit women into the Naval Coast Defense Reserve: "History of Women in the Navy," Navy Department Press Release, Jul. 30,1942.

194 –   **"grab the children and beat it into the woods"**: Edward Robb Ellis, *Echoes of Distant Thunder*. New York: Coward, McCann & Geoghegan, 1975, p. 424.

only 3,500 men, nationwide, volunteered: Ernest Freeberg, *Democracy's Prisoner: Eugene V. Debs, The Great War, and the Right to Dissent*. Cambridge, MA: Harvard University Press, 2008, p. 54.

"a war between the exploiters and humanity": *Gloucester Daily Times*, Apr. 11, 1917.

a train from Boston brought in forty-one strikebreakers: *Glouces-ter Daily Times*, Apr. 16, 1917.

195 – send all available U.S. fighting vessels to serve in the North Sea: Henry J. James, *German Subs in Yankee Waters – First World War*. New York: Gotham House, 1940, p. 13.
Gloucester had a surprise visitor: John Dos Passos, *Mr. Wilson's War*. Garden City, NY: Doubleday, 1962, p. 284.

196 – "great groups of people gathered along the banks to cheer him": *Mr. Wilson's War*, p. 285.

197 – The blast leveled the north end of Halifax: Much has been written about the horrific munitions explosion in Halifax harbor. For a comprehensive account, see *The Town That Died: The True Story of the Greatest Man-Made Explosion Before Hiroshima—A Chronicle of the Halifax Disaster*, by Michael J. Bird. McGraw-Hill Ryerson, 1967.

The Embattled Pacifist
active member of a Keep Out of the War Committee: *New York Times*, Feb. 5, 1917.

198 – "We have settled into our little red cottage": Letter from Sloan to Henri, Jun. 17, 1917, from 252 E. Main St., Gloucester, quoted in *Revolutionaries of Realism: The Letters of John Sloan and Robert Henri*, pp. 232-233.
"to paint life from the street": *Gist of Art* (1939 edition), p. 251.

200 – enjoin the magazine from publishing its August issue: Zechariah Chafee, Jr., *Freedom of Speech*. New York: Harcourt, Brace, 1920, p. 47.
"subversive to authority and seditious in effect": *Freedom of Speech*, p. 47.
Burleson also suppressed *The Public* and *The Nation*: *Freedom of Speech*, p.107.

201 – the man who answers the call of the public: August Heckscher, *Woodrow Wilson: A Biography*. New York: Charles Scribner's Sons, 1991, p. 102.
"hiding his poltroonery": *Prodigal Father: The Life of John Butler Yeats*, p. 442.
"writes like an archbishop": *The Man from New York: John Quinn and His Friends*, p. 313.
"forget there ever was such a thing as tolerance": *Woodrow Wilson: A Biography*, p. 450.

202 – **"disloyalty active in the United States"**: *Woodrow Wilson: A Biography*, p. 398.
"Manhattan is a city of aliens": Alan Valentine, *1913: America Between Two Worlds*. New York: Macmillan, 1952, p. 113.
George Creel ... won approval to form a special propaganda arm: *Democracy's Prisoner: Eugene V. Debs, The Great War, and the Right to Dissent*, p. 45.

203 – **"Pay Envelope Stories"**: James R. Mock & Cedric Larson, *Words that Won the War: The Story of the Committee on Public Information 1917-19*. Princeton: Princeton University Press, 1939, p. 70.
Pershing's Crusaders: *Gloucester Daily Times*, Aug. 24, 1918.

204 – **she would be sentenced to two years in prison**: *Democracy's Prisoner: Eugene V. Debs, The Great War, and the Right to Dissent*, p. 62.
"this town is not for the war very enthusiastically": Letter from Sloan to Henri, Jun. 17, 1917, from 252 E. Main St., Gloucester, quoted in *Revolutionaries of Realism: The Letters of John Sloan and Robert Henri*, pp. 232-233.

Chapter Thirteen : Summer of the Periscopes
Toll of the U-156

205 – **"although the gaiety of the season is not up to the usual pace"**: *Gloucester Daily Times*, Aug. 10, 1918, p. 7.
recruited to "make good money" gathering sumac: *Gloucester Daily Times*, Aug. 7, 1918.
"Local Fishermen Hustle for Hoover": *Gloucester Daily Times*, Jul. 30, 1918.

206 – **the three-masted *Hattie Dunn***: *German Subs in Yankee Waters – First World War*, pp. 22-25.
***U-156*, under the command of Korvetten Kapitän Richard Feldt**: That Feldt commanded the *U-156* from Jan. 1, 1918 until it disappeared in the North Sea in September is confirmed by uboat.net and numerous other sources.

207 – **The U-boat shelled the tug and its row of barges**: *German Subs in Yankee Waters – First World War*, p. 81. The author, James, was an eye-witness to the attack. Also see *Echoes of Distant Thunder*, p. 424.
The plane was forced down in a gale: A.B. Feuer, *The U.S. Navy in World War I*. Westport, CT: Praeger, 1999, p. 138; *Cape Ann Shore*, Jul. 31, 1920, pp. 6-7.
The Gloucester schooner *Robert and Richard* was intercepted: *Gloucester Daily Times*, Aug. 1, 1918, p. 8; *Fast & Able: Life Stories of Great Gloucester Fishing Vessels*, p. 145; *German Subs in Yankee*

Waters – First World War, p. 91; *New York Times*, Jul. 23, 1918; "Record of Casualties to Vessels (1918)," pg. 56, in *Station Log Book* – Coast Guard Station No. 23 (Gloucester) – 2nd District, July 20th 1918 to Feb. 1st 1919.

208 – **an armed vessel would give a U-boat every excuse**: *German Subs in Yankee Waters – First World War*, p. 135.

209 – **the *Bianca* did not sink**: *German Subs in Yankee Waters – First World War*, p. 146.

dispatched to the bottom the schooners *Rob Roy* and *Muriel*: *Gloucester Daily Times*, Aug. 5 & 7, 1918, p. 1 headline on Aug. 5: "Three More Fishermen Fall Prey to German U-Boats"; *Fast & Able: Life Stories of Great Gloucester Fishing Vessels*, p. 61; *German Subs in Yankee Waters – First World War*, p. 93.

210 – **he recited in a casual, conversational tone**: The interview with Capt. Michael Clark is one of many in an oral history project conducted for Gloucester's Sawyer Free Library in the 1970s – when a few of the remaining sailing era fishermen could be found and persuaded to tell their stories. The audiotapes are an invaluable historical resource.

212 – **Kapitän Feldt employed an ingenious stratagem**: *Gloucester Daily Times*, Aug. 21, 1918, p. 1; *Fast & Able: Life Stories of Great Gloucester Fishing Vessels*, pp. 156 & 166; *German Subs in Yankee Waters – First World War*, p. 103; "Record of Casualties to Vessels (1918)," pg. 56, in *Station Log Book – Coast Guard Station No. 23 (Gloucester) – 2nd District, July 20th 1918 to Feb. 1st 1919*, p. 63.

What he was forced to leave behind: Cecile Pimental, *The Mary P. Mesquita: Rundown at Sea*. Decorah, ID: Anundsen Publishing Company, 1998, p. 48. Listed are Capt. Joseph Mesquita's personal effects lost when the *Francis J. O'Hara, Jr.* was sunk by the *U-156* in 1918.

twenty-two died, mainly in dories that failed to make it to shore: *German Subs in Yankee Waters – First World War*, pp. 108-109.

213 – **equipping its steam trawlers with wireless transmitters**: *Gloucester Daily Times*, Aug. 15, 1918, p. 8.

fled the doomed *Sennett* under U-boat attack: *Gloucester Daily Times*, Aug. 13, 1918, p. 1; U.S. Office of Naval Records and Library, United States Office of Naval Intelligence, 1920; "Victim or Participant? Allied Fishing Fleets and U-Boat Attacks in World War I & II," by Charles Dana Gibson. *Northern Mariner* I, No. 4 (Oct. 1991), 1-18.

214 – **"Get After the Submarines"**: *Gloucester Daily Times* editorial, Aug. 21, 1918.

215 – **"making great sacrifices to fight the war"**: *Boston Transcript* editorial quoted in *Gloucester Daily Times*, Aug. 19, 1918.

produce an Identification Card: *Treasury Decisions Under Customs and Other Laws*, U.S. Department of the Treasury, 1918, p. 81; *German Subs in Yankee Waters – First World War*, p. 74.

216 – **the *U-156* had destroyed thirty-four ships**: U-Boat.net, "Ships Hit by *U-156*." Of one hundred commercial vessels sunk by U-boats in North American coastal waters in 1918, thirty-five were fishing vessels ("Victim or Participant? Allied Fishing Fleets and U-Boat Attacks in World War I & II").

seventy-seven drowned crewmen: Lowell Thomas, *Raiders of the Deep*. Garden City, NY: Doubleday, Doran, 1928; *Fast & Able: Life Stories of Great Gloucester Fishing Vessels*, p. 245 (size of the crew confirmed by online sources).

Cows and Conspirators

217 – **"on East Main Street near Rocky Neck Avenue"**: *Gloucester Daily Times*, Aug. 16, 1918, p. 1.

purchased his *Spring Rain*: Heather Campbell Coyle and Joyce K. Schiller, *John Sloan's New York*. Wilmington, DE: Delaware Art Museum, 2007, p. 23; *John Sloan*, pp. 56-57.

"an ankle counted in those days": *Gist of Art* (1939 edition), p. 232.

218 – **She later acquired *Love on the Roof***: *New York Times*, May 8, 1988: John Gross review of exhibition, "John Sloan: Spectator of Life," at IBM Gallery, Madison Ave. and 56th Street, NYC.

"a true sense of Gloucester sun": John Sloan, unpublished notes, John Sloan Manuscript Collection, Delaware Art Museum, quoted in *John Sloan: The Gloucester Years*, p. 67.

219 – **The President wore "an outing suit of white flannel"**: *Gloucester Daily Times*, Aug. 17, 1918.

The President . . . was loath to leave the area: *Gloucester Daily Times*, Aug. 19, 1918.

"residents of Magnolia are discussing with indignation": Item in a Boston newspaper quoted in *Gloucester Daily Times*, Aug. 20, 1918.

220 – **a charge of sedition against Max Eastman**: *Carl W. Peters: American Scene Painter from Rochester to Rockport*, p. 304.

Floyd Dell ... was thrown out of the army: *Carl W. Peters: American Scene Painter from Rochester to Rockport*, p. 304.

221 – **Formed an "American Protective League"**: *Democracy's Prisoner: Eugene V. Debs, The Great War, and the Right to Dissent*, p. 96.

Allegedly Sylvester had made "disloyal remarks": *Gloucester Daily Times*, May 3, 1918.

charged that he had sent a "suspicious telegram": *Gloucester Daily Times*, Aug. 1, 1918, p. 1.

Neighbors had often seen Kunhardt walking alone: *Gloucester Daily Times*, Jul. 25, 1918.

222 – regarded as "slightly modified Eskimos": *Gloucester Daily Times*, Aug. 1. 1918, p. 7.

223 – arrested and sent to jail for "loafing": *Gloucester Daily Times*, Jul. 30, 1918.

"gaily flapping in reply": *Gist of Art* (1939 edition), p. 249.

"Why did I stop going to Gloucester?": Foreword to *The Red Cottage*.

224 – Sloan "used to rave" about Gloucester: *Stuart Davis in Gloucester*, p. 34.

225 – Henri's ecstatic descriptions of the Southwest: Foreword to *The Red Cottage*.

226 – among those showing the way to a better America: *The Red Cottage*.

Chapter Fourteen : View from a Distant Shore

A Plaque in a Park

227 – "tall, lean and swarthy": unidentified newspaper clipping, 1919, Solomon Jacobs scrapbook in Cape Ann Museum.

"If flying machines are going to be used": unidentified newspaper clipping, 1919, Solomon Jacobs scrapbook in Cape Ann Museum.

"snugged in the parlor of his house": *Boston Daily Globe*, Oct. 24, 1920.

228 – The *Halifax Herald* had offered a cup and a cash prize: There is a good account of the 1920 fishermen's cup contest in *A Race for Real Sailors: The Bluenose and the International Fishermen's Cup, 1920-1938* by R. Keith McLaren. Boston: David R Godine, 2006.

229 – "A triumph for Americanism": *Fast & Able: Life Stories of Great Gloucester Fishing Vessels*, p. 187.

230 – The cause of death was listed as "apoplexy": *Gloucester Daily Times*, Feb. 9, 1922. "Death Takes Capt. Solomon Jacobs."

Two ministers eulogized: Solomon Jacobs obituary in *Gloucester Daily Times*, Feb. 13, 1922.

231 – The marble clock … that Sol donated in 1883: The duplicate marble clock may be seen today on the wall outside the mayor's office in Gloucester city hall.

a man of "great courage, determination, fearlessness, judgment and ability": *Fast & Able: Life Stories of Great Gloucester Fishing Vessels*, p. 117.

232 – "further enrich our conscious heritage": Proposal submitted by Salvatore "Sal" Favazza to Gloucester City Council in support of a park to honor Solomon Jacobs. *Gloucester Daily Times*, Oct. 21, 1974. Among the honored guests at the dedication was Alice Cox: Following a suggestion by Linda Johnson at the Cape Ann Museum library, Ms. Cox's neighbor, Paul Murphy, was queried by the author and provided this information.

The Stamp of Recognition

234 – "not a decent road west of Buffalo": "Artist as Rebel: John Sloan versus the Status Quo."

236 – "If what I am doing now were selling": *John Sloan on Drawing and Painting (Gist of Art)*, pp. 190-191.

"It is a bad sign for a man of my kind": Exhibition catalogue: *John Sloan – Paintings – Prints – Drawings*, Hurd Museum of Art, Dartmouth College, 1981, p. 9.

237 – "my work has made it utterly worthwhile": *John Sloan on Drawing and Painting (Gist of Art)*, pp. 190-191.

238 – *Glare on Gloucester Harbor*: Sloan note for the painting in Elzea Rowland, *John Sloan's Oil Paintings – A Catalogue Raisonne*, Vol. I, Newark, NJ: University of Delaware Press, 1991.

239 – "Five ... happy summers were spent in Gloucester": Note for *Dolly by the Kitchen Door*, *Gist of Art* (1939 edition), p. 248.

240 – "It is not necessary to paint the American flag to be an American painter": *John Sloan on Drawing and Painting (Gist of Art)*, p. 4.

"Art makes living worthwhile": *John Sloan on Drawing and Painting (Gist of Art)*, p. 35.

"dean of American painters": Sloan obituary in *New York Times*, Sep. 9, 1951.

241 – his admitted "Tabasco temper": "Artist as Rebel: John Sloan versus the Status Quo."

"Rebel with a paintbrush": Article on Sloan by Charles Poore in *New York Times*, May 21, 1950.

INDEX